THE COMPLETE GUIDE TO
TRIATHLON TRAINING

DATE DUE

Hermann Aschwer

THE COMPLETE GUIDE TO
TRIATHLON TRAINING

Meyer & Meyer Sport

ɔm Jedermann zum Ironman©
: Meyer und Meyer Verlag, 1996
Chilvers-Grierson

Die Deutsche Bibliothek – CIP-Einheitsaufnahme

Aschwer, Hermann:
The Complete Guide to Triathlon Training / Hermann Aschwer.
– Aachen : Meyer und Meyer, 1998
Dt. Ausg. u.d.T.: Aschwer, Hermann: Triathlontraining
ISBN 3-89124-515-7

© 1999 by Meyer & Meyer Sport, Aachen
Olten (CH), Vienna, Oxford,
Québec, Lansing/ Michigan, Adelaide, Auckland, Johannesburg
Internet: http://www.meyer-meyer-sports.com
e-mail: verlag@meyer-meyer-sports.com

Cover Photo: Horst Müller, Düsseldorf; Helmut Baur, Roth
Photos: Actions Sport 19, 57, 82; L. Anarell 99; C. Aschwer 9; S. Aschwer 55, 186;
A. Busch 178; R. Bistricky 75; A. Esser 205; B. Gorschlüter 82; H.Katzianer
13,23,140; Kettler 83; G. Mangold 66.193; H. Nowak 49; A. Pfützner 98,184;
Polar 30, 201; J. Schmidt 150; S. Schreiber 188; S. Schwenke 102, 138
All other photos and figures by Hermann Aschwer
Cover design: Walter Neumann, N&N Design-Studio, Aachen
Cover exposure: frw, Reiner Wahlen, Aachen
Type exposure: frw, Reiner Wahlen, Aachen
Typesetting: Quay
Editorial: Dr. Irmgard Jaeger, Aachen, John Cughlan
Printing: Burg Verlag & Druck, Gastinger GmbH und Co. KG, Stolberg
Printed in Germany
ISBN 3-89124-515-7

Contents

Foreword

Hermann embraces me, we shake hands and remain silent. Each sees the tears of the other - all has been said. Still you are alone - but not lonely, reduced down to yourself. You look into the the sympathising faces of two Hawaiian women and don't notice that they are still supporting you, almost carrying you in fact. Gently you are placed under palm trees, you feel yourself being stroked, caressed even. Wonderful childhood memories come back. All around you lie flower-crowned Hawaii finishers looking like helpless children. Only seconds ago you floated through a channel of yelling masses, now you are surrounded by an unreal peacefulness, the transition is almost ghostly.

Hermann and I have experienced this almost unreal scene in Hawaii many times. Hawaii is the highest level of triathletic existence - if only there weren't those damned qualifying rounds. Only they wear you down and eat you up.
I have stopped, Hermann still keeps going. We have remained friends.

He is one of the last dinosaurs of triathlon, in from the start. If anyone thinks Hermann cannot stop, he is wrong. He will stop when he has nothing more to say, and he still has much to say and to write.

He does not only have his own "Hawaiian adventure" but lets others share in it, helps, is always approachable. He is carried on by the pragmatic conviction that the "IRON" makes you physically and psychologically fit for your whole life. His motto is "Once iron, always iron", in every situation of your life.

Hermann is neither a philosopher nor a dreamer. Because he is a realist he gives you five years, assuming you stick to the path he has described in this book. That this path is not always fun, but sometimes even really hurts - he tells you that straight to your face too.

Perhaps you too will one day have the good fortune to be crowned with a Hawaiian Lei, wear a medal around your neck and be embraced by "a Hermann" at the finish line, and feel not only joy and pride, but perhaps also - at the end of this long path - a little humility as well.

Prof. Georg Kroeger
Hawaii finisher 1987, 1988, 1989

Successful Triathlon

I wish all women and men who have experienced triathlon themselves that they "finish" in all their races. That means: you have done it, you have successfully completed the event.

The feeling of euphoria you get near the finish line is worth struggling for.

Because women are no less successful than men in triathlon and realise performances just as impressive, I will take the liberty of referring to triathletes in the following text, whether women or men are meant.

More and more people of all ages are seeing the advantages of living active lives. This positive trend is not only apparent in the travel industry, with increasing numbers booking active holidays for their vacations, but is particularly noticeable in triathlon in this country.

Headlines such as "Triathlon, absolute madness" or "Triathlon, enjoying torture" and other completely unobjective headlines have meanwhile more or less disappeared. These days reports are still often full of astonishment but also show recognition of the sporting achievements of triathletes.

In particular with regard to the Hawaii triathlon, where reporting focussed mainly on the three German super athletes Thomas Hellriegel, Jürgen Zäck and Lothar Leder, it must be said that press coverage in recent years has become increasingly more objective and thus more convincing. Over 200 German Hawaii finishers, and their local newspapers, also contribute to improved media treatment, as do the increasing number of television reports.

The triathletes' achievements are admired, frequently discussed and not always, but increasingly often, comprehended.

Anyone who has experienced the 150,000 enthusiastic spectators every year in Roth can rest assured. Next year one or other of those spectators will themselves try to be amongst the finishers of a triathlon race. It need not, and should not be, a 226 km distance right from the start, but a novice triathlon also has its appeal. To reach this goal only a few months of endurance training are necessary, even for complete beginners. Anyone, however, who wants to go for the short, middle or even ultra triathlon distances will need several years of well thought out training.

I would like to accompany you on this interesting route, whether you are a leisure, competition or performance athlete. In doing so it is always my intention to give recommendations which can be put into practice in everyday training and competitive situations.

The training principles are generally valid for all triathletes.

The five stages from Novice to Ironman are for athletes who start as beginners and want to fulfill their ironman dream step by step. Triathletes who feel best over short and middle distances and in this way realise their sporting dreams will also find here many tips, recommendations and suggestions appropriate to their level. The same applies to those who come from other sports.

Extensive training schedules for the novice, short, middle and ultra distances make it easier to create one's own schedules.

In order to make the most of his or her individual capabilities in triathlon the reader will find comprehensive information on the decisive fundamental principles of triathlon training as a whole, with the various forms and types of training, far-sighted training planning and the very important aspect of mental training. Furthermore the book includes recommendations on the right equipment and clothing, correct nutrition, performance measurement one can carry out oneself, the most important blood values for triathletes and finding potential causes of injury.

At this point I would like to come back to the finisher idea. The main objective of every triathlon participant should be to finish. This means: "You have reached the overall goal and your own goal or - You've done it!"

This highest principle has its limits of course when one's health is placed at risk. Having finished a triathlon is still an honour for me even after over 100 races. The term "finish" should be used in sport much more widely than it is. All sports, with the exception of team sports, lend themselves to it. For example I was very impressed at the end of the Boston Marathon in 1984 when many passers-by asked me about the run saying "You are finished?". Coming from Germany I was more used to being asked my time. After just a brief reply like "Yes, I have" one would hear friendly words of recognition. In the States no one asked you about your time.

The same applies to Hawaii. Why shouldn't this sporting attitude with the Olympic ideal at its heart be possible here, too?

We triathletes should continue to set an example for other types of sport. The same applies to expressions such as defeat, vanquish, massacre or similar military sounding expressions when they are used with reference to triathlon. Why can't one say: left behind me, won, only had four athletes ahead of me etc.

Personally I feel equally uneasy about the German word for competition, "Wettkampf", which literally means a fight for a wager or bet. I find the terms "Wettbewerb" (competition in a non-violent sense), or just simply triathlon, to be

Everyone can be successful.

much more suitable. "Wettkampf" really does sound like fighting for a wager, and "Kampf" can quickly become "Krampf": nonsense! If, however, one sees here the struggle with oneself, then it is okay. But triathlon should never be a fight against others.

Having said that, I in no way wish to judge the idea of achievement, but rather to really underline the sporting fair achievement which even at the top need not be directed against others. In fact top achievements should be seen as being reached with the other athletes and not against them. What value would a triathlon victory have if the race only had one participant. The victor in a race needs sporting competition before he can win, without, however, having to defeat or "slay" them.

Not the victory but the Olympic ideal previously mentioned should be in the foreground.

The ladies of triathlon show their joy and satisfaction after reaching the finish line much more clearly than most of their male colleagues.

This leads to the question: What is actually success in a sportingly interesting competition like triathlon?

Do only the winning types have it, whose optimum environment allows them to be up front or win in all their races?

The answer from an experienced, enthusiastic and ambitious triathlete is no, definitely not. In triathlon every athlete is able to make a success of their sporting involvement. For me, in triathlon everyone is successful who achieves their own personal goal or even only a partial goal they have set for themselves. Whether that goal be: to jog 5 km without a break, to finish a novice triathlon, to reach the finish line in a short, middle or ultra distance triathlon, a marathon, a cycling race, a swimming race, to achieve a place in the middle of the field, to do well in one's age group or simply to reach a personal best time in swimming, cycling or running. No matter what goal one has set oneself, reaching it makes one a successful athlete.

The emphasis here is on "goals we have set ourselves". We athletes should be self-confident enough not to let our personal successes be reduced by know-it-alls or the media.

A perfect negative example of this is the partially absurd media coverage of the 1996 Olympic Games. Some of the journalists reporting would have had us believe that only the actual Olympic victors in each case were successful. Even a silver medallist was portrayed as a minor loser. Not to mention those who had dared to let themselves be eliminated in the pre- or intermediate rounds already. "Our" medal level was after all dependent on the number of gold medals. I cannot imagine that any of these reporters ever actively took part in sport themselves. This kind of petty-minded journalism always makes me feel very ill at ease.

Anyone interested in sport has an idea of how many athletes worldwide have worked towards these games. For years they have spared neither costs nor effort to intensively prepare themselves for Atlanta. Have neglected job, studies, friends and much more so they can get their chance. According to this view of things, any of them who missed out by fractions of a second, a centimetre or even a millimetre in the qualifying rounds and was eliminated must be an unsuccessful sportsman or woman. This is crazy to me.

In summary, to me a really successful triathlete is someone who has achieved his or her personal goals. Those people are thus unsuccessful who do not reach the goals they set themselves and who see their sporting rivals as personal rivals. The reasons are often a wrong approach. The goal strived for is set much too high. Here are some practical examples:

- The weekly training quota is set so high that through lack of time or other reasons it cannot be kept to.
- The expected place in a triathlon race is set at place 1-3 although one usually comes in at about place 40-50.

Success, and here I mean individual success, is the basis for the fun we should all have in triathlon. This is closely linked to our motivation for this sport triathlon. Briefly, the following are reasons for not having fun in triathlon any more:

• One trains too one-sidedly, too much, too little, always alone.
• The expectations placed on one are too great, the goals have been set too high.
• Starting in too many races, with full physical and psychological effort in each one.
• Unrealistic personal self-assessment.
• The sport is taken too seriously.

In spite of all our enthusiasm for the fascinating sport triathlon we should not forget: First and foremost the sport should be fun, physical and psychological well-being should be in the foreground. Apart from that, there are many things in life more important than swimming, cycling and running.

With this in mind I wish all those active in sport, especially the triathletes, the right view and a great deal of fun in our fascinating sport. For specific triathlon questions I continue to be available to all my keen readers and hope that this book contributes to further increasing the comprehensive knowledge desirable in triathlon.

I would like to express a deeply felt thank you to the great family of triathletes for the many many interesting hours I have had the privilege of spending with you in the last 15 triathlon years. This time and the numerous friends and acquaintances gained through it have given me priceless treasures.

Yours,
Hermann!

My address:
Dr. Hermann Aschwer, Ameke 40, D-48317 Drensteinfurt, Germany

Triathlon, The Endurance Sport

The term endurance has many definitions in sport science. Basically one can describe "endurance" as the ability to deal with a certain strain over a longer period of time without a major decrease in performance. For untrained people this means a strain of at least five minutes involving at least 1/6 to 1/7 of the total muscle systems of the body.

The three classic endurance sports, swimming, cycling and running, come together in triathlon. In duathlon they are cycling and running.

It is not without reason that triathletes are called "the kings of endurance sport". These three endurance sports are particularly suited as health and performance sport. Health sport has as its objective getting the body healthy and keeping it that way. The objective of performance sport is to induce the body to perform well or even exceptionally well.

The World Health Organisation describes health as a condition of
> physical
> mental and
> social well-being.

All three sport forms in triathlon can influence social well being. Mental well-being is also certainly encouraged. For maintaining physical well-being swimming, cycling and running are ideal.

These aspects also cover the term fitness, which can be equated with health, performance capacity, sportiness, and well-being.

Before a person does or considers doing triathlon, however, they have thought about the point of doing this kind of sport. Only when a sportsperson can see a reason for a leisure activity will he be prepared to stand by his convictions and be willing to overcome the problems and difficulties that are bound to arise.

When discussing the point of doing anything, however, it must be remembered that this will appear in a different light to each individual and also have differing priority.

Triathlon offers - more than almost any other sport - a multitude of opportunities for personal experiences:

- diverse experience qualities such as being alone, training in groups, in different kinds of countryside, in changing weather conditions, in a relaxed training mood, in a tense race atmosphere, at various training speeds, with the feeling of strength at the beginning of training and exhaustion at the end;
- varying performance demands and thus the experience of victories and failures;

- getting to know the latest new developments in cycling technology;
- joint training of young people, adults, women, men, people of differing ages and origin;
- consciously experiencing progress when training regularly;
- jointly experiencing races, i.e. the diverse experiences before and during a race, such as: systematically preparing for a triathlon race, experiencing and bearing the tension of the race, knowing and keeping to the rules of triathlon, starting alone and as part of a team, accepting failures, defeats and good performances, recognising the achievements of others.

Doing sport for the purpose of physical well-being is only possible by increasing one's capability for long term performance. Man is not a sprinter by nature but a long-term performer. Everyday stress cannot be dealt with through short-term maximum effort, but only through long lasting willingness to perform. For this reason endurance sports are already being supported by health insurance organisations. Prevention is better and cheaper than cure.

The physical proportion of health is largely determined by the efficiency of the heart and circulatory system. Of course the bone structure must be in order, mobility must not be allowed to wither away and a certain degree of speed ability is necessary.

The following impressive figures demonstrate that our lives represent an enormous long-term performance on the part of our heart and circulatory system. In a year an average adult's heart (resting pulse 80, working 100 beats per minute) beats:

42 million + 2.1 million = 44.1 million times.

In the same period the heart of a well-trained triathlete (resting pulse 50, working 70 + 1 hour daily sport at a pulse of 130) beats a total of:

26.3 million + 2.1 million + 1.7 million = 30.1 million times.

We see here that the heart of a triathlete who trains an average of one hour daily beats 14,000,000 times less in a year than the heart of an untrained person. There is no doubt that a reasonable amount of triathlon training develops stamina to a high degree, when a number of muscle systems are simultaneously involved in movement over a longer period of time.

Our "biological age", the condition of health a person is in, is not determined by the ability to carry heavy loads, to look good in a sprint or to carry out complicated moves on gym equipment, and most certainly not by an artificial tan on our faces. Rather, the quality of our health is determined by a good capability to perform over time. The well-known circulatory system researcher and sports doctor Prof. HOLLMANN summarises his scientific findings as follows:

"With a suitable form of physical training it is possible to stay 40 years old for 20 years."

Dr. Ernst VAN AAKEN, the worldwide recognised "high priest of running", propagates: "20 years younger through endurance training".

According to HOLLMANN, endurance training works against the aging processes; heart, circulatory system, breathing, metabolism, muscle systems and hormonal systems remain efficient. People stay younger than their actual chronological age.

BERG/KEUL have found in their research that 65 to 70 year old long-distance runners have the same ability to take in oxygen as 20 to 30 year old sport students. As oxygen intake is a measure of performing ability, this means that 65 year old endurance athletes have a similar sporting ability to untrained 30 year olds.

As a result of a diverse endurance training programme such as is the case in triathlon, people can enjoy the following advantages:
• Improvement in health
• Improvement of personal performance
• Prevention of illnesses
• Physical and mental freshness
• Retention of youthful vitality
• More zest for life.

Psychological Aspects of Triathlon

Can you imagine a triathlete who only swims, cycles and runs with his body and leaves his soul at home?

Only robots can do that. With people consisting of body and soul you cannot separate the two. Triathlon activates the whole person. At every training session every body cell profits from the increased oxygen supply. Triathletes can occupy themselves more intensively both with themselves and their surroundings. Not only the body but also mind and spirit are moved. Triathletes feel themselves as a "unit".

Body and mind are in symbiosis, in harmony and work together to their mutual benefit.

After a short training period the body warms-up, one feels better, is more alert, one feels how tensions disappear. Deep even breathing leads to liberating feelings. Fears are reduced and often disappear completely. The prevailing mood changes to the more positive side, and with this change, enjoyment of life increases. As someone who cycles or runs through fields, meadows and forests and swims in lakes, one feels a part of nature.

This is a very sublime and far-reaching experience. Regular endurance training forms and changes all aspects of a person. In triathlon demands are placed on people in their entirety: body, mind and soul. Feeling and thinking are just as important as the purely physical activity. Every athlete, assuming regular training, gains his own lasting physical and spiritual-mental (psychological) experiences. Naturally there are differences amongst sports-people in conscious perception. One person notices more, another less. As well as the mainly physical benefits of triathlon mentioned above, the three endurance sports also have a lasting influence psychologically in the following ways:

Together with increasing physical fitness a number of other aspects increase to the same degree, namely

- self-confidence,
- self-esteem,
- thinking ability,
- life energy, and thus
- love and ability to love,
- staying power,
- the ability to deal with and overcome difficulties.

In a word: endurance training improves the quality of life.

As already mentioned, the benefits of triathlon can only be experienced if training is regular and in appropriate amounts. For all endurance sports one needs a little patience in order to be able to train in a relaxed manner. Only then do such experiences manifest themselves – individually differing in degree of intensity from one person to another.

Basic Principles of Triathlon Training

Triathlon represents the adding together of three endurance sports. Not without reason do people speak of the "kings of endurance sport" when talking about triathlon and the ultra distance in particular.

Endurance is the ability to deal with long lasting strain over as long a period as possible without a major reduction in performance.

In addition to pure endurance, triathlon also calls for speed, strength, agility and coordination, i.e. technique.

In order for a triathlete to achieve optimum sporting performance, it is important to train specifically in all of these aspects in the appropriate relationship to each other. A sportsman who carries out a great deal of endurance training loses strength and resilience. On the other hand, too much strength training reduces endurance to a certain degree. Nevertheless, a certain amount of strength is necessary for swimming, cycling and running.

All three endurance disciplines have in common the requirement of a high level of basic endurance and stamina.

Basic Endurance

Basic endurance is the prerequisite for the development and forming of specific endurance. This basis is created through large amounts of training at low intensity. The building up of basic endurance for triathlon is done in winter and in the first phase of the preparatory period. This training can be in the sport itself, but need not necessary be. The organic basis for cycling can thus be created with long calm runs or cross country skiing. With a good endurance basis every triathlete is capable of training at increasing speed and covering more kilometres as the season progresses, without putting too much of a strain on himself.

Training basic endurance should mainly improve aerobic endurance.

General aerobic endurance is marked by working under "steady state" conditions, i.e. ensuring that the muscles used have a sufficient supply of oxygen when placed under dynamic strain. There is a balance between energy consumption and energy supply. The decisive factor here is the maximum oxygen intake capacity. The higher this maximum oxygen intake capacity is, the greater the aerobic endurance.

General anaerobic endurance, on the other hand, is the ability to maintain a high intensity of strain with less oxygen intake than is actually required. Anaerobic endurance is paraphrased by such terms as "speed endurance", "staying power" or "stability of pace".

Aerobic Endurance in Triathlon

Basic endurance should be established in the area of the aerobic threshold (2 mmol lactate). The intensity of strain should be chosen in such a way that the pulse is between 130 and 140 beats per minute. Strain leading to a pulse of less than 130 insufficiently activates the heart and circulatory system and only has a regenerative character.

In swimming, aerobic endurance is best carried out with the following training forms with medium strain:
- Distance swimming 1 to 3 kilometres
- Timed swimming e.g. 1 hour or 30 minutes
- Intervals 50 m intensive - 50 m relaxed without breaks betwen series. No maximum pulse.

This endurance training simultaneously gives one the opportunity to improve one's own swimming style and feeling for water (check on oneself).

Aerobic Training in Cycling

- Endurance training of 30-120 km, pulse 140-150 depending on triathlete's condition.
- Interval training e.g. 15 min. calm, 15 min. fast, 15 min. calm, 15 min. fast, Pulse up to 80% of maximum pulse rate.
- Maximum pulse rate about 220 minus age in years.

Aerobic Training in Running

- Jogging between 10 and 30 km at a calm, even pace.
- Dr. VAN AAKEN's LSD "long slow distance" run.

Easy interval training is also possible here e.g. 20 min. calm, 20 min. fast, 20 min. calm, 20 min. fast ....

Anaerobic Endurance in Triathlon

During anaerobic training oxygen consumption at high strain is greater than oxygen intake. For a short time the muscles function by using chemical processes which make it possible to release oxygen within the muscle itself. The amount of oxygen available in this way is fairly limited. Large amounts of harmful substances build up, the muscles harden and hurt. Movement obviously gets slower as a result. After this anaerobic strain oxygen must be "paid back" to the muscles. For this reason the term debt, oxygen debt, is sometimes used. The main reason for speed training is to experience the anaerobic feeling. If enough recovery phases are included in this kind of training, our body is capable of handling it. Triathletes who wish to specialise in short distances must do interval training to enter this anaerobic area more frequently than those preparing for the ultra distance. It is recommended that pulse measurement be used during anaerobic interval training as a control measure. It is, however, decisive that the current anaerobic threshold is known. This can be roughly determined by the Conconi pulse measurement method. More about this method can be found in the section on performance measurement in triathlon. Before every interval training it is necessary to carry out about ten minutes of warm-up swimming, cycling or running. In this way the body gets used to the form of strain in each case. Intervals at low intensity involve many repeats. If the degree of strain and distance are raised, the number of intervals is reduced and the length of the resting phases between them is increased.

Anaerobic Training

Swimming:
- Warm-up swimming, intervals, cool down swimming.
- E.g. 5 x 200 m, with 60 seconds breaks,
- 2 series: 5 x 200 m with 60 s breaks and 2 min. break between series.
- Pyramid swimming 50 m - 100 m - 150 m - 200 m - 250 m - 200 m - 150 m - 100 m - 50 m with 30 s break between each swim.
- 3 series 10 x 100 m with 30-40 s breaks, 2 min. break between series
- or 4 x 4 x 50 m, 5 s break, 60 s break between series.
- This last variation is very hard and requires good technique and a high degree of fitness.

Cycling:
- Warm-up cycling, intervals, cool down cycling.
- E.g. total distance 40 km. 4 sections à 5 km at speed, recovery breaks of 5 min. light pedalling between each section.
- Total length 40 km, 1, 2, 3, 4, 5 km at speed, followed each time by the same distance of easy pedalling.
- Total length 50 km, 2, 3, 4, 5, 6, 7, 8 minutes at speed, followed each time by the same period of easy pedalling.

Running:
- Warm-up running, intervals, cool down running.

- e.g. 6 x 1,000 m at 10 km best time speed, jogging break of 5 min. at 120 pulse rate.
- 2 x 1,000 m, 2 x 2,000 m at 10 km best time speed, jogging break 5 min.
- 1, 2, 3, 4, 5, 4, 3, 2, 1 min. at speed, followed each time by same period of light jogging,
- 2-3 x 5,000 m with 5 min. walking break each time.

"Fartlek" as Interval Training

Not every triathlete likes interval training with its constant repetition and fixed routes. The Swedish concept "Fartlek", which means something like "playing with speed", is a simple, natural form of speed training and can be incorporated in any run. During a run you accelerate until the next house, the end of the forest, the next building, or until any marking you determine for yourself. After this speed phase follows easy running or evenly paced jogging until recovery. If you feel like it, you do it again. The speed is determined by the athlete himself. Fartlek is intensive, free of restrictions and without prescribed distances and paces. The triathlete runs faster whenever he feels like doing so on the particular day. Fartlek is pace work, but in a playful and creative way. In addition it has the advantage that this entertaining variation requires no measured distance or 400 m track.

Fartlek finishes with easy cool down running and light stretching.

Calm enduring training creates the basis for every triathlete.

Performance Measurement in Triathlon

Anyone demanding special performance of his body must know what he can actually expect of it. For one person that may be a leading place in the Ironman in Hawaii, for someone else it may be successfully finishing a novice triathlon. Muscles and organs tune their level of fitness to everyday activities and for most people that involves little physical work. Anyone requiring more of their body must gradually accustom it to this. A doctor can best judge one's standard of fitness. He tests the heart, the circulatory system, metabolism and joints and can in this way discover damage of which the athlete is possibly not aware, but which could pose a danger to health if put under great strain.

This applies not only to beginners, but also for advanced performance athletes.

Therefore anyone doing triathlon should undergo a medical check-up. The greater the physical strain and the older the triathlete is, the more important regular medical checks are. For high performance athletes check-ups have long been accepted practice. Admittedly it is easier for them. There are special sports medicine examination places for them; often these are sports medicine institutions of universities, and these top athletes also usually have medical consultants and care on location.

The great majority of triathletes must find their own doctor, and they will not always find one who is also a sports medicine specialist. An ideal situation is when triathlon clubs have a member with extensive sports medicine knowledge.

A blood analysis with the values of importance to triathlon (see chapter Blood Component Values) can be carried out by any general practitioner. In any case he will know which specialists one can turn to if nesessary. Often general practitioners do not have the equipment for the simplest and at the same time most informative general examination. It is therefore advisable to visit a sports doctor. (They can be found in the yellow pages under "Doctor - Sports medicine".)

If an athlete wants to swim, cycle and run as fast as possible in triathlon, i.e. enter races on a performance oriented basis, training must be planned accordingly. Training researchers have established that in addition to the amount and frequency of training, intensity plays a decisive role in endurance training.

For beginners in endurance sport it matters little how they train, every kind of movement training leads to a measurable improvement in performance. At some stage the point is reached where more training no longer results in improvement. Now the amount and intensity of training must be precisely laid down according to the sporting objective. If training of basic endurance and fat metabolism is desired, optimum training intensity is around the aerobic threshold. If, however, speed endurance is to be improved, the anaerobic threshold is the decisive criterion.

There are two ways to find these thresholds: the ergometer test and the Conconi test.

Ergometer Test

Ergometry is the measurement of physical working performance. Erg is the physical unit for measuring work. For measurement a bicycle ergometer or a treadmill is used.

On the bicycle ergometer it is possible to carry out the following measurement without interruption of the strain applied:
- physical capacity in Watts,
- pulse rate,
- blood pressure,
- lactic acid level in the blood.

For triathletes the comparison with earlier ergometer tests is especially interesting, so this should be carried out at least once every spring. It is recommended that a blood analysis be carried out in conjunction with this test. In order to correctly judge maximum performance capacity, it is important that the triathlete exerts himself to the full in this test. As a rule that means that after an ECG at rest the strain on the bicycle ergometer begins at 100 Watt and is increased by 50 Watt every 3 minutes, until the athlete has reached his physical limit. All necessary measurements are made during exertion, including taking blood from the earlobe to determine the concentration of lactic acid.

The assessment of performance capacity, or level of fitness, is done using the formula: maximum performance in Watt, divided by current body weight in kg. For years now my personal value at the beginning of March has been 5.0 (400 Watt/80 kg).

The Institute of Sport Medicine at the University of Münster classifies performance capacity/fitness thus:

"The normal performance capacity of a man aged 20-30 is about 3 Watt/kg, of a woman the same age 2.5 Watt/kg. The values decrease by one per cent for every year over 30.

Performance guidelines:
- 3 Watt/kg - not endurance trained
- 4 Watt/kg - well-trained in popular sport
- 5 Watt/kg - very good endurance athlete
- 6 Watt/kg - absolutely top level athlete."

In order to judge one's physical resilience properly it is useful to look at comparative data from everyday life.

For a person with a normal weight of 70 kg the following values apply:
- 25 Watt walking very slowly
- 59 Watt walking normally
- 75 Watt walking quickly
- 100 Watt relaxed jogging.

Normal daily strain on a person, including in their occupation - without real physical strain - does not exceed 75 Watt.

Measurement of the level of lactic acid in the blood during the ergometer test is done in the last 15 seconds of each three minute exertion phase. For the intensity of endurance training the lactic acid level in the blood at the value of 4 mmol/l is especially important. It represents the so-called aerobic-anaerobic threshold.

The performance in Watt achieved at this value on the bicycle ergometer or running machine is called the threshold value and is a measurement of basic endurance. The threshold value can thus provide information on training condition resp. on aerobic endurance capability. The threshold value of untrained persons is lower than that of trained athletes. According to the University of Münster the threshold value of untrained men is about 2.5 Watt/kg.

A lactic acid concentration of 2 mmol/l is defined as an aerobic threshold, a level of 4 mmol/l as an anaerobic threshold.

Conconi Test

Measuring lactic acid is a complicated and costly matter, and can only be carried out in relatively few institutes. If the measurement is carried out directly after days of hard training it creates the illusion of an improvement in performance capacity. The reason is the more or less emptied state of the glycogen stores.

A method every triathlete can carry out themselves, assuming they have a pulse measurer, is the so-called Conconi test. This test, named after the Italian biophysicist Professor CONCONI, determines the anaerobic threshold just as the more complicated lactic acid measurement does. It can be carried out by a runner on a track or a cyclist on the road. On top of that, the test can be done in 30-40 minutes and provides directly available results which can be immediately incorporated into training practice.

On the running track the procedure is as follows: prerequisites are a 400 m track, a stopwatch, a pulse measurer and two people to record the data. With a Polar pulse measurer it is now even possible to carry out the measurements alone. The Conconi test on the running track should, however, be carried out at least two days after the last intensive training session, not during digestion and of course while wearing racing clothing. The test using simple pulse measurers has the following steps:

before the test, 3-4 km warm-up running. Here the pulse should not rise above 130. Measuring points in the stadium: 200 m and 400 m marks. The starting pace is very relaxed. Athletes who can run 10 km in 38 minutes or less begin with 60 seconds for the first 200 m. Otherwise one should begin with 70 seconds. Every 200 m after that the pace should be gradually increased, in each case by two seconds, until further acceleration is no longer possible.

At the 200 m mark the running time of the segment and the pulse - called out by the athlete - are recorded. From the regularly collected data the speed can be calculated $v = s/t$. With a distance of 200 m and the conversion from m/s into km/h the following values are arrived at:

$v = 200 \times 3.6/$time for the 200 m section;

e.g. $v1 = 200 \times 3.6/60 = 12$ km/h;

$v2 = 200 \times 3.6/58 = 12.41$ km/h.

These results are entered on a graph. On the horizontal axis the speed in km/h, on the vertical axis the corresponding pulse rates. The resulting coordinates are joined using a ruler. Two lines arise, however, a more steep one in the lower area, a flatter one above. Before the intersection of the lines the body is working aerobically, after it anaerobically.

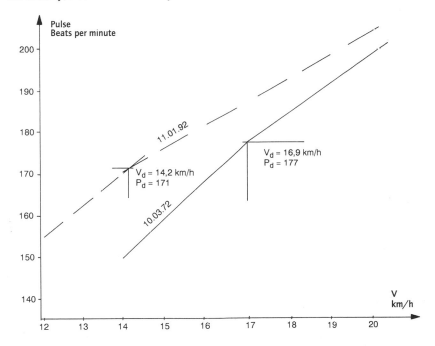

Pulse rate performance curve of 31 year old Frank Schumann

Conconi Test

11.1 Running time	t 200 m Time	Pulse	km/h Pulse v = 720 t	10.3 Running time	t 200 m Time	Pulse	km/h Pulse v = 720 t
0:59	59s	156	12.20	0:57	57s	143	12.63
1:54	55	161	13.09	1:48	51	153	14.12
2:49	55	159	13.09	2:39	51	151	14.12
3:43	54	162	13.33	3:28	49	153	14.69
4:37	54	165	13.33	4:17	49	157	14.69
5:30	53	167	13.58	5:04	47	164	15.32
6:21	51	171	14.11	5:49	45	166	16.00
7:10	49	173	14.69	6:34	45	172	16.00
7:57	47	176	15.32	7:17	43	173	16.74
8:43	46	179	15.65	8:00	43	176	16.74
9:27	44	185	16.36	8:41	41	181	17.56
10:09	42	187	17.14	9:22	41	186	17.56
10:51	42	190	17.14	10:01	39	189	18.46
11:32	41	193	17.56	10:39	38	191	18.95
12:11	39	195	18.46	11:15	36	195	20.00
12:50	39	197	18.46				
13:28	38	200	18.94				
14:05	37	202	19.50				

Conconi calls the pulse rate found at the intersection of the two lines the pd value and the speed the vd value. This means that a running pace up to the intersecting values can be maintained over a longer period of time without excess muscle acidity arising.

This test should be repeated at regular intervals of about four weeks: if there is improvement (shift to the right), the training can be continued; if there is stagnation or worsening (shift to the left), the training programme can be amended.

Conconi Test with Bicycle Ergometer

This is done as follows: 15 minutes warm-up cycling. Begin with 15 km/h or 75 Watt. Keep the strain constant for three minutes. At the end of the exertion phase note pulse and speed or wattage. Increase by 3 km/h or 25 Watt until complete exhaustion. Evaluation as before.

Conconi Test with Bicycle on the Road

Determination of the anaerobic threshold is also possible on a 30 to 60 second cycling circuit.

The anaerobic threshold represents the upper limit of aerobic capacity. The higher this anaerobic threshold is, the faster the triathlete is; also over a longer period of time. The anaerobic threshold is at roughly 85 per cent of maximum capacity. The accompanying example demonstrates that this is really only a rough estimate. Training below or at the anaerobic threshold guarantees maximum improvement of physical fitness. A strain above this limit leads very quickly to excessive exhaustion. There is thus a thin line between optimum training intensity and over training. If the anaerobic threshold is very close to the maximum strain e.g. 181:174, the athlete has a high level of basic endurance or stamina, in other words he is in very good shape. Here energy is provided aerobically for a very long time. If the difference between the pulse values is relatively great e.g. 181:150, there is room for improvement of the athlete's basic endurance. More about how this can be done is in the chapter: Basic Endurance.

Sporting Evaluation of the Conconi Curves Possible

The anaerobic threshold of athletes who are untrained, or are very well-trained, in speed endurance will be at a lower level of strain than that of someone very well-trained in endurance as a whole.

Anyone who regularly takes part in Conconi tests and compares the performance curves shown will see these changes:

- Flat curve

  A flat curve shows improved basic endurance. The anaerobic threshold is only reached after high performance (speed).
- Steep curve

  This can occur when one changes from mainly aerobic basic training to intensive anaerobic training.
- Shift to right or left

  A shift to the right indicates an improvement in performance, a shift to the left is a worsening of performance.
- No kink

  In late November my personal curve had no kink in it. This indicates a lack of speed endurance and anaerobic capacity. In the regeneration phase this is not surprising.

Conconi's Training Recommendations

CONCONi and LENZI have calculated intensities of strain for long distances after a Conconi test. The pulse value at the anaerobic threshold is assumed as 100 per cent.

Method of training:	long jog	70-80%	90 - 150 minutes
	slow jog	80%	50 - 90 minutes
	medium jog	85-90%	30 - 50 minutes
	fast run	95%	20 - 30 minutes
	speed run	97-103%	10 - 20 minutes

According to K. HOTTENROTT the following pulse rate and speed values are possible during races:

Race	Vd in %	Pd in %
Marathon	88	92
10 km	94	100
5 km	100	102

All of the 65 people tested by K. HOTTENROTT had specifically prepared themselvs for their particular distance and achieved the above mentioned values. For a 10 km run this therefore means: after optimum preparation the pulse value should be exactly 100% of the Pd value determined in the test beforehand. The speed should be 94% of the Vd value.

For 31 year old Frank SCHUMANN the values to be reached in a 10 km run on 15.3. should have been:

Pulse value   100% of 177 = 177
Running speed   94% of 16.9 km/h = 15.89 km/h

How often particular training intensities should be chosen for a certain triathlete is determined by consideration of the training phase and the current physical condition of the athlete.

Precise pulse rate measurement with the aid of a pulse measurer

Training Forms

There are triathletes who like to place demands on themselves in regular training and in this way achieve their performance. Others only train according to their gut feeling and let things come as they will. Finally there are athletes who see everything very casually and are as good as they can be with their own method.

Training by Feeling

Relying only on one's feeling in triathlon is more than risky in two ways.

On the one hand the athlete runs the risk of not being able to make the most of his sporting abilities owing to monotonous and slow training. This actually happens more rarely. What more often happens is that training is carried out too intensively over long distances. In the younger triathlon generation in particular, endurance training is understood as a "full steam ahead" from the first to the last kilometre. In some cases the result of their daily exhausting training sessions is regular disappointment after races. The individual times in the longingly wished for triathlon race are no better than in normal training. The reasons are obvious. These athletes have "shot their bolt" in training already and cannot improve themselves further in competition. These symptoms are observed particularly frequently among athletes who train alone or in cases where attention is not paid to differing abilities within a group and everyone is oriented to the strongest athlete. It is clear that the others want to, or "have to", prove themselves. In training at least they want to be as fast as their top athlete. With an attitude like this athletes will not enjoy endurance sport for very long. What fun is it when every run, every cycle tour turns into a speed rush?

Others, training alone, feel themselves constantly under pressure and think that only through hard, intensive training can I become faster and manage to keep up with the great competitor. These people not only injure themselves frequently, they actually burn out physically and psychologically.

As can be seen, successfully training and relying on one's gut feeling is a very risky game, unless the triathlete provides himself with a very precise picture of his strain level in training by carrying out pulse measurements at regular intervals. Another possibility is to carry out training sessions with staggered intensity. Both methods together with a sufficient amount of self-criticism can provide for balanced training. For beginners, however, this is likely to be especially difficult. Unless, that is, these still inexperienced athletes come across a training partner who has both experience and specialised knowledge.

Training with Staggered Intensity

In this form of training the best performance in each case in the particular discipline is 100%.

Examples:

Swimming:	1,000 m in 15 min.	= 1:30 min. per 100 m
	1,000 m in 20 min.	= 2:00 min per 100 m
Cycling:	40 km in 1:00 h	= 40 km/h
	40 km in 1:06 h	= 36.36 km/h
Running:	10 km in 35:00 min.	= 3:30 min./km
	10 km in 40:00 min.	= 4:00 min./km

Basic endurance training is carried out in the region of 65-90% of the best time in each case. Running 10 km in 40:00 min. = 4:00 min./km at 90% intensity means a kilometre average of 4.44 min., which corresponds to 4:24 min./km. At an intensity of 70% that would be 5:12 min./km (see Table 1).

Basic endurance training is linked with long training distances. According to NEUMANN/PFÜTZNER, this is more than 2,000 m in swimming, more than 80 km in cycling and more than 20 km in running. Extra long training sessions are done at the lowest level of intensity (65-70%).

Interval training is done in the region of 100%, e.g. 6 x 1,000 m running, 10 x 100 m swimming, 5 x 3 km cycling. Training of the fat metabolism should be carried out in the intensity area of 65-70%.

In order to differentiate the levels, not only numerically but also language wise, in the training schedules I take the following graduation as a base:

100% = race speed	80% = brisk training
95% = very hard training	75% = easy training
90% = hard training	70% = calm training
85% = very brisk training	65% = very calm training

Which intensities are possible in competition? These are of course dependent on the distances.

Over the short distance these are:
swimming >= 95%, cycling >= 95% and running 90%.
Over the middle distance:
swimming 90%, cycling 90% and running 90%.
Over the ultra distance:
swimming 90%, cycling 90% and running 80%.

Table 1:

Running Best time over Times per	10.000 m: 1.000 m	35:00 3:30	40:00 4:00	45:00 min 4:30
Intensities in %	100	3:30	4:00	4:30
	95	3:40	4:12	4:43
	90	3:51	4:24	4:57
	85	4:01	4:36	5:10
	80	4:12	4:48	5:24
	75	4:22	5:00	5:37
	70	4:33	5:12	5:51
	65	4:43	5:24	6:04

Swimming Swimming best times over	1.000 m:	14:00	18:00	22:00 min
Intensities in %	100	14:00	18:00	22:00
	95	14:42	18:54	23:06
	90	15:24	19:48	24:12
	85	16:06	20:42	25:18
	80	16:48	21:36	26:24
	75	17:30	22:30	27:30
	70	18:12	23:24	28:36
	65	18:54	24:18	29:42

Cycling Cycling best times over	40 km:	40	38	36	34 km/h
Intensities in %	100	40.0	38.0	36.0	34.0
	95	38.0	36.1	34.2	32.3
	90	36.0	34.2	32.4	30.6
	85	34.0	32.3	30.6	28.9
	80	32.0	30.4	28.8	27.2
	75	30.0	28.5	27.0	25.5
	70	28.0	26.6	25.2	23.8
	65	26.0	24.7	23.4	22.1

When training with staggered intensity, the training weeks must of course also be considered. Those who do not wish to rely on gut feeling but who do not have a pulse measurer available should also stagger the training weeks with respect to the training intensity. This is dependent on the training period.

So far as the intensity and the amount of training is concerned, I like to create three categories of training weeks:

"N" - the "normal" training week

"H" - the "hard" training week

"R" - the "regenerative" training week At the beginning of the year, during the preparatory period, the N and R weeks alternate.

Beginning with N:R through N:N:R to N:N:N:R.

The athlete obviously needs a little sensitivity to make sure that the total strain of training, work and private obligations is not too high. During block training H weeks appear for the first time. Then, however, in the proportion: N.H:R, resp. H:H:R during a two week training camp in southern regions (northern hemisphere)

For the competition period the combination is: N:H:R.

After triathlon races it should be:

After a short triathlon: R:N:H

After a middle triathlon: R:R:N:H

After an ultra triathlon: R:R:R:N:H

More details can be found in the training schedules.

Training by Pulse Measurement

The training of a triathlete can best be regulated with regular pulse measurement, i.e measurement of the heart rate. Our training increases the demands on the body. The whole organism adapts to these changed conditions. This fact can be observed in the heart, circulatory system, blood, lungs, muscle systems and the metabolism. Triathlon only leads to an adaptation of the organism however when a certain stimulus threshold has been reached. If the strain is too high it can cause injury and over time lead to physical and psychological damage.

How much strain should you put on yourself as a triathlete in order to get the greatest possible training result? Maximum performance capacity or fitness can serve as a yardstick, this can be seen from the pulse. The more beats per minute, the harder the heart muscle is working. As a comparison the average strain on a person is about 30% of their maximum performance capacity. To increase performance you need to train at an intensity of 50-80%.

The following influence the optimum pulse: age, fitness, sex, heart size and the total constitution of the athlete.

The heartbeat can be measured as follows:
- At the pulse: two or three fingers are placed on the inside of the wrist below the thumb, e.g. the pulse beats are counted for 15 seconds and multiplied by 4. The result is the pulse in beats per minute.
  Example: when measuring the pulse at rest 12 beats are counted in 15 seconds. This equals a pulse at rest of 12 x 4 = 48 beats per minute.
  After training 35 beats are counted in 15 seconds.
  This equals a pulse under strain of 35 x 4 = 140 beats per minute.
- At the throat: middle and index finger are placed sideways on the throat, a little below the jaw.
- With a pulse measurer: this measurement with a so-called pulse coach provides the most exact readings. This method is becoming popular not only among top athletes. These devices (priced from 199,- DM upwards) provide the possibilty to read the pulse at any time during training. On top of that you can have the pre-set minimum and maximum pulse announced with a beep. More expensive devices can even be connected to a computer in order to show the pulse graphically.

Pulse at Rest

A triathlete's pulse at rest is very much dependent on the size of the heart. If the heart is 500-600 cm³, the pulse at rest is 75, if the heart is 700-800 cm³ it is 62, if the heart is 950-1,000 cm³ it is only 50 and if the heart is 1,000-1,050 cm³ it is only 45 beats per minute. If the pulse at rest is under 40, the heart size is more than 1,100 cm³.

Because women have smaller hearts than men their heart beat at rest and under strain is higher.

The pulse at rest is measured early in the morning in complete calm in bed. Untrained healthy people have a pulse at rest of 65-80. Endurance trained athletes have a pulse at rest under 60, in the middle range even 40-50 beats per minute.

There is, however, no direct relationship between a low pulse at rest and sporting performance capacity.

Especially during the main training phase, every triathlete should regularly check his pulse at rest. If it is 5-8 or even 10 beats per minute higher than usual, then only regenerative training should be done. In Hawaii the situation is different. Because of the climatic conditions a higher pulse at rest is to be expected.

During swimming the pulse is on average 10-15 beats per minute slower than during running. Because of their lack of technique weak swimmers frequently do not achieve high pulse readings.

In cycling, pulse readings vary as a result of wind or hills more than they do in running.

Pulse readings in triathlon are thus a yardstick for the amount of strain. Up to a certain pulse rate the body gains its energy "aerobically" with the help of oxygen. Above this border rate energy is gained "anaerobically" without oxygen. This is accompanied by the production of lactic acid which collects in the muscle and leads to tiredness.

With the right training this threshold can be pushed upwards. This means that the muscles take longer to tire. The athlete can achieve higher performance over a longer period of time. The optimum training stimulus lies under this border rate. This is in turn dependent on age.

Table 2 gives guidlines.

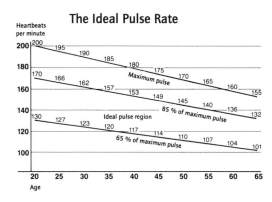

The aerobic region roughly covers the region between 65 and 85% of the maximum pulse, the anaerobic region covers the pulse readings between 85 and 100% of the maximum pulse.

So: aerobic region: about 65-85% of maximum pulse reading,
anaerobic region: about 85-100% of maximum pulse reading.

The anaerobic part of training is greater for athletes who race short distances than it is for athletes who race long distances. For older people too the anaerobic part of training should be less. The number of years of training and the number of training sessions also have an influence on the anaerobic proportion of training. But be careful! With increasing training intensity comes increased risk of injury.

Summary:

One can more or less carry out the determination of the anaerobic threshold (particulary important to triathletes) oneself during training with the help of a pulse measurer (exact terminology: heartbeat rate measuring device). The use of a pulse measurer does not mean that one should ignore one's own feeling when training.
A pulse measurer is not necessary for every training session.

Never train mindlessly according to a pulse formula (e.g. 85% of maximum pulse). The longer the training session is, the lower the pulse rate must be.

An example as illustration:
Assumption: using the Conconi test the approximate values have been confirmed. At which pulse values should a) a 25 year old athlete and b) a 45 year old athlete train?

(a) Approximate value: maximum pulse = 220 - age = 220 - 25 = 195.
  Rule of thumb: anaerobic threshold = 85% of 195 = 166 = pd 100 %
  Training recommendation according to CONCONI:
  5,000 m run at 166 pulse (fast jog)
  Improvement in aerobic endurance resp. basic endurance
  Time up to 1 hour: 85% of 166 = 141
  Time over 1 hour: 80% of 166 = 133
  Regeneration up to 45 min. 75% of 166 = 124

(b) Approximate value: max. pulse = 220 - 45 = 175
  Rule of thumb: anaerobic threshold = 85 % of 175 = 149 = pd 100%
  Training recommendation according to CONCONI:
  5,000 m run at 149 pulse (fast jog)
  Improvement in aerobic endurance resp. basic endurance
  Time up to 1 hour: 85% of 149 = 127
  Time over 1 hour: 80% of 149 = 119
  Regeneration up to 45 min. 75% of 149 = 112

At which pulse and which speed can one now run in various running races?
    According to the research by K. HOTTENROTT of the University of Marburg already mentioned, after optimum preparation these values are:

Marathon run: 92% of Pd and   88% of Vd
10 km run: 100% of Pd and   94% of Vd
5 km run: 102% of Pd and 100% of Vd
100 % Pd = pulse reading at the anaerobic threshold.
Vd is the matching running speed.

Recovery, or Minor Regeneration

By "minor regeneration" we mean the break between training stimuli, in contrast to the major regeneration that takes place in the transitional period.
    The break between two training sessions has an enormously important role for triathletes. In this period the body should recover from the previous training

session. If the break is too short, this invariably leads to over training. Breaks that are too long reduce performance. Both are a disadvantage to performance oriented athletes. The art of balanced triathlon training lies in finding the right proportion of training strain and recovery. Hard training days must alternate with light days. In the same way hard and light training weeks must be alternated. In finding the right balance one must not only consider the trainings themselves but also things such as occupational, family and other private demands. In other words, the entire environment of the athlete.

Creating a balanced training programme is thus quite a difficult undertaking. For this reason the following training suggestions need to be adapted by every triathlete to their own personal situation.

The following characteristics typify a balanced training programme:
a) the pulse at rest in the morning is practically constant,
b) one has the motivation to train.

Regeneration after Competition and Training

Regeneration or quick recovery is of great significance to triathletes. Those who regenerate quickly can begin their normal training programme earlier. They train more effectively and are thus capable of higher performance than those who already need a break of several days after hard training. When the sporting exertion is over, the used up energy reserves have to be refilled as quickly as possible. Used up protein has to be replaced. Sweating has led to a disruption of the water and electrolyte 'household'. Lactic acid and urea, the metabolism breakdown products, need to be removed as quickly as possible. Sufficient resting time leads to complete regeneration. The natural recovery period can be shortened if appropriate measures are taken. When the body receives liquid after the race, it is important to note that the sweat loss needs to be compensated for not only with water, but also with important minerals, e.g. with mineral water + apple juice + Kanne Brottrunk (a lactic acid fermented drink, see p. 219 and p. 231). After a triathlon or intensive training of one and a half hours close to the anaerobic threshold, the body's supplies of glycogen are exhausted. If a mixed diet follows, it takes about three days to replenish the glycogen stores, whereas with carbohydrate rich nutrition (see chapter: Nutrition of Triathletes) the extremely important replenishment only takes one day. After two or three days on a carbohydrate rich diet the stores are in fact too full, which is described as "super compensation".

The circulation in tired and exhausted muscles is worse as a result of the development of lactic acid and urea. Light to medium activities after the sporting exertion support the supply of oxygen and thus the circulation in the tired muscle systems.

For these reasons active regeneration is considerably more effective than passive regeneration. It therefore makes sense after a triathlon to jog around slowly for about 15 minutes, to slowly cycle around for 30 minutes and then to do some light stretching exercises. If you have the opportunity to take a 20 minute bath at 34°-37° within the first three hours after intensive exertion, or to visit a sauna or whirlpool, then do this. The physical stimuli improve the circulation of the muscle systems and thus help shorten the regeneration time.

After a race, the training sessions on the following days should be only of very low intensity. Swimming and cycling should be given preference to running as these sport forms put less strain on the body. Swimming has the shortest regeneration times because in races the strain on the muscles is relatively short.

Those who allow their body no regeneration and who also increase their training too quickly as well as participating in many competitions will sooner or later run into the problem of over training.

Over Training

Anyone doing triathlon in a performance oriented manner should take a close look at the risk of over training. Over training is the term used to describe a clear reduction in performance without being organically ill. It can be ascertained from the concentration of urea in the blood. If this value is above 50, the athlete is over trained.

Athletes are particularly at risk who:
- train too hard,
- train with too much intensity,
- do not allow themselves sufficient regeneration,
- participate in too many races,
- do not consider their occupational and private commitments when planning their training,
- do not have a sufficiently broad basis for their intensive training, i.e. have neglected basic endurance training,
- take the sport too "seriously".

Typical symptoms of over training are:
- higher pulse rate by 10-15 beats, higher blood pressure,

- lack of concentration, depression,
- unusually distracted behaviour, inability to relax,
- sweating at night, diarrhoea, constipation,
- frequent colds, fever,
- lack of strength in training,
- difficulty going to sleep,
- restless sleep at night,
- lack of desire to train, apathy,
- muscle and joint pains,
- questioning sports training,
- lack of appetite, loss of weight,
- drop in performance despite increased training.

Which measures are necessary to overcome over training, and what must be done to avoid it? Without any order of importance, these points are relevant:
- Only train regeneratively, i.e. in the lower intensity region 50-60%.
- Allow for more rest days.
  Take the addage "Sport should be fun" seriously.
- Train with more enjoyment, do not force it.
- Join a group that trains calmly.
- Have a "change of scene", i.e. take a holiday or short break.
- Only enter races after several months preparation with training in the lower and middle regions of intensity.
- Go without alcohol and nicotine.
- Reduce the amount of training to 50% in competition period.
- Absolutely carry out regeneration weeks after races.
- Keep a training journal, so you can monitor yourself.
- Choose a sufficiently long transitional period, one month for every decade of age.
- Get enough sleep, at least seven hours.
- Vary your training.
- Do not take every triathlon "deadly seriously", there are more important things in life than triathlon.
- Do not extend the triathlon season further with other races (cross country, marathons) or if you do, then "just for fun".
- Do not enter too many triathlon races in a season.
- Do not "go to the limit" in every triathlon you enter.
- Be able to miss a training session now and then without a bad conscience.
- After injury, increase training strain slowly.

Training Records

For every triathlete training records should simply become routine. While it is not of significance for triathlon itself, it is very important as an aid towards achieving optimum training progress. If you have written down your training sessions and preparations for earlier events, you can trace these back over several years and make better decisions as to how best to train and to plan for races. If, for example, you are excessively tired, you may find possible reasons in the training records and can thus make changes to the amount of training while there is still time, and so eliminate negative consequences. Training records help you not to make the same mistake twice. At the same time they give you a reassuring feeling like having money in a savings account. Every swimming, cycling and running kilometre represents a credit in your account which annually earns interest in the form of improved triathlon results.

Not only the amount of training is important when making entries, but also the intensity. Also important now and then are data such as body weight and pulse rate.

For both pulse and weight you should always measure at the same time of day, e.g. weight in the morning after ablutions, pulse at rest before getting up.
Under "Notes" you should write down anything that is important or could be important, such as the weather - wind, rain, gradients, new shoes or going to bed late. Weekly performance should never increase rapidly, therefore these details are of great importance.

Training Planning

Triathlon training which is monotonous in intensity and amount does not allow the athlete any major improvement in performance. On the other hand, athletes who divide the year into periods with varying amounts and intensity of training experience considerable improvements in performance. A systematically structured year has three periods of differing length:
• Preparatory period
• Competition period
• Transitional period
The individual periods are also individually different in length for triathletes with differing ambitions.

For beginners the following periodisation is recommended.
(northern hemisphere):

Preparatory period:	February - May	4 months
Competition period:	June - September	4 months
Transitional period:	October - January	4 months

For competitive athletes the following periodisation is recommended.
(northern hemisphere):

Preparatory period:	February - May	4 months
Competition period:	June - October	5 months
Transitional period:	November - January	3 months

For performance athletes the following periodisation is recommended.
(northern hemisphere):

Preparatory period:	January - May	5 months
Competition period:	June - October	5 months
Transitional period:	Nov. - December	2 months

Older athletes, who on the whole need longer regeneration than younger athletes, should allow one month per decade of their life for the transitional period. Through this longer transitional period one also finds it easier to maintain the motivation for the coming sporting years. Fortunately endurance sport is a kind of sport that every healthy human being can carry out up to a very great age, this particularly applies to triathlon.

I can still see before me the presentation ceremony at the world championship in Muskoka, Canada in September 1992. In the M70 three American athletes jumped up onto the pedestal with a zest I wish some 20 year olds had. Another possibility is to take a so-called year of active rest after a number of intensive years.

Preparatory Period

The first section of the preparatory period is for creating basic endurance or stamina. This provides the basis for intensive training in the second section and in the competition period. At low to medium intensity the amount of strain is systematically increased. Nevertheless you must always remember recovery and regeneration as discussed above.

Training is mainly done by the long-term method. Because of the weather conditions, running and swimming will be trained most. Cross-country skiing and cycling on rolling devices also improve basic endurance. General fitness can also be improved through strength training in these months. Because of our weather conditions in the northern hemisphere at this time it is recommended for ambitious athletes to divide the winter-spring training into so-called blocks. An example: January swimming month, February running month, March cycling month. It is also possible to postpone everything by one month or to swap the running and the swimming month. More on this in the training recommendations.

A note before we start on training in the weakest discipline. This should be given preference, especially in the preparatory period. Unfortunately there is a slight catch here: this discipline is usually the least fun. There is a simple formula against that: make sure you train your weakest discipline in a suitable group. Here you overcome the initial difficulties more easily because the motivation in the group is greater and you yourself are distracted from your own lack of enthusiasm by easy going conversation in the group. Once you reach a certain standard in your weakest discipline you start to really enjoy it after all.

You have the best chances of achieving success if you train your weakest discipline at least three times a week. The second section of the preparatory period (6-8 weeks) is marked by a reduction of the amount and an increase in the intensity of training. Interval training, Fartlek in running or occasionally open cross-country races are possibilities for additional training variations.

When cycling in groups you can occasionally race to a town sign. Short distance triathletes also practise changing jerseys. Combination training, especially the change from cycling to running, are added to the programme in April. This helps deal with the transitions in competition better. Possible variations in combination training cycling-running:
- short, fast cycling unit + longer, more relaxed running
- longer, more relaxed cycling + short, quick run
- short, quick cycling + short, quick run.

In the whole preparatory period it is important to change between weeks of normal, hard and regenerative exertion (see training types). During the entire preparatory period there should always be one training session per week which lasts longer, but at reduced intensity. This does not necessarily apply to beginners. This could be a long run or a cycling tour of several hours. This trains the using up of fat energy, of particular importance to endurance athletes,

e.g.	Short distance triathlon:	20 km running or 80 km cycling
	Middle distance triathlon:	25 km running or 100 km cycling
	Ultra distance triathlon:	28-30 km running or 130-150 km cycling

Competition Period

For ambitious triathletes the competition period runs over 4 to 5 months of the year. It begins in late May with the first open air swimming pool triathlon events and runs until September, or October for those with Hawaii as their major objective.

No triathlete can be in top form during this entire period. It is therefore advisable to set oneself two, or at the most, three triathlon highlights.

In the first part of this period there are preliminary competitions. These give the athlete the opportunity to test fitness, material and also various tactics and nutritional habits in the field. Between the first test triathlons there will be a certain amount of intensive training, except for the last three days before events. Hard training sessions are followed by easy ones, and hard weeks by normal and easy or regenerative weeks. After every race it is important to make sure of sufficient regeneration. This is of course dependent on the length of the triathlon, on training condition and on the age of the competitor. Atheletes in very good training condition regenerate quicker than others. Younger athletes regenerate faster than older athletes. The intensity of the race also plays a role here. If this was 90% instead of the usual 100%, the recovery time will be considerably shorter.

For athletes with good endurance training, regeneration after a short distance triathlon will take about a week. After this they can train normally, but not hard. This does not, however, apply to beginners at all. After a middle distance triathlon regeneration takes two to three weeks, after an ultra distance triathlon it can take up to three or four weeks. In this time of course one should not participate in further events. Although I know this, I must confess that I personally have also "sinned" in this respect. The number of races per year is decided first and foremost according to their length, but also according to training condition, age and attitude. By attitude I mean the following:

There are a number of triathletes who go into races in a completely relaxed way and you can really see how they enjoy triathlon. That includes simply enjoying measuring their own ability with others in a fair competition, not fighting against them. Then there are others who take the whole thing extremely seriously, who think that triathlon is the most important thing in the world and put themselves under immense psychological pressure. They do not see at all that our sport is supposed to be fun. Once you have found your form in the course of the season and had it confirmed in races, you will mainly train very easily between further events. The amount of training will be reduced.

Transitional Period

The really quiet months for triathletes begin directly after the last race of the season. As this is usually also the last highlight of the season, the "tyres are flat" now, so to speak. Every triathlete now looks forward to the coming months of easy training. In this transitional season it is in no way advisable to quickly add on the beginning cross-country season. This might not cause any problems in the first one or two years, but sooner or later the body will claim its rest time in the form of injuries which often refuse to go away. Triathletes simply need major regeneration at the end of a season that has taken a toll on their strength. Now there is time to dedicate oneself to hobbies and pastimes which have not received enough attention over the years owing to lack of time. These hobbies should particularly include interpersonal contacts, i.e. increased contact with friends, acquaintances and of course one's own family. The transitional period varies in length for ambitious athletes. Beginners and older people should allow themselves a longer time out than young, professionally training athletes. In a nutshell, in this time the triathlete should recover both physically and psychologically and thus gather strength and motivation for the following season. The motivation factor is often underestimated.

No one who is not motivated can perform well. Motivation is a prerequisite for success in triathlon. It creates the willingness to train systematically.

Training is playfully relaxed and of a minimum amount. A few kilograms of winter fat are the right (external) sign of good regeneration for many triathletes. Naturally the extensive nutrition of the preparatory period must also be reduced, for the daily energy requirement is much less. One should also not omit a critical review of the whole season. Questions like: was the preparation correct, were the seasonal highlights well-chosen, did the triathlon results match my ability, was the amount and intensity of training right, did I successfully balance work, private life and sport, etc. Questions and more questions, to be answered critically.

Not to forget the most important question: were effort and benefit in the right proportions for me personally? In order not to forget these hopefully honest answers, it is worth noting them in writing in your training book. Without daily training records it is not possible to answer the questions outlined here.

Training and Competition Tips

Swimming

Swimming is the triathlon discipline which requires the most effort technically. A swimmer with good technique uses up much less energy than one who swims mainly with strength. If possible, technique training should take place under the direction of a swimming trainer after warming-up in a calm state. If there is no swimming trainer available, a suitable person among the triathletes themselves should observe training and call for any necessary changes.

As these days almost exclusively the crawl is swum, I will now go into some detail on basic crawl techniques. In my book "Handbook for Triathlon" I have already described extensively (pages 45 to 55, German edition) how to change successfully from breast stroke to crawl, and also the advantages and disadvantages of the crawl. The following points are therefore those which every triathlete should consider and constantly check. These are:

- make your body long, i.e. lie as high and horizontally in the water as possible;
- pull in your stomach;
- face in the water up to the forehead;
- swim with elbows high;
- bring the hands forward just above the water and turned slightly outwards;
- movement above water must be relaxed and easy;
- fingertips enter the water first, slightly outside the body axis; the arm is stretched;
- the surface area of the hand pushing down should always be maximum possible:
- the shoulder of the arm carrying out the stroke goes deeper into the water and adds to the pressure;
- after "grasping" the water the arm stroke should begin in reverse S form and get faster and faster;
- the movement is carried out by the hand, the elbow remains "still", it must not move backwards out of the way;
- at shoulder joint level the pressure phase begins;
- at the end of the arm stroke the hand still pushes back at hip level;
- ideally the arm should be almost stretched out: thumb - middle - thigh;
- one should only grasp quiet, still water, i.e. one practically pulls oneself along the water and then finally pushes away from it;
- the head is only turned to the side; it should not be turned away from the body axis;
- if the head is held too high the hips and legs sink accordingly and increase resistance;
- in open water one should therefore only briefly look at the objective after every 5-10 strokes;
- in triathlon foot kicking should only be used a a stabiliser; therefore swim with the feet across each other and turn the big toes slightly inwards;
- three phase breathing improves the situation in the water.

If there is no swimming trainer available, there are several ways to check one's swimming technique:

Training group members take turns to sit on the pool edge observing and correcting team members. While swimming one should take the opportunity to tell colleagues of mistakes observed under water.

Finally we triathletes have the possibility of watching very good swimmers training and memorising their potentially perfect crawl technique and later visualising it during training. That means: reeling off the perfect swimming style so far as this actually exists – before one's inner eye and then transferring it to one's own movements. Another method is to practise swimming movements in front of a mirror. Trainers' experience has shown that swimmers in front of a mirror make the same mistakes as in the water. In front of the mirror it is possible to train techniques and check on oneself, e.g. whether the hand is below the body axis or the elbow remains up front, or whether the pressing phase is maintained until the arm is stretched out.

In our highly technical age there is of course also the option of the video camera. After someone else has filmed several lengths of training, the pictures should be viewed on a screen during the same training session. In this way one can criticise oneself and, especially important, immediately make improvements. Mistakes must be eradicated as soon as they are noticed, otherwise they establish themselves more and more strongly. Those who swim properly leave the water with a good pulse rate and can make the best of their opportunities in the following disciplines.

The following calculations will show every triathlete why it is worth constantly polishing one's technique in order to glide through the water like a dolphin.

Fresh water has a density of 1.00 kg per litre, human beings have a density of 1.05 after breathing out. Breathing in increases the volume at the same weight, so that density is now only about 0.97. In this phase you cannot sink, unless larger parts such as head and shoulders are above water. It is well known that thrust in water is largest when all parts of the body are in the water. A person with

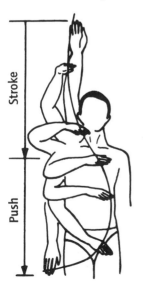

a relatively large amount of body fat has a lower density than a slim, wiry person. Fat just has a lower density than muscle fibre. With my height of 1.87 m and my weight of 77 kg (summer) I personally have to cover 802 body lengths over 1,500 m and 2,064 body lengths over 3,860 m. Over 3,860 m that is 77 kg x 2.064 = 158,928 kg = 158,928 tonnes. With every body length I thus have to push 77 kg of water aside. Over 1,500 m that is a water mass of 77 kg x 802 = 61,754 kg or about 62 tonnes. So, almost 62 tonnes over a short distance and 159 tonnes over the ultra distance. After these numbers, is it any wonder that swimming is such a slow way to move forwards? The calculation of the energy required of the swimmer is somewhat different.

Correct arm movement seen from below.

Frictional, front and eddy resistance must also be taken into consideration. This little game with numbers about the amount of water swimmers must push aside is designed to show how important it is to keep frontal resistance as low as possible by having as good a position in the water as possible. Having the lower body sink too deep in the water because the head is too high, and the hips bending off to the side, increase the frontal resistance and thus reduce speed in the water.

Swimming Training

The first triathlon discipline, swimming, is often the least loved. For this reason it is often given too little attention during training. Unfortunately I too belong to this category of triathlete. Instead of 7 km per week I just manage half of that on a yearly average.

I have, however, sworn to improve next season because while writing this book the advantages have become clear to me. Unfortunately there is often a gap between our knowledge of something and actually doing it.

It is not without reason that top people like Kalli NOTTRODT among others swim 15-20 km per week.

The advantages of extensive swimming training:

- Less risk of injury through excessive strain on joints, tendons and ligaments than in cycling and especially running.
- Short term anaerobic strain in water pushes the aerobic-anaerobic threshold further into the higher pulse region and allows the body higher performance capacity in cycling and running.
- In addition to the opportunity to improve technique and swim faster, extensive swimming training causes one to see every swimming distance in triathlon as easy so one can then go on to the cycling and running sections at full steam.
- In swimming it is not only a question of "When will I come out of the water?", but also "How will I come out of the water?".

In spite of all the useful tips and hints it must not be forgotten that for many athletes it takes up a great deal of time visiting swimming baths that may be 20 km and more from their homes. Because of impractical work and opening times it is often only possible to swim in overcrowded baths. It is understandable when athletes who must train under such conditions say: "I will train the bare minimum in swimming and concentrate more on cycling and running training."

This often unfavourable situation does not, however, contradict in any way the advantages of extensive training. They happen to be a reality and unfortunately, or as a comfort to all triathletes, thank goodness, all athletes must put up with unfavourable conditions of some kind in their environment.

Which swimming opportunities should triathletes use?

- Training groups in a swimming or triathlon club.
- The early morning. Many baths open at 6 a.m., and at this time people usually swim in a very disciplined manner.
- The evening after 7 p.m.
- In summer lakes are often available. For safety reasons always swim in twos and threes. Beginners who feel insecure in open water, or are even afraid, should train in open air swimming baths. In order to reduce these fears in open water, swimming in the area for non-swimmers, or quiet "bathing" in the company of a rubber boat or lilo can be helpful.

Performance oriented triathletes should master the crawl. There are many advantages:
- Fastest swimming stroke.
- Safest swimming stroke during mass starts because less space is required than for breast stroke.
- Spares the leg muscles for more effective use in cycling and running.
As a disadvantage one could mention that orientation is more difficult. For changing from breast stroke to crawl (or freestyle) the transitional period or the summer holidays are a good time, at a swimming lake.

In open air swimming baths one has the opportunity to observe one's own arm strokes.

Further Tips and Hints on Swimming Training

It is also advisable to practise three phase breathing outside the competition period. Three phase breathing means that after every third breath you breathe alternatively to right or left.

This more effective swimming technique can also be worked on in the winter months without the pressure to perform.

Three phase breathing has the advantages of better orientation and a more favourable position in the water. Learning this technique should be done without a stopwatch or other pressure, but at a quick pace so that the hips do not bend away or the body sinks.

Remember: you do not learn to drive a car at 130 km/h!

Generally the Following applies to the whole season:

- The effectiveness of the arm strokes can be measured by simply counting the number of swimming movements per length.
- Never work against the water, but with it.
- Try to find swimming partners of the same speed ability.
- To check your own technique swim a few lengths practising four or five phase breathing. These breathing exercises are important and make three phase breathing easier. Check your own arm strokes under water.
- Whether doing sprints, easy endurance swimming or bathing, always watch out for optimum technique.
- Swimming paddles in training give a good feeling for a clean stroke and push phase.
- Try to always stay relaxed when swimming. Include a few easy lengths too. Often these are not so slow after all.
- Always train with variety, i.e. never swim the same intervals twice in one week.
- Never fall into a monotonous rut. If you always swim the same distances at the same speed you will never get faster.
- Warm-up and cool down swimming exercises are well suited as special arm stroke exercises.
- Begin and finish swimming with changes of position.
- Shortly before finishing swimming have a 1 x 50 m training race.
- Include a longer endurance swim at least every second week, e.g. 1,500 m, 2,000 m, 2 x 1,000 m, 3 x 1,000 m. Either with as even a pace as possible, as in a triathlon, or else the first half of each length more powerfully, followed by the second half more quietly and longer. Fartlek in the water with changes of frequency.
- Whenever possible train swimming in groups. In the mid to long-term always swimming alone can be demotivating.

- Use open water swimming for quiet endurance swimming, never swim alone. Measure intervals by counting the arm strokes, e.g. 50 fast strokes, 20 easy strokes.
- Only wear neoprene suits during training in cool water temperatures and a few times before races. Constantly training in a neoprene suit reduces swimming times in triathlons because the training effect is not great enough.

Suggestions for Training

Generally: Stretching + 300 m warm-up + training + 200 m cool down + stretching.
Intervals: 8 x 200 m alternating very quickly/calmly
     5 x 100 m with 30 s break between + 500 m timed + 100 m
     pyramid swimming with 30 s breaks
     50/100/150/200/250/200/150/100/50 m   ·
     3-4 x 500 m relaxed and very quickly, alternating
     200, 300, 500, 300, 200 m with 30-60 s breaks
Additonally: technique training with pull buoys, board, paddles
Test to check condition: 1 x each month 30 minutes for beginners, 60 minutes for well-trained athletes
    This endurance swimming should be carried out at maximum intensity without interruption.
    Particularly recommendable as group training owing to higher motivation.
Endurance swimming: beginning and finish as above:
2,000 m, 2 x 1,000 m, 4 x 500 m, 1,500 m, 3,000 m
In a lake: Beginning and finish as above:
Endurance swimming,
     100 strokes quickly, 100 strokes relaxed,
     200 strokes quickly, 100 strokes relaxed.
     1 x lake width very quickly, 1 x lake length relaxed,

Special competition tips for swimming
- Arrive very early.
- Check out the starting area well before the start.
- Make sure you understand the exact course well before the start. Which buoys must you swim around?
- 10 minutes before the start do warm-up swimming.
- Locate orientation aids plenty of time in advance (buoys, buildings, towers, trees in the background and similar).
- Place yourself realistically in the starting field.
- Try as quickly as possible to get into a good swimming position - one in which you can swim realatively unhindered. I personally accept longer distances to get this.
- Find your own swimming rhythm.

- Do not swim at the shoulder level of other athletes because the stirred up water can easily get in your mouth during the breathing phase. It is better to swim at the other's hip level. It supports optimum gliding in the water.
- Head for your own orientation marks. Do not rely on the person in front of you.
- After every 5-10 double three phase breaths orientate yourself briefly.
- Concentrate on your own technique.

SPEED TABLE   SWIMMING

Distance	100 m average							
	1:10	1:15	1:20	1:25	1:30	1:35	1:40	1:45
200 m	0:02:20	0:02:30	0:02:40	0:02:50	0:03:00	0:03:10	0:03:20	0:03:30
400 m	0:04:40	0:05:00	0:05:20	0:05:40	0:06:00	0:06:20	0:06:40	0:07:00
600 m	0:07:00	0:07:30	0:08:00	0:08:30	0:09:00	0:09:30	0:10:00	0:10:30
800 m	0:09:20	0:10:00	0:10:40	0:11:20	0:12:00	0:12:40	0:13:20	0:14:00
1000 m	0:11:40	0:12:30	0:13:20	0:14:10	0:15:00	0:15:50	0:16:40	0:17:30
1200 m	0:14:00	0:15:00	0:16:00	0:17:00	0:18:00	0:19:00	0:20:00	0:21:00
1400 m	0:16:20	0:17:30	0:18:40	0:19:50	0:21:00	0:22:10	0:23:20	0:24:30
1600 m	0:18:40	0:20:00	0:21:20	0:22:40	0:24:00	0:25:20	0:26:40	0:28:00
1800 m	0:21:00	0:22:30	0:24:00	0:25:30	0:27:00	0:28:30	0:30:00	0:31:30
2000 m	0:23:20	0:25:00	0:26:40	0:28:20	0:30:00	0:31:40	0:33:20	0:35:00
2200 m	0:25:40	0:27:30	0:29:20	0:31:10	0:33:00	0:34:50	0:36:40	0:38:30
2400 m	0:28:00	0:30:00	0:32:00	0:34:00	0:36:00	0:38:00	0:40:00	0:42:00
2600 m	0:30:20	0:32:30	0:34:40	0:36:50	0:39:00	0:41:10	0:43:20	0:45:30
2800 m	0:32:40	0:35:00	0:37:20	0:39:40	0:42:00	0:44:20	0:46:20	0:49:00
3000 m	0:35:00	0:37:30	0:40:00	0:42:30	0:45:00	0:47:30	0:50:00	0:52:30
3200 m	0:37:20	0:40:00	0:42:40	0:45:20	0:48:00	0:50:40	0:53:20	0:56:00
3400 m	0:39:40	0:42:30	0:45:20	0:48:10	0:51:00	0:53:50	0:56:40	0:59:30
3600 m	0:42:00	0:45:00	0:48:00	0:51:00	0:54:00	0:57:40	1:00:00	1:03:00
3800 m	0:44:20	0:47:30	0:50:40	0:52:50	0:57:00	1:01:10	1:03:20	1:06:30
4000 m	0:46:40	0:50:00	0:53:20	0:55:40	1:00:00	1:04:20	1:06:40	1:10:00

Distance	100 m average						
	1:50	1:55	2:00	2:05	2:10	2:15	2:20
200 m	0:03:40	0:03:50	0:04:00	0:04:10	0:04:20	0:04:30	0:04:40
400 m	0:07:20	0:07:40	0:08:00	0:80:00	0:08:40	0:09:00	0:09:20
600 m	0:11:00	0:11:30	0:12:00	0:12:30	0:13:00	0:13:30	0:14:00
800 m	0:14:40	0:15:20	0:16:00	0:16:40	0:17:20	0:18:00	0:18:40
1000 m	0:18:20	0:19:10	0:20:00	0:20:50	0:21:40	0:22:30	0:23:20
1200 m	0:22:00	0:23:00	0:24:00	0:25:00	0:26:00	0:27:00	0:28:00
1400 m	0:25:40	0:26:20	0:28:00	0:29:10	0:30:20	0:31:30	0:32:40
1600 m	0:29:20	0:30:40	0:32:00	0:33:20	0:34:40	0:36:00	0:37:20
1800 m	0:33:00	0:34:20	0:36:00	0:37:30	0:39:00	0:40:30	0:42:00
2000 m	0:36:40	0:38:20	0:40:00	0:41:40	0:43:20	0:45:30	0:46:40
2200 m	0:40:20	0:42:10	0:44:00	0:45:50	0:47:40	0:49:30	0:51:20
2400 m	0:44:00	0:46:00	0:48:00	0:50:00	0:52:00	0:54:00	0:56:00
2600 m	0:47:40	0:49:50	0:52:00	0:54:10	0:56:20	0:58:30	1:00:40
2800 m	0:51:20	0:53:40	0:56:00	0:57:20	1:00:40	1:03:00	1:05:20
3000 m	0:55:00	0:57:30	1:00:00	1:01:30	1:05:00	1:07:30	1:10:00
3200 m	0:58:40	1:01:20	1:04:00	1:05:40	1:09:20	1:12:00	1:14:40
3400 m	1:02:20	1:05:10	1:08:00	1:09:50	1:13:40	1:16:30	1:19:20
3600 m	1:06:00	1:09:00	1:12:00	1:14:00	1:18:00	1:21:00	1:24:00
3800 m	1:09:40	1:12:50	1:16:00	1:18:10	1:22:20	1:25:30	1:28:40
4000 m	1:13:20	1:46:40	1:20:00	1:22:20	1:26:40	1:30:00	1:33:20

Cycling

Cycling takes up the greatest proportion of the total time of every triathlon distance. The same applies to regular cycling training. Therefore one should consider: "Are there opportunities for me to do part of my time cycling training when doing other things e.g. on my way to work?" In the afternoon or evening you can extend the journey home as you wish and thus gain considerable time. When cycling, most of the body's weight is borne by the buttocks. Thus the strain on the holding and supporting apparatus of the body is small. Even when standing on the pedals the orthopaedic strain is considerably less than when running. For these reasons active recovery training can be carried out on a racing bike. The same applies to swimming. Regenerative training, after races or hard training sessions, should last 45-60 minutes at the most. Relaxed and easy peddling is called for. Because of the low level of orthopaedic strain on the body in cycling especially long training sessions are possible. This is particularly important for triathletes who do the ultra distance. If a body is only ever put under strain for one or two hours, it will have great problems when called on to endure nine, ten, eleven, twelve or more hours of exertion. Cycling is more suitable than any other sport for training the metabolism of fat.

As a rule after two and a half to three hours the glycogen supplies have been emptied so much that the body turns to burning fat in order to get energy. This biological process can create quite considerable problems for athletes. Triathletes who frequently break through this threshold in training hardly notice the change from glycogen to fat utilisation in competition.

Fat Metabolism Training

Fat metabolism is of great importance, in particular to medium and ultra distance triathletes because there is only about 2,400 kcal of energy in the glycogen supplies. Fat metabolism makes energy from fat combustion available for sporting movement. This is needed when the glycogen supplies are insufficient. We humans have huge potential available to us in the fat reservoirs of our bodies. With my body weight of 78 kg in summer and a fat content of 14.5% (measurable by a doctor) this is 11.31 kg of fat. 1 kg of fat provides 9,000 kcal of energy. That means that theoretically 11.31 x 9,000 = 101,790 kcal of energy is available to me from fat combustion. At an energy consumption of a maximum of 1,000 kcal per hour in a triathlon theoretically more than 100 hours of movement are possible. In competitions, which are longer than the "basic" ultra distance the energy consumption per hour of course sinks considerably. Apart from that, such distances, are not first and foremost an energy problem.

Fats, however, only burn in the fire of carbohydrates. This means that at certain intensities the combustion of glycogen and fats takes place in parallel. Therefore triathletes must take into consideration that fat metabolism only takes place at slow or medium intensity. Under this relatively low strain fat metabolism, with the aid of enzymes or fermenters, only takes place in those muscle fibres which are active during slow to medium exertion (ST and FTO endurance fibres). So, the more the muscles are trained in aerobic endurance, the larger the local energy reserve is as a result of fat metabolism. If one trains at higher intensity the wrong muscle fibres (speed fibres FTG), and the wrong metabolism channels (carbohydrate metabolism), are trained. Carbohydrate metabolism under use of the speed fibres is addressed in interval training. Pulse rates during fat metabolism are usually around 130. Because each group of muscles needs to have its own fat metabolism training, the following is recommended:

In swimming fat metabolism is trained during warm-up and cool down swimming, also in calm endurance sessions and between intervals. Fat metabolism training presents the least problems in cycling. Only a little intensity (with medium exertion) is necessary, over a period of more than 1 1/2 hours. The pulse should be about 130.

The same applies to running training. At a pulse rate of about 130 fat metabolism is trained in the lower jogging region over a period of 2-3 hours. Combined fat metabolism training with 2-3 hours of cycling under medium strain, and a calm 12 km run directly after cycling, is very effective.

Nutrition during Cycling

A short distance triathlon is already a full grown endurance discipline, the middle and long distance triathlons even more so of course. The body uses up lots of energy in these. This energy must be partially replaced during the course of the race. In swimming this is usually not possible, except over a double ironman distance where the swimming is often carried out in open air baths. During running solid nutrition can be taken in to a limited extent, but because of the time available it can hardly be converted into energy.

It is therefore most sensible for athletes to eat and drink while cycling. If possible this should be easily digestible, e.g.: bananas, biscuits, low-fat high-protein energy bars such as PowerBar, Kanne Kraftriegel, and abundant drinks. I have always found my energy drink very good, consisting of Kanne Brottrunk + apple juice + Kanne Fermentgetreide (fermented grain). As many organisers provide electrolyte drinks that are very concentrated and lead to diarrhoea, my advice is to drink a bottle of water for every bottle of electrolyte drink consumed. In the course of a 180 km ride every athlete should eat some bananas, biscuits and energy bars, in small portions and well-chewed, accompanied by sufficient liquids. All of this must of course be practised during long training rides.

Aerodynamics

Good aerodynamics reduce air resistance. To achieve this it is not enough to merely possess an ultra modern, ultra expensive racing bike and then neglect all other important factors. First of all one thing: air resistance doubles with speed. In concrete terms that means: at a speed of 42 km/h air resistance is already twice as high as at 30 km/h.

Thus it is important to consider further points such as:

- Close fitting cycling clothing.
- Keeping the knees close to the crossbar and parallel to the frame.
- Handle bars as low as possible.
- As much of the forearms as possible resting on the triathlon handle bars.
- Mount cycling bottles behind the saddle.
- For short distances carry a drinking system if practical.
- Keep upper body as still as possible. In the higher gears the upper body begins to rock.

Some other important things about cycling training in brief:

- Always ride with a helmet.
- Have spare tubes with you.
- Mount a number of bottle holders on the bike.
- Try to keep to optimum rpm of 100-110.
- Take sufficient liquids and food on longer training rides.
- Always have something edible with you to avoid hunger stops.
- Change gear early enough on upward gradients.

Good aerodymnamics are a great advantage.

- In the first two months of the preparatory period only cycle with the chain on the smaller cog.
- Sunglasses protect against sun, insects and wind.
- First increase the amount of training, then the intensity.
- In one day you can carry out endurance training after strength training - but not vice versa.
- Keep to normal, hard and regeneration weeks.
- When doing interval training make sure you have 15-20 minutes of warm-up and cool down cycling.

Safety on the Racing Bike

In triathlon races, wearing a helmet is compulsory. Two statistics show how right and important this is. In 1991 in the "old" federal states of Germany alone more than 700 cyclists died on our roads. 64,000 were injured, some badly. It will be obvious to anyone that at 51%, head injuries top the sad list of injuries. We athletes on our racing bikes are particularly at risk, in an accident our head and shoulders go down first. It must therefore be clear to every triathlete that a helmet should be an essential part of their standard equipment. This applies of course not only to races, in which the roads are mostly closed off to other traffic, but even more so to our numerous training rides.

In today's traffic density our motto must be:

NOT A SINGLE METRE WITHOUT A HELMET!

In addition, with our helmet we triathletes set an example to other cyclists. Fortunately this realisation has been accepted by most when the safety of children is concerned. Anyone who is of a different opinion may change their mind on reading about this sad incident: A 46 year old triathlete lent his cycling helmet to a younger colleague for a triathlon. He himself then wanted to ride his racing bike a mere 800 m to the cycling track to cheer his protegé on. On the way there he was hit by a car and injured so badly that two and a half years later he is still in a coma. Helmets with a TÜV seal are not enough for triathletes. Triathlon helmets must satisfy either the American ANSI Z 90,4 or the Snell norm. It is also important to make sure the size is right. With the help of small foam pads it is possible for everyone to have a helmet that sits and protects optimally.

Basic Training in Spring

It would be ideal if we could keep on cycling in the months from November to February. In our latitudes this is usually only possible on the unloved rolling devices or occasionally on weekend excursions. The second variation is no better, namely to stop

The helmet must fit too.

cycling completely in the cold and uncomfortable part of the year and put more effort into running and swimming. This is the version I have chosen for more than fifteen years.

In March, when the sun is already higher in the sky again, it is time to say: "At last, back on the bike". For me this is a motivational factor that is not to be underestimated. Or is it just my bad conscience saying: 'You haven't sat on your bike for four months now, get going!' Many will know the feeling. On days when the temperature is over plus five degrees Celsius the bike is taken out for the daily journey to work. In especially good weather the journey home is lengthened a little. On the weekends this is sometimes supplemented with a 90 or 120 minute ride to prepare for the cycling block. Several times now this has taken place on the "cyclist's island Mallorca".

If you want to place such an emphasis on cycling, you should use every opportunity beforehand to get at least 700-800 cycling kilometres behind you before you head south. Only then can you be sure that the extensive basic training will actually pay off.

Basic training means that longer cycling trips at low intensity are practised. This is all done on the smaller chain cog to train round pedalling. Those who plan a two or even three week cycling block in southern climes should consider the following.

This important training phase serves only the purpose of basic training and thus provides the basis for targeted training work shortly before and during the competition period. In long, calm trips of up to several hours duration, endurance performance capacity is mainly improved and metabolism trained. Low gears and pedalling frequencies of between 100 and 110 are important here. Wherever possible upward gradients should be managed in low gear and sitting on the saddle. If you pedal standing up you mainly heave yourself up the hill with strength and your own body weight.

Owing to metabolic processes in the body, the third day should always be an active rest day. Very relaxed pedalling for 1-2 hours is advisable.

I must warn against letting every quietly planned training ride turn into a race that often leads to total exhaustion. Despite intensive warnings I experience the same dilemma around me year after year. At least half the triathletes who come to Mallorca each year to do basic training are simply "finished, worn out" after a week at the most. On the third day at the latest an endurance session is no longer enough for these hotheads, there has to be a speed session as well. And what kind? E.g. 50 km single trip at a 38 average, in bad weather. You have to show what you can do.

After 6-7 days their fire is totally burnt out. In the second week many cannot even train every day because of the injuries.

The other days are then "wasted". The body gets its rest phases through injuries and colds.

Cycling Block

How could such a cycling block be put together? Here are two examples from my experience.

My starting situation in each case was 800 cycling kilometres altogether beforehand and 60 to 70 kilometres of running per week.

My training objective: still be able to train normally on the last day. In other words, not cutting back but a build up training should be achieved.

Important parameters were my morning pulse at rest, and my training feeling. If my pulse at rest was 4-5 beats per minute higher there was only a short, more relaxed cycling session.

In 1991 these three weeks in Mallorca were the basis for my first double ironman. Total covered in the 22 days: 2,000 cycling kilometres, 3.4 swimming kilometres in the ocean and 181 running kilometres. This includes participation in the Arenal Marathon Run on the second day in stormy and rainy weather. This run was done at a good speed, but nevertheless not "to the limit".

Frank SCHUMANN, a 31 year old triathlete from Warstein, and I cycled the whole 2,000 km together, harmoniously and chatting as we rode along next to each other. While we were doing so our families enjoyed the sun on the beach at Cala d'e Or.

22.3.   Arrival and 9 km loosening up run.
23.3.   30 km cycling
24.3.   Marathon run in storm and rain 2:53 hours
25.3   Sightseeing tour west coast, rain
26.3.   105 km cycling   25.4 km/h, evening 10 km loosening up run

27.3. 127 km cycling 26.5 km/h, 1,000 m swimming
28.3. 91 km cycling 27.2 km/h, evening 14 km run in 1:10 h
29.3. 145 km cycling 27.0 km/h
30.3. 58 km cycling 23.5 km/h, evening 14 km run in 1:10 h
31.3. 105 km cycling 25.8 km/h, pulse at rest constant 48
Week's performance: 631 km cycling/38 km running/1,000 m swimming

1.4. Rest, evening 18 km in 1:30 h
2.4. 192 km cycling 26.5 km/h,
3.4. 100 km cycling 26.5 km/h, evening 14 km running
4.4. 120 km cycling 27.5 km/h, 1,200 m swimming in the ocean
5.4. 90 km cycling 27.5 km/h, evening 9 km running
6.4. 130 km cycling 27.5 km/h, 1,200 m swimming pool, ocean
7.4. 145 km cycling 28.6 km/h, evening 14 km run in 1:05 h
Week's performance: 777 km cycling/55 km running/2.4 km swimming Pulse
at rest daily 47-48

8.4. Rest day
9.4. 240 km cycling 27.5 km/h, 2 breaks à 15 minutes
10.4. 88 km cycling 26.3 km/h, evening 14 km running, pulse at rest 53
11.4. 128 km cycling 27.5 km/h, evening 14 km running, pulse at rest 48
12.4. 106 km cycling 29.3 km/h, evening 9 km running, pulse at rest 46
Return home from Mallorca

For triathletes who only compete over short distances, more or less the same applies. Their training sessions can be 30-40% less extensive. But here too basic endurance and fat metabolism training have absolute priority.

The intensity of basic endurance training in cycling should be between 65 and 80% of best performance, and in the pulse region of 115-135. My pulse rates were always between 110-120. Younger athletes of course have correspondingly higher pulse rates.

In order to comment further on intensity, the following calculation is necessary. 2,000 km on 20 training days is an average of 100 km per day. My best performance over 100 km should be about 36 km/h. Average speed on Mallorca 27 km/h: that is at any rate 75% of my best performance. Orientational values for distances of 100 km per day are shown in the table below.

Best performance over 100 km in km/h	Average speed to be cycled in km/h		
100%	65%	75%	85%
40	26	30	34
38	24.7	28.5	32.3
36	23.4	27	30.6
34	22.1	25.5	28.9
32	20.8	26.3	27.2

Bicycle Interval Training

To get used slowly to competition speed after doing basic endurance training one should begin with interval training before the first triathlon. But be careful, the danger of over straining in intensive sessions is not to be underestimated. For more on this see Anaerobic Training, p. 22.

A high-tech product with optimum aerodynamics. The smooth surfaces cause little turbulence.

A delightful way of training change in pace is Fartlek on the bike. The game with speed already familiar from running can be ideally transferred to cycling.
After a 15-20 minute warm-up phase one sets a goal at will, e.g. the next entry to a town, the next tower, for a section to be ridden quickly. This little game can be repeated as often as desired.

For training trips in groups in which a number of increases in pace are planned, I can strongly recommend the following.

"Scoring Place Name Signs"
This is done as follows: Every time a training group draws near to a town, one of the participants starts a sprint without any kind of command. With a surprise attack out of the slipstream he tries to reach the place name sign first. Because none of the athletes knows who will start an escape attempt at what time, humorous playfulness on and with the bikes develops. The first attempts can begin 800 m, 1,200 m or even 2-3 km before the town.

As soon as one cyclist takes off the others try to catch up and also to win the place name sign point. The imaginary finishing line is at the level of the sign. This method is great fun. To prevent this Fartlek leading to a higher and higher basic speed, one of the group must ensure that the pace is always returned to what is comfortable for the group.

Fartlek in cycling can be trained all year round after calm basic training in spring. It introduces variety to training and saves staring at the clock.

Some basic principles of interval training:
- Before every interval training there should be warm-up-cycling.
- Get used to the desired speed slowly.
- Begin with short distances.
- Orient intervals towards the season's objective.
- Ensure variety in the intervals, frequently change length of strain and intensity.
- Carry out interval training regularly.
- Make interval breaks long enough, continue to pedal easily in the breaks.
- After every interval training there should be a cycling excursion.

Race tips for cycling
- Attach start numbers to a rubber band, in front for running, at the back for cycling.
- Place your bike ready in a suitable gear and with a full drink bottle.
- Start with high pedalling frequency.
- Start taking in liquid early.

- Eat solid nutrition in small chunks.
- Never cycle "dry", accept drinks early enough.
- Optimum rpm 80-90.
- On hills change gear in time, never "drag yourself" up the hill.
- Choose close fitting cycling clothing.
- In cool, damp weather carry a thin raincoat under your cycling tricot "just in case".
- Ride the last few minutes with somewhat less "pressure" in order to loosen up the muscles for running.
- Only undo and take off your helmet in the change over zone. Undoing the chin strap too soon can lead to disqualification.

SPEED TABLE   CYCLING

Distance	Speed 20 km/h	22 km/h	24 km/h	26 km/h	28 km/h	30 km/h	32 km/h	34 km/h	36 km/h	38 km/h	40 km/h
10 km	0:30:00	0:27:16	0:25:00	0:23:04	0:21:25	0:20:00	0:18:45	0:17:38	0:16:40	0:15:47	0:15:00
20 km	1:00:00	0:54:32	0:50:00	0:46:09	0:42:51	0:40:00	0:37:30	0:35:17	0:33:20	0:31:34	0:30:00
30 km	1:30:00	1:21:49	1:15:00	1:09:13	1:04:17	1:00:00	0:56:15	0:52:56	0:50:00	0:47:22	0:45:00
40 km	2:00:00	1:49:05	1:40:00	1:32:18	1:25:42	1:20:00	1:15:00	1:10:35	1:06:40	1:03:09	1:00:00
50 km	2:30:00	2:16:21	2:05:00	1:55:23	1:47:08	1:40:00	1:33:45	1:28:14	1:23:20	1:18:56	1:15:00
60 km	3:00:00	2:43:38	2:30:00	2:18:27	2:08:34	2:00:00	1:52:30	1:45:52	1:40:00	1:34:44	1:30:00
70 km	3:30:00	3:10:54	2:55:00	2:41:32	2:30:00	2:20:00	2:11:15	2:03:31	1:56:40	1:50:31	1:45:00
80 km	4:00:00	3:38:10	3:20:00	3:04:36	2:51:25	2:40:00	2:30:00	2:21:10	2:13:20	2:06:18	2:00:00
90 km	4:30:00	4:05:27	3:45:00	3:27:41	3:12:51	3:00:00	2:48:45	2:38:49	2:30:00	2:22:06	2:15:00
100 km	5:00:00	4:32:43	4:10:00	3:50:46	3:34:17	3:20:00	3:07:30	2:56:28	2:46:40	2:37:53	2:30:00
110 km	5:30:00	5:00:00	4:35:00	4:13:50	3:55:42	3:40:00	3:26:15	3:14:07	3:03:20	2:53:41	2:45:00
120 km	6:00:00	5:27:16	5:00:00	4:36:55	4:17:08	4:00:00	3:45:00	3:31:45	3:20:00	3:09:28	3:00:00
130 km	6:30:00	5:54:32	5:25:00	5:00:00	4:38:34	4:20:00	4:03:45	3:49:24	3:36:40	3:25:15	3:15:00
140 km	7:00:00	6:21:49	5:50:00	5:23:04	5:00:00	4:40:00	4:22:30	4:07:08	3:53:20	3:41:03	3:30:00
150 km	7:30:00	6:49:05	6:15:00	5:46:09	5:21:25	5:00:00	4:41:15	4:24:42	4:10:00	3:56:50	3:45:00
160 km	8:00:00	7:16:21	6:40:00	6:09:13	5:42:51	5:20:00	5:00:00	4:42:21	4:26:40	4:12:37	4:00:00
170 km	8:30:00	7:43:38	7:05:00	6:32:18	6:04:17	5:40:00	5:18:45	5:00:00	4:43:20	4:28:25	4:15:00
180 km	9:00:00	8:10:54	7:30:00	6:55:23	6:25:42	6:00:00	5:37:30	5:17:38	5:00:00	4:44:12	4:30:00
190 km	9:30:00	8:38:10	7:55:00	7:18:27	6:47:08	6:20:00	5:56:15	5:35:17	5:16:40	5:00:00	4:45:00
200 km	10:00:00	9:05:27	8:20:00	7:41:32	7:08:34	6:40:00	6:15:00	5:52:56	5:33:20	5:15:47	5:00:00

Running

Training in running has special significance for triathletes. In our latitudes it is possible to train running, as well as swimming all year round without any major costs.

Another advantage of running is that this third triathlon discipline can be practised in all weathers, except perhaps thunderstorms, at any time of the day or year and in any surroundings. Unlike cycling, regular training can be carried out in the autumn and winter months even in darkness, rain and snow.

If you run from home the often annoying travel time is eliminated. In addition, running is the most energy intensive of the three endurance sports in triathlon. Later in the year, when the weather is cold and wet, it is advisable to give running preference to cycling. An hour of running is more effective than cycling for one or two hours with the risk of catching a cold. Furthermore, uphill running trains strength for cycling.

A sensible training combination for running:
Main competition July
Endurance   Interval training   6 weeks
Endurance   Speed endurance   6 weeks
BASIC ENDURANCE   3 MONTHS

Basic Endurance

The three month training phase creates the basis for the whole season. Basic endurance represents the foundations of the house under construction (triathlon), which is extended on the first floor with speed endurance and on the top floor with interval training. During the first three months you run in the aerobic region or the "steady state". This term stands for oxygen balance, i.e. as much oxygen is taken in as is needed for providing energy.

Further orientation values: this basic training is about 15% below the aerobic-anaerobic threshold or at a lactic acid value of 1.5 mmol/l. Be aware that this aerobic-anaerobic threshold, which should now be checked every month using the Conconi test, changes constantly.

Endurance training should be done in such a way that you can hold a conversation at the same time without any effort. That should be a maximum of 65-75% of maximum performance.

Here is a brief example:
a) Using pulse rates:

Athlete aged 20 years: max. pulse c. 220 - 20 = 200
Approximation: anaerobic aerobic threshold
200 x 0.85 = 170
170 x 0.85 = 145 training pulse, roughly

Athlete aged 40 years: max. pulse c. 220 - 40 = 180
Approximation: anaerobic aerobic threshold
180 x 0.85 = 153
153 x 0.85 = 130 training pulse, roughly

b) Using maximum performance capacity:
10,000 m best time = 38 min. = 3:48 min./km
65-75% of this means 5:45 - 5:00 min./km
10,000 m best time = 35 min. = 3:30 min./km
65-75% of this means 5:20 - 4:40 min./km

In this three month phase many kilometres should be run in the aerobic region. On the other hand, a popular run can provide for more variety in training, but it should be run at less than full exertion, just as part of training. If training is in blocks (swimming, running, cycling block), the amount of training from week to week will change automatically. If this is not the case, you could change the amount stepwise.

Long distance triathletes

e.g.	1st wk 50 km	2nd wk 60 km	3rd wk 70 km	4th wk 80 km
	5th wk 50 km	6th wk 70 km	7th wk 80 km	8th wk 90 km
	9th wk 50 km	10th wk 80 km	11th wk 90 km	12th wk 100 km

Short distance triathletes could graduate the amount this way:

e.g.	1st wk 40 km	2nd wk 45 km	3rd wk 50 km	4th wk 55 km
	5th wk 40 km	6th wk 50 km	7th wk 55 km	8th wk 60 km
	9th wk 40 km	10th wk 55 km	11th wk 60 km	12th wk 65 km

Block Training

Long distance triathletes

January:	Swimming month 1st - 4th week as before
February:	Running 5th wk 50, 6th wk 80, 7th wk 100, 8th wk 120 km
March:	Cycling 9th - 12th wk 50 - 60 km

Short distance triathletes

January: Swimming month 1st - 4th week as before
February: Running 5th wk 45, 6th wk 55, 7th wk 65, 8th wk 75 km
March: Cycling 9th - 12th wk 30 - 40 km

With this form of training you should always have the feeling that you can run faster. Altogether your total fitness should be improved. This is achieved through longer and especially through long, calm and even runs. Hard training in this period does more damage than good.

Speed Endurance

The foundation for the development of speed endurance has been laid in the previous months through long calm runs. You can now quietly build up on this foundation. But watch out if you think you can do this without a foundation. Your "house will fall down" when you strain it in competition, and all the training effort will have been for nothing. Anyone who has not managed their three months quiet training phase will need to keep working on their foundation in April. They may not quite reach their top performance in July, but they will also not risk failure by having to give up. Runs in hilly territory are particularly suited to developing speed endurance and resilience. Once or twice a week, for older people once a week, is more than enough, because in April cycling training has been correspondingly increased. When training on hills you reach the anaerobic region. For hill training a 10 - 15% gradient over a length of 500-600 m is suitable. At 85 % of performance capacity, that is a little more than the 10 km competition requirement, you run up the hill in short steps on the balls of your feet. Shortly before the end of the hill you increase the rhythm. At the top you loosely run 500 m and aferwards you trot down the hill. Speed endurance training is begun with four to five hill runs and is increased every week. Long distance athletes and older persons do this once a week; short distance athletes twice. In addition of course long aerobic runs are continued. Another opportunity to train the transition to interval training is:

Short distance specialists 2 x 10 min. or 3 x 7 min. at top pulse rate and each time 5 min. jogging break until pulse < 110. 2 x per week at the most. Long distance specialists 2 x 15 min. or 3 x 10 min. at 90% of top pulse rate and each time 5 min. jogging break. If the feeling for the strain is good, the times can be extended by a few minutes. This must be seen from the point of view of coordination with cycling and swimming training. These runs, which serve speed endurance, can be sensibly carried out in combination training after an easy cycling session of 30-50 km. Through these training forms, maximum oxygen intake capacity is improved. This manifests itself in that the oxygen breathed in is used better and thus the athletes's performance improves.

Interval training means being able to "clench your teeth ".

Interval Training

Interval training, also called speed training, is not suitable for beginners. They will get faster without doing interval training, i.e. just by doing endurance training. Performance oriented triathletes who have been doing endurance training for several years can handle interval training better. Speed training puts the body under great stress and increases the risk of injury. Therefore at the first sign of over training one should immediately replace interval training with very calm endurance training The positive side of speed training is, however, that by getting used to competition speed, athletes become capable of running further and faster. After doing the six week interval training and the triathlon it is of course advisable to stop and return to basic improvement again. The greater the foundation, the higher the competition strain it can later bear. Interval training is usually done on a track. You can also do it on a course that has been measured with a wheel on a country or town road. This applies especially to those who do not like running on an ash or synthetic track or simply do not have one near their home. Short distance triathletes carry out e.g. the following 1 x per week, in addition to 15 minutes warm-up and cool down, in each case at 90 % of the intensity of their best time:

1,000 m best time 3:00 min. 90% = 3:18 min.

2,000 m best time 6:20 min. 90% = 7:00 min.

3,000 m best time 9:50 min. 90% = 10:50 min.

5 x 1000 m, 1 km jogging break up to a pulse of <110

or 3 x 2,000 m, 1.5 km jogging break

or 2 x 3,000 m, 2 km jogging break

or 400 m - 800 m - 1,200 m - 1,600 m - 1,200 m - 800 m - 400 m jogging breaks of the same distance in each case. Another variation of interval training is Fartlek, described earlier. Finally, pyramid training. Here you run 2, 4, 6, 8, 6, 4, 2 minutes quickly and you jog the same time in between. It is also possible to do 1, 3, 5, 7, 5, 3, 1 minutes. For triathletes who prefer the middle and ultra distances, longer intervals are more suitable.

The speed here is 85% of the best time in each case or else at 10,000 m speed, e.g.

6 x 1,000 m, jogging break up to pulse <110

or 3 x 2,000 m, jogging break 1 km up to pulse <110

or 3 x 3,000 m, jogging break 2 km

or 2 x 5,000 m, jogging break 2 km

Pyramid training could be done in this way:

6, 8, 10, 8, 6 minutes with the same time as jogging break in each case.

The speed sections in Fartlek are also longer here than for short distance athletes. Between training runs on the track or elsewhere you should run as often as possible in a relaxed manner in the aerobic region. For short distance triathletes, the long distance runs should be 10 to 15 km long. Ultra triathletes choose distances between 12 and 25 km. It is advisable to do a run at lower intensity once a week over a distance of 25 to 30 km.

For athletes who want to train 70 km per week in four sessions I recommend the following proven combination:

12 km and 15 km, which includes an interval training of 6 x 1,000 m or 2 x 5,000 m, 18 km and 25 km. Principle: The longer the distance, the lower the speed. The 12 km can be included in alternating training. Alternative: alternating 12 km, 15 km, 18 km, 21 km, and 12 km, 15 km, 18 km, 29 km.

In addition to these runs, once a week speed training of 8 x 8 seconds at top speed with 100-200 m jogging break in between should be included in training. Because here phosphate conversion should be activated, there is no reduction of glycogen to lactic acid in such short periods (< 10 seconds). Interval training must of course be stopped early enough before the competition period. (see training schedules.)

25 km and Marathon Runs for Whom?

After creating the endurance basis in the first months of the year, the period around the end of April is a good time to practise what you have learnt. For short distance triathletes a 25 km run or a half marathon of 21.1 km can be attractive and sensible. There is then plenty of time to recover before the season begins in June. Such a run is very useful mentally because you can show you have sufficient staying power before the season has begun assuming, of course, that the run was divided up correctly and successfully finished. Although a 25 km run is shorter than a short distance triathlon so far as the time is concerned, it is harder because of the one-sided use of the muscles. It requires a longer period of regeneration. Such a welcome test run need not be run "to the limit". I advise anyone who has done an intensive cycling block, during which they only did easy running, to follow this with a few days of regeneration, and then increase running training for two weeks. The 25 km run then rounds off this interim running block. In these two weeks short distance triathletes should try to include three times two hours of easy running in addition to the other training elements. The targeted competition speed should be run 1 x per week over 10 km. Ten days before the 25 km run another variation is advisable: 3 x 5 km at race speed with 6 minutes jogging break between each run. For runners who plan to do the 25 km in 1:40 h the following rule of thumb applies:

The 10 km phase time during the 25 km run should only be two minutes slower than the 10,000 m best time.

E.g. 10,000 m best time 38 min., phase time during 25 km run 40 min., targeted final time 1:40 h.

Marathon Run for Middle and Ultra Distance Triathletes

For middle and ultra distance triathletes a marathon run in spring is strongly recommended. If you do not attempt too much and cover the 42.195 km well, this run gives you confidence and self-assurance for the coming triathlon season. This run brings not only physical but also psychological advantages, which I find especially important for beginners. The fear of the marathon run in the ultra distance triathlon melts in spring with each of the 42.195 km. Mentally strengthened, the athlete can begin his 226 km in the summer.

How can a marathon run be incorporated in spring training?

With the basic endurance training of the first few months of the year the athlete has created the basis for the 42.195 km run. The month of running and cycling has had its effect. Particularly the long cycling sessions of over 100 km and runs of over two hours have trained the switching over to fat combustion. After the cycling emphasis in late March/early May, three weeks of special preparation for the marathon are sufficient to ensure a personally good time is run. The cornerstones of this preparation are three runs over 33 km. Two of them should be run in the last three weeks. One run can certainly be incorporated in training several weeks earlier already, such as in bad cycling weather.

These runs, in which the necessary metabolism adaptation is trained, use up the glycogen supplies and then switch over to "brutal" fat combustion. This low point, which occurs during a marathon at between 30 and 35 km, should be only touched on. At this point, which is critical for athletes who do not yet have much endurance training, there are no more glycogen reserves left in the muscles being used. The organism must get the necessary amounts of glycogen from its own substance by converting protein. This is usually linked with a loss of intensity, meaning lower speed. Only athletes very well-trained in endurance notice this conversion. During these 33 km runs, which train metabolism adaptation and getting used to such long strains, it is important to choose only a very calm pace.

Drinking is also important during such long runs. Unlike in a marathon, however, you should not take in liquid every 5 km right from the start, but initially train being in a state of shortage. In a 33 km training run it is enough to take in liquids at 22 and 28 km.

What Marathon Time Is Possible?

Triathletes, who in addition to running also swim and cycle, need to do considerably less running kilometres per week than athletes who only run. Be careful, therefore, of training plans devised for runners.

Nevertheless, my experience shows that STEFFNY's rule of thumb also applies to triathletes: Best time over 10,000 m x 4.66 = maximum achievable marathon best time.

10,000 m best time	Maximum achievable marathon best time
45:00 Min	3:35 h
42:30 Min	3:22 h
41:00 Min	3:15 h
40:00 Min	3:10 h
39:00 Min	3:05 h
38:00 Min	3:00 h
37:00 Min	2:55 h
36:00 Min	2:50 h
35:00 Min	2:45 h
34:00 Min	2:40 h
33:00 Min	2:35 h
32:00 Min	2:30 h

Triathlete Training for 2:59 h, 3:15 h and 2:44 h

Marathon in 2:59 Hours

Three hours is a magic barrier in marathon running. For many athletes doing it in less is an appealing and motivating sporting achievement. To do this a basic speed of 37-38 minutes over an actual 10 km distance is necessary. Actual because often popular runs are said to be 10 km, but are in fact shorter or longer. For this reason the 10 km time should be based on an athletic association run. These officially measured runs really are exactly 10,000 m long. In addition to the basic speed mentioned, there should be running training four times a week. After the running month, February with about 80 km per week, this is reduced in the cycling month March to 50-60 km. The last six weeks before the marathon run could be structured like this (without other training sessions):

1st week:		Emphasis still on cycling
2nd week:		Emphasis still on cycling, 1 x 15 km easily, 1 x 8 x 1,000 m in 4:00 min. per kilometre and 1 x 25 km very calmly in 2:20 h
3rd week:	Tues.	15 km in 1:00 h
	Wed.	1:20 h easily
	Thur.	10 x 1,000 m in 4:10 min./km
	Sat.	30 km in 2:30 h
4th week:	Tues.	12 x 700 m track, 2:55 min with 2 min. breaks
	Wed.	12 km easily
	Thur.	18 km easily
	Sat.	25 km in 1:52 h in 4:30 min./km
5th week:	Tues.	10 x 700 m track, 2:55 min, 2 min. breaks
	Wed.	18 km easily
	Thur.	15 km 1:00 h
	Sat.	33-36 km in 12 km/h, 5:00 min./km
6th week:	Mon.	15 km easily
	Wed.	on/off 5,000 m in 19 min. glycogene run
	Fri.	30 minutes jogging
	Sat.	40 km cycling
	Sun.	Marathon run 2:58 h, 21 min. every 5 km section.

Marathon in 3:15 Hours

For 3:15 h the plan could be like this:

Prerequisite: 10,000 m best time 41 minutes 25 km in 1:50 h

1st and 2nd week		Cycling emphasis with 1 x 15 km, 1 x 8 x 1,000 m in 4:20 min./km 1 x 25 km very calmly in 2:25 h
3rd week:	Tues.	14 km in 1:00 h
	Wed.	12 km easily
	Thur.	10 x 1,000 m 4:30 min./km
	Sat.	30 km in 2:40 h
4th week:	Tues.	10 x 700 m in 3:15 min. each with 2 min. breaks
	Thur.	18 km easily
	Sat.	25 km in 2:00 h quickly
5th week:	Tues.	10 x 700 m in 3:15 min. each with 2 min. breaks
	Wed.	18 km easily
	Thur.	14 km in 1:00 h
	Sat.	33-36 km at 11 km/h, 5:30 min./km
6th week:	Mon.	15 km easily
	Wed.	on/off 5,000 m in 21 min. glycogen run

Fri.	30 min. jogging
Sun.	Marathon run 3:15 h, 23 min. per 5 km section.

Marathon in 2:44 Hours

For 2:44 h the plan could be:

Prerequisite: 10,000 m best time 35:00 minutes This plan which I actually carried out shows how you can achieve your objective with 75 km a week.

2nd week of March:		7 km swimming (S), 150 km cycling (C)
	Tues.	2 x 12 km running to swimming baths 1 h each
	Wed.	13 km 1:00 h
	Sat.	36 km 3:12 h
	Sun.	12 km in 56 min.
3rd week of March:		5 km S, 130 km C
	Tues.	2 x 12 km, each 59 min.
	Thur.	15 km in 1:00 h
	Fri.	Flight to Mallorca
	Sat.	24 km in 1:51 h, 73 km cycling in 2:45 h
	Sun.	78 km cycling in 3:14 h
4th week of March:		1 km S, 536 km C
	Mon.	24 km 1:53 h, 50 km cycling
	Tue.	16 km 1:13 h, 102 km cycling 3:40 h
	Wed.	8 km 0:40 h, 144 km cycling 5:30 h
	Thur.	8 km 0:39 h, 100 km cycling 3:30 h
	Fri.	16 km 1:14 h, 85 km cycling 3:14 h
	Sat.	55 km cycling 2:05 h
	Sun.	Marathon run on Mallorca 2:48, very even run, second

half exactly the same speed as the first.

At this point my best time was 2:45:51. After the Mallorca marathon the desire to do 2:44 was very great, as at this time the qualification for the German Marathon Championships was 2:45:00.

1st week of April:	1 km S, 623 km C	
	Mon.	10 km 0:52, 81 km 27.5 average
	Tue.	160 km 26 average
	Wed.	8 km 0:44 h, 100 km 24 average, strong wind
	Thur.	200 km 24 average, stormy
	Fri.	24 km 1:45 h, return flight from Mallorca
	Sat.	15 km 1:00 h
	Sun.	82 km cycling

2nd week of April: 6 km S, 100 km C
    Mon.   6 x 1,000 m in 3:25 min./km, 5 min. jogging break
    Tue.   26 km in 2:05 h
    Thur.   15 km in 1:08 h
    Sat.   10 km popular run 35:40 min.
3rd week of April: 7 km S, 300 km C
    Mon.   34 km in 2:40 h
    Thur.   18 km in 1:18 h
    Sat.   7 x 1,000 m 3:40 min./km
    Sun.   24 km in 2:00 h
4th week of April: 4 km S, 244 km C
    Tue.   19 km, of which 5 km in 18:30 min. glycogen run
    Thur.   16 km in 1:16 h
    Sun.   Marathon Hamburg, 2:44:21 best time
Average running performance since beginning of year 75 km per week.
Three weeks later first short distance triathlon of the season.

SPEED TABLE   RUNNING

Time	1 km	3 km	5 km	10 km	15 km	20 km	25 km	30 km	35 km	Marathon
2:55	8:45	14:35	29:10	43:45	0:58:20	1:12:55	1:27:30	1:42:05	2:03:04
3:00	9:00	15:00	30:00	45:00	1:00:00	1:15:00	1:30:00	1:45:00	2:06:35
3:05	9:15	15:25	30:50	46:15	1:01:40	1:17:05	1:32:30	1:47:55	2:10:06
3:10	9:30	15:50	31:40	47:30	1:03:20	1:19:10	1:35:00	1:50:50	2:13:37
3:15	9:45	16:15	32:30	48:45	1:05:00	1:21:15	1:37:30	1:53:45	2:17:08
3:20	10:00	16:40	33:20	50:00	1:06:40	1:23:20	1:40:00	1:56:40	2:20:39
3:25	10:15	17:05	34:10	51:15	1:08:20	1:25:25	1:42:30	1:59:35	2:24:10
3:30	10:30	17:30	35:00	52:30	1:10:00	1:27:30	1:45:00	2:02:30	2:27:41
3:35	10:45	17:55	35:50	53:45	1:11:40	1:29:35	1:47:30	2:05:25	2:31:12
3:40	11:00	18:20	36:40	55:00	1:13:20	1:31:40	1:50:00	2:08:20	2:34:43
3:45	11:15	18:45	37:30	56:15	1:15:00	1:33:45	1:52:30	2:11:15	2:38:14
3:50	11:30	19:10	38:20	57:30	1:16:40	1:35:50	1:55:00	2:14:10	2:41:49
3:55	11:45	19:35	39:10	58:45	1:18:20	1:37:55	1:57:30	2:17:05	2:45:16
4:00	12:00	20:00	40:00	1:00:00	1:20:00	1:40:00	2:00:00	2:20:00	2:48:47
4:05	12:15	20:25	40:50	1:01:15	1:21:40	1:42:05	2:02:30	2:22:55	2:52:18
4:10	12:30	20:50	41:40	1:02:30	1:23:20	1:44:10	2:05:00	2:25:50	2:55:49
4:15	12:45	21:15	42:30	1:03:45	1:25:00	1:46:15	2:07:30	2:28:45	2:59:20
4:20	13:00	21:40	43:20	1:05:00	1:26:40	1:48:20	2:10:00	2:31:40	3:02:50
4:25	13:15	22:05	44:10	1:06:15	1:28:20	1:50:25	2:12:30	2:34:35	3:06:22
4:30	13:30	22:30	45:00	1:07:30	1:30:00	1:52:30	2:15:00	2:37:30	3:09:53
4:35	13:45	22:55	45:50	1:08:45	1:31:40	1:54:35	2:17:30	2:40:25	3:13:24
4:40	14:00	23:20	46:40	1:10:00	1:33:20	1:56:40	2:20:00	2:43:20	3:16:55
4:45	14:15	23:45	47:30	1:11:15	1:35:00	1:58:45	2:22:30	2:46:15	3:20:26
4:50	14:30	24:10	48:20	1:12:30	1:36:40	2:00:50	2:25:00	2:49:10	3:23:57
4:55	14:45	24:39	49:10	1:13:45	1:38:20	2:02:55	2:27:30	2:52:05	3:27:28
5:00	15:00	25:00	50:00	1:15:00	1:40:00	2:05:00	2:30:00	2:55:00	3:30:59
5:05	15:15	25:25	50:50	1:16:15	1:41:40	2:07:05	2:32:30	2:57:55	3:34:29
5:10	15:30	25:50	51:40	1:17:30	1:43:20	2:09:10	2:35:00	3:00:50	3:38:01
5:15	15:45	26:15	52:30	1:18:45	1:45:00	2:11:15	2:37:30	3:03:45	3:41:31
5:20	16:00	26:40	53:20	1:20:00	1:46:40	2:13:20	2:40:00	3:06:40	3:45:02
5:25	16:15	27:05	54:10	1:21:15	1:48:20	2:15:25	2:42:30	3:09:35	3:48:33
5:30	16:30	27:30	55:00	1:22:30	1:50:00	2:17:30	2:45:00	3:12:30	3:52:04
5:35	16:45	27:55	55:50	1:23:45	1:51:40	2:19:35	2:47:30	3:15:25	3:55:35
5:40	17:00	28:20	56:40	1:25:00	1:53:20	2:21:40	2:50:00	3:18:20	3:59:06
5:45	17:15	28:45	57:30	1:26:15	1:55:00	2:23:45	2:52:30	3:21:15	4:02:37
5:50	17:30	29:10	58:20	1:27:30	1:56:40	2:25:50	2:55:00	3:24:10	4:06:08
5:55	17:45	29:35	59:10	1:28:45	1:58:20	2:27:55	2:57:30	3:27:05	4:09:39
6:00	18:00	30:00	1:00:00	1:30:00	2:00:00	2:30:00	3:00:00	3:30:00	4:13:10

Tips for Running Training
- Arrange the training programme as follows: Warm-up running ten minutes, stretching, training session followed by cool down and stretching exercises. Never run to the training finish line at full speed.
- Have several pairs of running shoes and change them constantly.
- Treat all parts of the body that rub each other with vaseline or fat.
- Clothing should be close fitting, but not tight.
- On long runs train taking drinks.

A few notes on interval training:
- Interval training should have a tiring effect, but not be totally exhausting.
- Let your pulse sink to 110 between intervals.
- Each week slightly increase the number of intervals.
- Restrict interval training for short distance triathlons to eight weeks. For ultra distance triathlons keep it to twelve weeks.
- Warm-up training is very important here, cool down training equally so.
- Careful, most injuries happen during speed training.

Tips for the Race
- Set realistic goals and partial goals.
- Start loosely and relaxed.
- If possible make sure your shoes have velcro fasteners or Tanka clips (rucksack fastener).
- Drink regularly especially in heat.
- If you get cramps, stretch the muscles until the cramp goes.
- When the going gets hard, think positively and consciously be aware of your environment.

Triathlon in the Heat

Being a summer sport triathlon is carried out even in very high temperatures andsometimes also high humidity. Both factors, temperature and humidity, affect performance ability quite considerably, especially when both occur at the same time. These performance reducing factors are not only found in Hawaii. We need only think of the European super summers of the early Nineties. Only a quarter of the total energy production in triathlon is actually needed to move forward. The rest is released as heat. This heat can massively increase body temperature. At high temperatures the heat must leave the body through perspiration. Thus people who sweat quickly are at an advantage. They release body heat more quickly, and lose a great deal of minerals and trace elements. The blood must transport the heat to the skin surface, which in turn places a further strain on the circulatory system, in addition to that of oxygen intake and supplying energy. This costs additional energy, which is then no longer available for moving forward. Furthermore, more blood, which has been taken away from the muscles, must flow through the skin in order to ensure optimum release of heat is achieved. All this has the effect that at high temperatures you cannot cycle and run as fast. High humidity leads to poorer vaporisation of our sweat. The cooling effect is reduced because the sweat stays on the skin longer. The result is that the body temperature rises still further. The consequences can be muscle cramps, profuse sweating, general tiredness, states of exhaustion such as headaches, nausea, dizziness or even uncontrolled movement, fainting and unconsciousness.

What can one do about this?

- While cycling start drinking early, before you start to feel thirsty.
- Prepare ahead by drinking a lot on the day before the competition. No alcohol, however, for this encourages urine production and leads to loss of liquids.
- Take in more liquids just before the race starts.
- Drink frequently while cycling in order to prepare for the marathon and the long distance races. The stomach can only let 800 ml (0.8 l) per hour of liquid pass through it. When running, however, loss of fluids can be much higher.
- Drink a lot on reaching the finish line.
- Darkly coloured urine indicates a fluid deficiency.
- During the race watch out for the above mentioned signs of overheating. Simplest solution: reduce exertion.

  - Only start if you are well prepared.
  - At every refreshment station cool headand neck, arms and legs with water.
  - Wear light coloured clothing and hats.
  - Ensure sufficient acclimatisation, in other words, arrive in plenty of time.
  - When it is hot, only train in the early morning or late evening

For training the same preventive measures apply.

Drinking at an early stage and wearing a hat are a "must" in excessive heat.

Triathlon in the Cold

In our latitudes, but also elsewhere, triathletes can encounter races in cool temperatures. You can protect against cold water with a neoprene suit. When the water temperature is below 15 degrees the DTU rules forbid swimming, rightly so. After all, sport should serve health and therefore any health risks should be avoided.

Most heat is discharged via the head, so it makes sense to take special measures. The simplest way is to wear two bathing caps. Wolfgang ARNOLD, a former water polo player and swimming 'crack', wears a "pimpled" bathing cap such as women wore 20 years ago under his competition cap in cool temperatures. The sealed in air cushion prevents too much cooling down. I prefer a neoprene cap which, although it makes me look like I'm about to rob a bank, serves its purpose completely. With this hood, over which I pull the official bathing cap, I do not find it so difficult to sink my head into water that is 17 or 18 degrees cold.

For short swimming distances, however, it is often enough to smear on cold protection grease (milking grease). Training outside, cold showers, regular visits to the sauna can lead to a degree of insensitivity to the cold. When the water is cool, and on top of that the air as well, one should in any case definitely make sure of having dry cycling clothing. Anyone who immediately jumps onto his bike and

In the cold long, dry clothing is needed for cycling.

races off with a wet upper body and a wet T shirt when the air temperature is below 15 degrees should not be surprised at having kidney trouble the next day. Are not these few minutes worth having potential mid or long-term health problems? Yes, of course, I know, the class victory, the prestige, the club mate ...., is that all worth more than my health? On top of that, there is one thing we should not forget: Sport is supposed to be fun, isn't it....?

The Most Important Training Principles for Triathletes

- Train regularly.
- Give training preference to your weakest discipline, if possible in a group.
- Have fun training, do not force it.
- If you want to prepare well for races, train double the planned triathlon distance every week in the last two months before the race.
- Increase training slowly.
- First increase the amount of training, then the intensity.
- Make sure training camps are sufficiently well prepared.
- Eat consciously, as much protein and as little fat as possible.
- If you listen to your body often, you will develop a feeling for the appropriate strain in training and competition.
- Pay close attention to small injuries.
- Always ensure plenty of variety in training. Never do the same training session twice in one week.
- Alternate normal, hard and regenerative training phases as required.
- Plan for enough resting days.
- Never consider training recommendations as dogma. Always consider the total strain of sport, job and private life.
- The break between two training sessions should always be at least four hours.
- The longer the training session, the lower the intensity.
- An intensive running session should be followed by an easy cycling or swimming session as both place less strain on one's "moving parts".
- There should be at least 24 hours between two intensive training sessions.
- In the last week before an event train loosely, relaxed, regeneratively and less.
- Short distance triathletes can once again include intervals in the last week in a shortened form in order to train their feeling for speed.
- Take in food and liquids early enough in both training and events.
- Drink cola only in the last running kilometres.
- One day before the event, drink much and eat little.

- The day before a triathlon eat early enough. Food takes about 8-15 hours to be properly digested.
- Only use proven material in a triathlon.
- Ultra distance triathletes should enter their last "serious" short distance triathlon 4-6 weeks before their seasonal peak.
- Triathlon races are won in the mind, so show mental strength.
- After a change of location dedicate the third day to active rest.
- Don't become a training world champion!

Reasons for this are often: training too hard, too little regeneration, too abrupt increase in amount of training, expectations too high, training too hard in the last week before a triathlon, not loosely enough, i.e. too grimly.

Possible Training Pattern

Tue., Wed., Thur.	with increasing total strain
Fri.	partial recovery with greatly reduced exertion
Sat., Sun.	two days of strain
Mon.	day without training for complete recovery
Alternatively:	Tue., Wed. increasing strain
	Thur. partial recovery with reduced exertion
	Fri., Sat., Sun. great strain

Basic endurance training 1.5 mmol/l lactic acid
"aerobically" with the following pulse rates:

Swimming	150
Cycling	130-140
Running	130-150

Speed endurance training (threshold training)
"anaerobic-aerobically" lactic acid 3-4 mmol/l:

Swimming	150-180
Cycling	150-170
Running	150-170

Interval training
"anaerobically" lactic acid > 6 mmol/l:

Swimming	max. pulse
Cycling	170 - max.
Running	170 - max.

Terms:	Intensive training equals speed in a triathlon
	Extensive training equals speed considerably below triathlon level

Stretching for Triathletes

By stretching we actually mean a stretching after preceding tenseness. Stretching is designed to improve suppleness, mobility and flexibility of the relevant moving systems. Regular stretching prevents problems with tendons, ligaments and muscles.

Stretching exercises should be incorporated into every training session in order to compensate every potential contraction of the muscles. Every physical strain is made possible by muscle contractions (contraction = shortening). In triathlon there are therefore frequently muscle contractions in the strained body parts in swimming, cycling and running.

A contracted muscle is, however, capable of less performance and is more prone to injury. An elastic and strengthened muscle system increases resistance to these often long lasting strains and thus reduces the likelihood of injury quite considerably. Improved mobility and flexibility improve moving technique. In running, the length of one's stride is increased, which of course leads to better running times. The loosened movement in swimming allows a better swimming technique. The same applies to cycling.

When Should Stretching Exercises Be Carried out?
- Before and after swimming.
- Before and after cycling.
- After the ten minute warm-up running phase and after cool down running.
Beforehand easy jogging, hopping, jumping to prepare the circulatory system and the muscle systems.

How Should You Stretch?
- All exercises should be done slowly in a loose and relaxed manner. At the same time relax mentally.
- Slowly stretch the muscles to your personal pain threshold.
- This is reached when you feel a tingling in your muscles.
- Stay in this stretching position for ten seconds, breathing normally.
- When the first stretch is finished, stretch a little further. Maintain this renewed tension for another ten seconds.
- Stretch larger muscles longer than smaller ones.
Afterwards, slowly release the tension.
Repeat each exercise 3 x.
Avoid any sudden or springing movements, they hinder rather than improving the stretching ability of the muscles. After stretching one group of muscles (agonist),

always address the opposite muscle group (antagonist), e.g. thigh front, thigh rear. If you have pains and injuries avoid stretching.

During stretching it is important to wear loose, comfortable training clothing that also protects you from catching a chill. Because stretching characteristics vary from one person to another, every triathlete should concentrate on optimally improving their own personal mobility.

Exercises before and after Swimming Training

The mobility of the shoulders, the hip area, the vertebrae and the ankles are especially important in swimming. The more supple the triathlete, the more "fishlike", elegant and thus efficient are his movements in the water.

Exercises before and after Cycling

Those muscle groups which are mainly static (resting) during cycling should be intensively stretched. This considerably reduces the tendency to tenseness. For cycling this means stretching the leg, back and arm muscles.

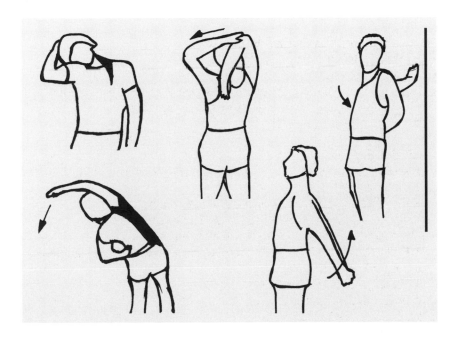

Stretching before and after swimming

The highly strained muscles should be stretched in particular after cycling training. This leads to faster relaxation and regeneration. Stretching the most strained muscles, i.e. those most prone to contraction, makes these more relaxed and elastic, delays tiring in particular and also often helps prevent cramps.

Here are some exercises for cycling which should be carried out both before and after cycling:

Stretching exercises for cycling/running, before and after training

Exercises before and after Running Training

Especially in running, good mobility provides for an economical running style. This means the running movements are rounder, the risk of injury is less and the length of stride gets longer.

An impressive example:

In a marathon run over 42,195 m about 30,000 strides are necessary. If the length of these strides is increased by only 3 cm (2%) through better mobility, this finally makes a difference of 30,000 x 3 cm = 90,000 cm = 900 m - an improvement in running time of about four minutes. At 5 cm that would be 1,500 m already.

With loose and stretchable leg muscles higher speeds can be kept up longer. Especially before and after intensive running sessions stretching must be carried out. In this way contraction of the muscles is prevented and regeneration improved.

Strength Endurance

In the first months of a competition year, in the preparatory period, strength endurance training can foster comprehensive athletic training of a triathlete. Good strength endurance is decisive for resistance to tiring during long lasting repetitive exertion as it is experienced over several hours in a triathlon. Triathlon training is not meant to create musclemen by training maximum resilience, that would just be ballast on the bicycle and when running.Therefore it is important to do strength endurance training with small doses of resistance over a longer period of time and to carry out numerous muscle contractions. In an exercise repeated many times even the athlete's own weight provides suitable resistance.

Cycling standing up improves strength endurance.

Why does a triathlete need a high level of strength endurance?

When cycling standing up or against a strong head wind, more strength is needed than when cycling in an optimum aerodynamic position. When running strength endurance training helps make it easier to carry one's body weight and provides for improved stretching of the legs. In particular the calves, the front and back of the thighs and the buttock muscles are placed under strain. Just as they are when walking.

In swimming, athletes can better overcome increasing water resistance as they increase their speed, through greater strength in the arm, shoulder and back areas.

Altogether strength endurance training in combination with stretching has the following benefits:

- Greater resistance to strain of the moving parts of the body through stronger muscles, tendons and bones. The strain in the three endurance sport types can be withstood longer.
- Cycling and running can be done faster and longer.
- Swimming strokes are stronger through stronger muscles.
- Muscles with a better blood supply tire more slowly.
- Improvement of movement coordination.

General Remarks on Strength Endurance Training
- For ambitious triathletes a certain amount of regularity is recommended in order to stabilise the strength attained.
- Training must be built up slowly. The muscles and tendons need time to adjust to the exertions. In this way the risk of injury is kept as low as possible.
- Before every strength training session a warm-up phase of 15-20 minutes is necessary, because warm loose muscles are less prone to injury.

This warming-up can be done by:

Easy running, which can be extended by up to an hour.

Easy pedalling on the rolling device or ergometer.

Skipping and gymnastics.

- If you wish to visit a studio, you should carry out all exercises precisely under supervision. The strain in strength endurance training should only ever be 50% of maximum strain. Each exercise should include a series of 10 to 40 repeats. 2-4 series are advisable.

This kind of training is ideal in pairs. While one is doing his exercises the other takes a break between series. Both can observe each other and make corrections if necessary. A triathlete does not, however, actually need a training studio to carry out suitable strength endurance training. With a rope for pulling on, and light dumbbells, it can be carried out anytime at home.

For swimming training in a pool paddles are recommended. With these it is possible to do strength training during normal swimming practice. Using paddles,

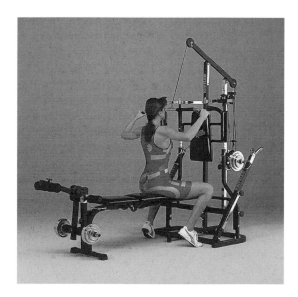

Butterfly exercises to strengthen the chest muscles and the front shoulder muscles (delta muscle)

whose larger surface creates more water resistance, strength training is carried out in the form of intervals.

If the hands together with the paddle blades do not enter the water properly, the paddles are torn out of one's hands. More frequent swimming with paddles is recommended in the preparatory period in particular. In order to increase the development of strength you can make the conditions more difficult and thus increase frictional resistance for the muscles. When swimming this can be done by wearing a T-shirt, when cycling by using a heavy training bicycle or simply by cycling up hill in higher gears. Similar effects can be achieved when running by wearing especially robust training footwear. The strength necessary for endurance capacity is developed to a considerable extent through the endurance training itself. In addition to the two variations that can be carried out in the water, namely swimming with paddles and/or a T-shirt, triathletes and swimmers also have the option of dry training.

This includes training by pulling on a fixed rope and light dumbbell training. A rope can easily be secured in any dwelling, usually in a stairwell. When pulling down on the rope, make sure the movement is the same as that when swimming. Stand where the rope is already a little tense. Bending your upper body forwards, stand with legs apart and grasp the loops of the rope. With every pull hold your elbow high as in swimming; in the beginning phase let it "stand still". Do not form a fist as the movement is then harder to control. Strength endurance training now consists of long series at low strain. A series should include 30, better still 50, 80 or 100 pulls. There should be 5-10 series with breaks of 1-2 minutes between series. Further ways of varying the strain are a greater distance from the fixed point, shorter breaks, and a higher number of pulls and series.

For triathlon beginners, but also for advanced triathletes, training to increase general strength in the upper body is helpful. Circle training, combining various strength exercises in one training session, is particularly suitable for this. No limits are placed on the athletes imagination in developing such combinations.

The main thing to make sure of is sufficient variety: Pull-ups, press-ups of all kinds, standing up from a horizontal position on one's back, lifting stomach and legs when lying on one's stomach etc. With these exercises triathletes can improve their general strength in their own homes.

Light Dumbbell Exercises
- Raise the dumbbells alternately with arms outstretched in front of the body. The palms of the hands should face downwards.
- Raise two dumbbells at the same time at the sides to shoulder height.
- Lying on the back, obliquely raise a weight with the legs.

- Lying face down on a table up to the hips, raise the upper body extending over the table edge until it is horizontal. Do not go any higher. This strengthens the back muscles.

Apart from this, strengthening can be carried out when cycling by going up gradients in high gears, and when running by wearing heavy training shoes and more clothing.

Strength endurance can also be trained in winter through cross-country skiing. This trains many of the muscles used in swimming. The use of double poles and diagonal stride are especially suitable.

Mental Training

In triathlon, especially over long distances, the development of willpower and mental discipline are very important. These too must be trained. I understand the term "mental" as meaning using our mind, our reason or intellect. In other words, those processes involving our thinking capacity. The term "psyche", which is definitely closely linked with this, is more related to the area of feeling, the spiritual sector.

First of all let me share with you the opinion of a professional in this field, Dr. Barbara WARREN, a sports psychologist who is a consultant to many top American stars in her practice in San Diego. After I got to know her and her twin sister Angelika CASTANEDA in Hawaii, in California, in her homeland Austria and in Roth, she was immediately prepared to give me her expert opinion in writing.

"The Mind, an Important Factor in Sport
In order to be able to do sport at all you have to know what part the mind plays in successes and failures. How do we get where we are, how do we deal with the way we think about ourselves, and how do we react to stress and concentration? Our achievements in life always consist of the mental images we have in our mind's eye.

As humans we can change our lives by exchanging the thoughts in our minds for other thoughts. I learned my basic principle in working with athletes in my own practice from my trainer Noel MONTRUCHO:
See it - feel it - allow it.

With these words we can not only put our mind in the mood to do something, but also to win. Mental memory and trying things out take us straight to the finish line, but only if we do it passionately.

The sports psychologist Dr. Barbara Warren (left) with her twin sister Angelika Castaneda from San Diego. Next to them Tom Warren, the "Ironman legend". He has participated in every Ironman event in Hawaii to date and in 1979 he actually won.

Our body cannot differentiate between a real experience and one which only exists in our imagination; in trying things out we determine a cycle of successes.

This of course runs parallel with neuro-muscular practice. We can be winners if we transpose our God given talent together with a maximum of precise knowledge used in sport on to an optimum preparation of mind and body.

In my practice I work with the breaking through of barriers which sportsmen and sportswomen have set themselves. I show them how to deal with themselves as a winner. I tell them how to avoid sabotaging their own victories, and I know that winning must be learned.

How can our mind intervene concretely in our preparations and of course in our triathlon?

Certainly there are many successful possibilities. After much consideration I have decided to simply describe to readers my individual mental preoccupation with triathlon in some detail. With regard to my first ultra distance triathlon and my first far-reaching Hawaii experience I have already described these mental components in my book "Mein Abenteuer Hawaii-Triathlon".

May I call my mental dealing with triathlon successful?

As I have so far finished in all of my more than 150 triathlon events, and have seldom ended a race dissatisfied, I feel I can let this statement stand for itself without any exaggeration. The same applies to my roughly 60 marathons and the many other running events since 1980.

I am often asked why I have been doing triathlon for 15 years and can still motivate myself again and again. This probably has much to do with the passion mentioned by Barbara Warren, both in the theoretical preoccupation with the sport of triathlon and of course on the practical side, in training.

The theoretical preoccupation with the opportunities triathlon offers us, but also with its limits and its dangers, is actually so interesting and comprehensive that I could write a book of more than 500 pages if I were to present extensively all the problems touched on, or associated directly and indirectly with the sport. Because, however, I wish to pass on my knowledge and experience in as concrete, vivid and practical a form as possible, some problems can only be covered briefly.

That I have not lost my appetite for the physical preoccuupation with triathlon can be put down to the fact that I have always placed, and still place, great emphasis on calm endurance training. My training is not very intensive - yes, I know, often not intensive enough.

On the other hand I orientate myself to the following statement, which I have found from experience to be true: "Not the length but the intensity of training strains the body unfavourably."
Or: "No race is too long, but some are too fast."

It is clear to me that a day on which I take part in an ultra distance triathlon is not necessarily the healthiest day in my life. On the other hand it represents that extra something and motivates me to live 355 days a year more consciously and healthily than most people in our part of the world as a result of my nutrition and my endurance training.

I like to compare a race day with another day of celebration. Then too we sin against our health through excessive consumption of food and drink. But if you lead an especially healthy life on the other days of the year, surely you can "sin" a few times a year with a good conscience, don't you agree?

In addition to calm endurance training there are several other factors which in my opinion help maintain motivation in triathlon:

In the autumn and winter months I tend to allow for a four month regeneration period. In this time I catch up on things that were somewhat neglected in the summer months, such as music, intensifying friendships and acquaintanceships, planning travel, going through the slides and photos of summer trips, and above all browsing through books of the Fifties. For me such old books are still the nicest presents there are. This often completes a circle in the world of my thoughts. As a 13 and 14 year old school boy I would start dreaming whenever I read a story that took place outside Germany. Although I never left our region of Münsterland, I developed concrete impressions of Austria, Italy, America, Australia and other countries. In my imagination I spent many hours there. And today I have the great fortune to have seen and experienced most of these countries. The long winter evenings are ideal for such daydreams. During this really long regeneration time I recover physically, mentally and spiritually very well. In spring I again look forward very much to my sport, just as I look forward in autumn to the long evenings.

I only run 2-3 x per week and swim 1-2 x. I stop cycling altogether until the first rays of February sun return. Here are two examples of how much I adjust myself mentally and physically to this period of active recovery: As soon as the last race of the season is over I no longer swim the 1,000 m in 19 minutes as in the competitive period, but in 21-23 minutes. The willingness to achieve faster training times is simply no longer there. In running it is the same. I have difficulty maintaining my five minute speed per kilometre. Even if I forced myself, after the season is over, I no longer manage to train at my usual training pace. For a while I can really "let myself go" sportwise.

The past years have shown me that this was exactly the right thing to do. When my head says it is time for a break, my body cannot and does not want to go on. "First the head and then the legs", that's it.

In the winter months it is time to critically review and take stock. What should I do differently next year etc. Fortunately our triathlon sport is so diverse that even I change some things each year. Additionally, for years now I realise again and again: Hermann, as well as running, cycling and swimming you should also do strength training, more stretching, more ..., more ...! But unfortunately, no, thank goodness, there are other things in my life which are actually more important than fascinating triathlon.

Another major aspect which makes sure my motivation returns, and which can equally apply to other athletes, is that I have more or less succeeded in incorporating my training into my daily schedule. From February or March until October I cycle to work daily on my racing bike. 2 x 19 km daily means 4,000-4,500 kilometres annually just through cycling to and from work. In the afternoon I can extend the ride home easily without delay arising by travelling to the cycling location. Thus the most time consuming part of training is practically taken care of and no longer requires great attention. Equally important to maintaining motivation is the fact that on principle I always plan my holidays and my travel first, and then my races. Not the other way round. It has always been natural to me to take my family on sporting trips as far as possible. Compensation for the bother that triathlon directly or indirectly causes them, such as laundry, mowing the lawns ... etc.

That was a brief look at my environment, which I draw on to maintain and renew my motivation. Finally, every year there are several new, appealing and perhaps spectacular races which I can add to my season's programme. In Germany, Europe and the world triathlon offers so many interesting events that I can see no danger to my motivation in the coming years (why not decades?).

How Can I Use My Mind, My Psyche Properly for My Races?
Personally, in my many triathlon races I have found:
"The longer the distance and with it the race duration, the more decisive is psychological, mental strength."

For the psychological preparation of "my" triathlon, of "my" big day, a positive basic attitude is essential, from which my "passion" stems for everything I do in connection with the race.

With my personal goal in mind: to finish a triathlon for the first time, an ultra distance triathlon over 226 km or even to qualify for Hawaii, I have set myself a great challenge. This must now be met.

The question of "why" must be clearly answered before the actual sporting activity. 15 reasons for the so fascinating sport of triathlon have already been extensively covered in my book "Handbuch für Triathlon". Now, during the training phase, doubts about achieving one's sporting goals should be responded to positively, for example:

"In training I am able to do the short distance, the middle distance or even the ultra distance. If Hermann can do it in his training, so can I. He only needs to accompany me." I promise anyone who trains according to my recommendations that I will "mentally" be with them and support them, especially when there are critical moments. The whole thing becomes much simpler when I consider this triathlon as a three course menu.

Entrée:	1.5 km or 3.86 km swimming
Main course:	40 km or 180 km cycling
Dessert:	10 km running or a marathon

I wish all triathletes bon appetit.

So that the dessert is not too bitter and does not spoil "my" whole meal, it is absolutely advisable to lose the fear of the 10 km or marathon run. This is very easy.

Before the triathlon, either in spring or autumn or in the preseason, a number of calm runs over the particular distance are undertaken. For the marathon distance this is an absolute must. This is simply part of sensible basic endurance training. It is decisive, however, that when doing this run you do not destroy your motivation for the rest of the season by starting the first half like a world champion and then in the second half only just making it by crawling along and forcing yourself on. It is better to be a few minutes slower, but calmer. This run should build you up, not wear you down. That applies both physically and mentally. So, now we have already removed our fear of running. We do exactly the same with swimming. Without looking at the clock the swimming distance is covered once or twice before the event, simply easily and relaxed.

Cycling actually creates the least problems. Here too you can roll along the triathlon distance on an especially nice day with a cycling team mate. A few breaks along the way do no harm.

In a state of fear I cannot achieve my real performance capacity in a race, I can only do this in a state free of fear. The prerequisites can be created through well thought out training.

Where else can fears arise in triathlon and how can they be dealt with?

- Fear of not getting to the cycling "check-in" and the swimming start on   time:
  The answer here is to arrive early and to put the jerseys etc. in the appropriate bags at home already. Pack your cases and bags the evening before departure at the latest and use a check list (see page 140) to make sure you have everything.
- Fear before the swimming start:
  Turn up in plenty of time, avoid bunches - even if it means swimming a few metres more, having spare goggles in your swimming trunks can calm you down amazingly, do a warm-up swim and check the goggles, ensure you are tense but free of fear.
- Always remember:
  I am supposed to be having fun, this is not a "struggle" for me here today.
- Fear of the chaos in the change-over zone:
  Before the start study the locations and mentally go through the procedure several times.
- Fear of being kicked:
  In crawl or freestyle unlikely. In breaststroke keep more distance sideways.
- Fear of a swimming, cycling or running time that is too slow:
  Always set yourself two goals. A very good and a satisfactory time.
- Fear of a flat tyre in the cycling section:
  Practise changing the tube several times at home. Clean your racing bike intensively and in doing so inspect all important parts.
- Fear of ....
- Fear of ....

Be an optimist, not a pessimist!

The difference becomes quickly clear in the forms of expression.

The pessimist always answers: Yes, but ....

The optimist alwas answers: BUT YES!

Apart from this, remember my two problem solving theories in my book "Adventure Sports – Ironman – Der Hawaii Triathlon". There it says:

"THERE IS A SOLUTION TO EVERY PROBLEM."
"MAKE THE BEST OF EVERY SITUATION!"

So, instead of seeing everything black on black and pessimistically, and thus robbing yourself of a great deal of the joy of the race, it is highly advisable to see things positively, optimistically.

Experts have also found that failure in races is usually linked with negative thoughts, while successes are linked with positive thoughts.

In difficult situations this could be the scenario:
- "If I get a flat tyre, it will be fixed in five minutes. This compulsory break will give me renewed strength", or
- This momentary phase of weakness will pass. Just keep calm. I have handled greater problems than this. Besides, the others will have their problems too, and by then I will be up and running again", or
- On a steep hill, do not moan and complain, but approach the matter with healthy aggression, such as "come on hill, I'll eat you up today, I'll get you - even if you have something against that. In a minute there is a racing descent, then it's a matter of: "Only flying is more fun..."
- In the bike park: "Let the others have their paraphernalia; with my bike I've ridden a 38 average before; everyone has to peddle; I'll get past one or the other."
- Concentrate on your strengths, be conscious of them. Accept your own weaknesses, but do not be obsessed with them. All your concentration should be dedicated to your strengths.
- Don't put yourself under too much pressure, for this hampers you. Rather, become aware of what is really more important in life. Such as health, joy, fun ....!

The methods athletes use mentally and physically to prepare themselves for and to participate in a race are as numerous as the triathletes themselves.

I will therefore describe here my personal physical and mental preparation for a race. This too should not be copied without question, but should be extended taking into account one's own strengths and avoidance of one's own weaknesses.

The extremely interesting article "Dealing With Your Personality Structure - A Factor Of Success" by Prof. Georg KROEGER in the appendix of this book demonstrates how to become aware of one's own strengths and weaknesses.

In my opinion the basis for successful and satisfying sporting activity is on the one hand the physical preoccupation with triathlon (my sporting emotions) and the resulting mental willingness as a prerequisite for, on the other hand, the physical activity, i.e. training.

As someone who participates in his sport passionately, but not professionally, but rather as an intensive performance oriented hobby, my personal situation naturally has great significance. This probably applies to 99.9% of all triathletes. For the small number of professionals, on the other hand, it is a completely different matter. That is, however, not a subject to be dealt with here.

This becomes especially obvious with regard to the amount of training. Everyone knows that in the main training period, and during the season, there is a great need for willingness to compromise, in order to at least partially do justice to all interests according to their importance. There is no question that one's occupation has absolute priority. Therefore comprehensive training is done at the expense of one's private life, often of the family. It is important to provide well in time for the prerequisites for unstrained training. The necessary compromises should be agreed on in winter. Reaching them is not always easy.

But it is certainly easier than having to "sneak in" every hour of training the whole season long and then having a really bad conscience about doing one's sport. Under these conditions it is extremely difficult to maintain the enjoyment of sport needed to perform well.

I cannot advise anyone to seek the ideal world of sport and at the same time be responsible for destroying a friendship, a partnership or even a family. I see the following opportunities to involve one's partner and family in triathlon:

- Plan the season together in the quiet winter months.
- Bring predictable repairs to the house or appartment forward to the winter months.
- Do not necessarily plan relaxation holidays according to races, but races according to vacations. While travelling to or from a holiday destination it is often possible to include an interesting triathlon one always wanted to participate in.
- Integrate your partner, your family, in triathlon activities. Go to events together, combine triathlons that are further away with a visit to friends, a short holiday, a sightseeing tour or a long weekend.
- Spring training in southern climes is excellent for travelling together. Because there is no work pressure there, one still has enough time for doing things together in spite of training. In a training camp there should be days of rest too.

So, carry out your training with as little friction as possible on the private side. As can be seen, with good will it is always possible.

Relaxed behaviour is even a guarantee of success in training. With early planning of the seasonal highlights there is enough time left to prepare oneself psychologically for the new challenges. This is the prerequisite for the necessary training motivation. In triathlon too the head goes before the legs.

In good time after the regeneration period of several months I set myself partial goals, as the season itself is still some way off. After all the seasonal highlights are the actual major goals of the season. These in turn provide motivation for the necessary systematic endurance training. Partial goals, e.g. the obligatory spring marathon, support the major goals and also make sure that training never becomes monotonous and boring.

Of decisive importance here is how realistic the goals and partial goals one sets oneself are. If I reach the goals I have set myself, they motivate me further. If I have set them too high and do not reach them, that leads to a loss of motivation. If goals are constantly set too high and not reached, the result can only be demotivation. This endangers systematic training and with it success in competition. If, on the other hand, goals are set too low, this leads to insufficient pressure in training.

Realistic intentions are thus important also as a prerequisite for psychological preparation. A useful method can be to set two goals. One set high in case everything goes very well. You should keep this to yourself and not tell everyone a second goal in case things do not go so well. You can and should discuss this lower, but realistic intention with your team mates. Keep the first one hidden like a joker in a card game.

The goal set in triathlon cannot be first place for everyone. Only a small number of athletes are in the running for this. A personal best performance in swimming, cycling, running, a top placing in one's age category, qualification for a championship or simply a good race are plenty of motivation and incentive.

Motivation is in fact one of the main pillars of good mental preparation. In addition, self-confidence, fear and relaxation are further important mental aspects for endurance athletes. In triathlon, motivation, which is nothing other than our various motives for our will, why we do what we do, can be differentiated into race and training motivation.

The motivation to take part in a triathlon race is with certainty different to that which leads to regular training. While in a race things are involved such as challenge, recognition, genuine experience, getting a placing or simply the fact that we want to measure ourselves against others, in training it is more a matter of the joy of exercise, enjoying the countryside, diversity, health consciousness, sensible use of leisure time and contact with like-minded people. The latter includes training in groups.

This usually takes place during cycling and running in the aerobic region, which invites one to chat. If a group stops talking that is usually a sign that they are no longer training in the aerobic region. In these training sessions which often last several hours there is a place for discussions of every kind. Whether sport, politics, travel, private matters - everything can be discussed and provides involuntarily for diversion. Information on sporting conditions in races and in particular recognition of sporting achievements of sporting colleagues have the effect of both building them up and motivating them.

The diversity of triathlon training also offers each of us the opportunity to run, cycle or swim alone. In doing so I can give my thoughts free rein, find myself, think in peace or simply enjoy the beauties of nature. Here too it is easy to involve one's partner and family. Having a cycling escort while running can be very entertaining. A healthy degree of self-confidence is a part of the mental strength of a triathlete. This should increase with the last months and weeks of training before a race. Believing that my training was not only right but ideal for me strengthens this self-confidence.

I create my race plan taking my surroundings into consideration. This leads to real anticipation of the triathlon. I find joy in wanting to manage this race, to wrestle with the problems and difficulties that arise in the course of it and finally to overcome them. In this respect the triathlon later presents the opportunity to celebrate a number of small victories which at the finish line add up to a large personal victory. This anticipation of the great Day X then provides for the necessary tension needed to reach great achievements.

To put it another way, if you have conscientiously and calmly done your homework (training), you can enter the exam (triathlon) full of self-confidence. In order to make the great Day X a personal success you must of course consider the many technical and organisational aspects described later in this book. I go into important races with the following attitude:

- Realistic estimate of my ability.
- It is a race for me with others, not a struggle against others.
- I am swimming, cycling and running for myself.
- The other triathletes are competitors, not opponents to be "beaten, rubbed out or put down".
- The triathlon today should be fun. Enjoyment and fun gliding in the water, rushing on the bike and enjoying the running.
- I am not afraid of any discipline, but I have respect with regard to the distances and their length.
- This triathlon gives me an opportunity to prove my ability to myself.
- This is "my" race.
- What others do is completely uninteresting to me.
- I will orientate myself only to my body, my feelings and my mind.
- The inner tension helps my race motivation and my sporting performance.
- The most important objective in this triathlon is, as always, to finish. The second is to realise my plan, and the main objective of my plan is to achieve my best time.

For the above reasons I look forward to the race and can calmly await it. Nevertheless I know all too well that feeling before the start: I must have forgotten everything. But I'm sure everything will turn out fine after the start signal.

This self-assurance grows more and more with every triathlon. On top of that, at absolutely every start I am certain: Hermann, today you will learn something new again. So far it has always been like that, why should today be any different. This way I am well prepared for all kinds of crazy things happening.

With the start signal the light tension is released and I try as quickly as possible to get to a position on the edge where I have room to swim. My principle: better to swim a few metres more at my own pace than to get into a panic in a large bunch. Always swimming conscious of the fact that afterwards two more full grown endurance sports follow, I neither run out of oxygen nor get in a panic. Although my thoughts sometimes wander, I try to concentrate on my swimming style. Because I have already had bad experiences with drafting (follow the leader) because the person in front of me went the wrong way, I no longer rely on others, every 5th to 10th stroke I take a quick glance towards the interim target I am heading for.

When it is cold in long races I dress dryly on principle. Cycling 180 km in a wet bathing suit is not very comfortable. Personally I cannot handle the cold very well and therefore I take no health risks, even though getting changed costs time and placings.

When cycling I reel away at my own speed and do not bother at all how fast or slowly the other athletes are going. I am doing my own triathlon, I rely on my gut feeling. This has never betrayed me. In short triathlons I sometimes do allow myself to be torn away and try to follow an athlete I know at a reasonable distance, perhaps keeping him just in sight. A remark at this point about the most unsporting practice of riding in a slipstream. Anyone who does not want to ride in a slipstream will always find a way of competing fairly even at the risk of having to drop back a few metres. It is annoying I know, but I comfort myself with the thought that this slower ride means a slight saving of energy. Then it is a case of either: save your strength for the running or I will start a sprint in order to set myself at a distance.

To me, demonstrating mental strength means sticking to my principle: I am running my race and I will not be drawn into rushing by anyone else. Over the long distances this takes its toll heavily in the running, of that I am certain!

The running tactics over the short distances are somewhat different. Here you can take a small risk now and then. Over the ultra distance there is no place at all for such games. Here the motto is: wait, the results are decided after the running, not after the swimming or cycling.

In the second section I notice positively if I am within my time plan or even ahead of it. My motivation grows constantly and releases new energy. I observe the spectators and look forward to my new projection. On the long distances I set myself several intermediate goals, e.g. in cycling the 60 km, 120 km, 150 km marks, in running the 5 km sections. Over short distances, on the bike it is the 10 km points and in running the even kilometres. It is especially important to cycle or run ahead of the partial goals you set yourself. If you are forever riding or running behind them the fun will soon go out of it, doubts will arise: "Why am I actually doing this? Do I need this? Can't I live without triathlon?" etc. Then you are already on the way to giving up, to failure. Thousands of reasons can be found for giving up triathlon. Afterwards comes great frustration. The reason then is not the training but having set goals that are too high and unrealistic. The frustration of messed up races can then be so great that athletes let triathlon be triathlon. Without that something extra, training then can become dull, and the complete exit from the sport is preprogrammed with all the negative consequences for the heart and circulatory system. That does not necessarily mean that every endurance athlete has to take part in races. Whoever decides to do endurance training without participating in triathlons has just as much benefit.

Every athlete has problems in the running stage. A brief change to a slower "gear" and the desire to finish always help here. Every time you overcome a low phase it is a small victory. By the time the finishing line is crossed, the many small victories become an overwhelming personal victory. Everyone who crosses the finishing line is a winner and has the right to feel that way.

Whether or not others are satisfied with my performance does not interest me at all. Decisive is whether or not I am satisfied. This self-assurance is part of being a triathlete.

Even if the time does not quite match our expectations, what does that mean in relation to the weather, the route, the problems etc.?

For me another important factor after the race is the feeling: "Today I did my best. That which was possible under today's conditions and with the training I did." Then I accept my performance and am satisfied. My satisfaction, my feelings of happiness at the finish line, compensate for the small unpleasantnesses on the way to this, my personal victory. According to my experience, optimum psychological race preparation expresses itself this way:

Impatient expectation of the starting signal combined with slight joyful tension or excitement. This continues in the race with clear and conscious orientation. You have the triathlon under control. Thus your personal energy can be channelled properly. The triathlon is experienced consciously with all its ups and downs. For me this is really the heart of a highly interesting sporting activity.

The only possible consequence is a good result for the particular triathlon. Combined with this is a motivational push for daily training.

On the other hand, psychological race preparation that reduces performance capacity shows itself this way:

Excessive nervousness, haste, uncontrolled activity, racing pulse, strong urge to urinate, excessive psychological pressure. In triathlon this can cause you to lose your head (e.g. going along with every attack made by other athletes) and tactical lack of control. Failure is inevitable. One often even experiences cases where highly talented athletes put themselves under so much pressure before decisive races that the body "takes" an illness or injury and they are thus literally freed from having to start.

The second form of reduced performance expresses itself in: total calmness, lack of enjoyment, inability to order one's thoughts, or even the wish to withdraw from the race. The result in the race will be a lack of willpower with all its negative consequences. Exit from the sport is predictable.

Triathlon for Men Only?

Women and Triathlon

As already mentioned in my opening remarks, everything in this book of course applies equally to men and to women, although mainly the masculine forms are used. This is not meant to be discriminatory, but merely a simplification of language.

These days we do not need to say much about the ability of women in particular in endurance sport. This of course applies to triathlon as well, in fact especially. Just think that in 1992 a woman like Paula NEWBY-FRASER finished in Hawaii with a time of 8:55 h, only 9.4% slower than Mark ALLEN at 8:09 h.

Dr. VAN AAKEN has already proven that women are not sprinters, but endurance performers. A woman is not a muscle machine, but a metabolic athlete. She is more dogged and patient than the average man. In training she is easier to motivate and trains more diligently. On average she has a lower weight, lower water content in the body and a lower proportion of muscle. In a man this is 40%, in a woman only 23%. Altogether comparable performance by women in triathlon and in marathons can be assumed to be about 10% above the time of men.

In the book "Richtig laufen mit Galloway", Meyer & Meyer Verlag Aachen, there is a chapter by Barbara GALLOWAY on this highly interesting question of "women and endurance sport", in which the peculiarities of women in endurance sport are treated in some detail (pages 143-157, German edition).

The chapter covers such topics as structural differences, possible problems with menstruation as well as sport and pregnancy.

On the following pages I would like to let three women with completely different ambitions have their say. From whose writings one gets a very good idea of their attitude to triathlon.

Gerda W. from Hamm, in the age category W35, is a busy woman. As well as looking after a husband, a 16 year old daughter, a house and garden she has a full-time job. As team leader of a Runners Point shop, her work is also linked with sport. In addition she runs her sports club. Anyone with so much "sportiness" who is always in a good mood must be involved with heart and soul.

"How did I get into triathlon - and above all: how do I manage to combine sport, family and job?

Thinking about this question it became clear to me that I have already changed much in my life so I can do triathlon. Originally I tried to keep fit with regular jogging. Soon after I began regular participation in popular runs. Because my husband is a keen cyclist we began occasionally going on weekend cycling tours together. On vacation we often went swimming with our daughter. A club colleague suggested I take part in a novice triathlon. At first I thought it a crazy idea. But an attempt can't do any harm, I thought.

Thus one day our whole family took part in the Drensteinfurt Novice triathlon. During preparation I had realised that I found the training appealing and diverse. After that there were other events we took part in. Meanwhile triathlon is not exactly the focal point of my life, but it does play an important part. That is not

always easy, because although the experience and insights I gain through the sport help me in my work in the sports shop, the daily working time until 6.30 p.m. is anything but helpful for my sporting activity. As far as possible I cycle the 6 km to work. If the family is not to be neglected it is easy to see that I would be "stuck" without their support. Together with my husband I have devised a system of sharing work in the

Natascha Badmann

household which allows both of us to train regularly. We do most of our training together and thus have a chance to talk about other aspects of our family life. Obviously I will never become world champion this way. But I experience all the benefits of regular sporting activity and at the same time experience how sport enriches our life as a family."

The second remarkable woman I would like to cite and from whom we male triathletes can learn much, is an athlete who has been involved in endurance sport for decades.

Gudrun S. of Suhl in Thüringen, an ever happy athlete in the age category W50, already has a "picture book career" in cross-country skiing behind her. In 1964 and 1968 she successfully participated in the Olympics, including a fifth placing in the 5 km ski cross-country in Grenoble. For some years now the sports teacher has been doing cross-country skiing in winter and triathlon in summer, together with her partner and 18 year old son. As a matter of course she shares her experience in the Thüringen Triathlon Association and in the organisation of the Rascher Bergsee Triathlon in Suhl. In her age category she is always up near the front, without being grim about it. In triathlon she prefers short distances so far, while in cycling or cross-country skiing she finds longer courses attractive.

Her excellent contribution:
"Motives and thoughts of a long distance woman"

I almost always train cycling and cross-country skiing alone. While doing so I think about all sorts of things, for some years especially about why I actually do it, why I have managed to be active for so many years, always to find motives to bring myself to carry on again and again, in spite of some pains and minor injuries, how I manage to find the time necessary for training and racing ...

A scientifically founded basic principle is that needs, experiences and current

Gudrun S.

emotions determine the attitudes and actions of a person in a certain situation. Over many years I have succeeded in gathering knowledge and experience regarding my physical abilities and potential, to find out what I like, what does me good, but also what I should avoid because it does not do me good. It is important not to copy anyone else, because when you observe yourself you quickly find out what is beneficial to your well-being, your health and your performance capacity. After long patient practice you will recognise that it gets easier and easier to weaken negative emotions, strengthen positive ones, limit conflicts, survive them better and accept realities.

Prof. Dr. F.KLINGBERG, at the time Director of the Institute for Brain Research at the then Karl Marx University in Leipzig, wrote: Do not say you have no time. Time is impersonal. Everyone has it. Time is unlimited, only the processes of life take place in fixed and limited periods of time. This applies particularly to processes of consciousness. If you do not live very consciously, you do much which is unnecessary, experience much which you do not really want, make mistakes and have to repeat or begin again, in other words you waste time. Having time for yourself and time for others are two independent factors. If you only have time for yourself you isolate yourself. If you only have time for others you disintegrate. If you never have time for yourself you will not be satisfied in life.

We women especially should think about this, for in long runs, triathlons and cross-country skiing women are still a small minority. What motivates then to dare participate in a 100 km ski cross-country? For months you preoccupy yourself mentally and physically with this distance. At the beginning it is a bold intention. But gradually you begin to grasp that and the thought will not let you go. Of course it is an adventure. I can hardly imagine a life without extreme situations. At 70 I will never again be able to do what I do now. But I can do something which is an extreme situation at 70. Probably I am a little addicted to such things. There will always be a few extreme adventures in my life.

Who is without ambition about such a long distance? I do not believe there are sports persons without ambition. For many their running time is what spurs them on. At an advanced age we should of course distance ourselves from this approach, for physical health is worth more than finishing a distance, much more than a good running time. One can only advise ambitious sportsmen and sportswomen to listen to their bodies now and then and check how the muscles are getting on, whether there is any "squeaking or rubbing" anywhere.

PROF. Dr. ISRAEL told us: Our moving apparatus is the only human organ that can be voluntarily influenced, therefore it has to be protected from the unreasonableness of its owner. In an ultra long distance run, in a marathon, we are in an exceptional situation. We can no longer be reached through our consciousness. At the most our consciousness tells us: 'I've had enough, what's the point, I'm going to stop.' The thing is to outwit this consciousness which rationally signals the senselessness of an undertaking. This includes: No negation! I.e. replace negative thinking with positive thinking. Not: 'At 80 km I still won't have any pain', but rather: 'At 80 km I am still feeling really great.' Despite intensive sporting and mental preparation I still occasionally experience a certain fear of all that lies ahead of me. In the meantime I am convinced that this fear is necessary and that all who charge into this adventure without a second thought will fall flat on their faces. Sooner or later strength runs out. Then you need your mental strength which has often helped you in these situations, made you "get a move on". With every single step you come closer to your goal, the goal of your dreams. Kilometre 80, only another 20 km, just a fifth of the distance. You sense that you have the opportunity to fulfil a dream. And then you feel an undescribable, uncanny shiver down your spine. The feeling carries you along towards the finish. Then comes the hope of a good conclusion. All tiredness, all heaviness and all pains too are no longer felt. Now they make room for a glorious feeling of satisfaction, a deep sense of gratification. Feelings that make it worth running, running on and on. I had dreamed of running 100 km, now it has become reality. A dream you do not experience often.

Nevertheless, afterwards you are totally burnt out and glad you do not need to run any more. And then it really gets on your nerves that you cannot turn off your mind. You try to calm down, but you are so high that you have another sleepless night ahead of you. Yes, such a long distance will always remain a highlight in your life."

The third woman is Willtrud B. from Kirchheim-Teck. A committed triathlete who

knows what she wants. In 1992 when she had just moved up to W30 it was her most successful year up until that time. As a teacher she even had the courage to take a year long break from her career after her "breakthrough in Roth" in 12:41 h, in order to find out about the world with and through triathlon.

Willtrud B.

In the Ironman Canada she then reached a great achievement of 10:52 h, which she crowned with 11:21 h in Hawaii in 1992. Her training plans from the last six weeks before the ultra triathlon of Penticton show how she prepared her 10:52 h in Canada. Before that though let us read the interesting description by W.B. of "HOW" and "WHY" exactly triathlon.

"For me triathlon is a fascinating sport. Several years ago friends encouraged me to participate in a novice triathlon. It was really great fun, and that is how it all started. Training was extended from year to year, training camps were included in annual planning. The whole thing got more and more interesting and my motivation for training and longer distances in competition increased. After my first 'Ironman' event in Roth in 1990 I discovered my preference for the longer distances. The training, the preparations, simply everything in triathlon is a lot of effort. On the bottom line, however, it is all worth it and you get so much back in different ways. Such a race is a great, but always calculable, experience and adventure. That is why you have to get the training, the mental preparation and the material right.

By mental preparation I mean that I constantly preoccupy myself with the event and keep on imagining it again and again. I think through every single situation and reconsider it. I try always to think positively while doing this. I believe that is

very important, for in such long races much is decided in the mind. It is, however, not always quite so simple to combine family, friends, occupation and sport. The right attitude makes many things possible and there is never time for boredom any more. For me it is always a new challenge to experience my own limits in races and also in training. Every race is different and you learn something new from every race. During an ultra triathlon I occasionally reach a point where I ask myself "Why?"

The fastest woman in triathlon: Paula Newby-Fraser

"This is where the mental preparation comes in. The body is tired, now the mind has to be so much clearer. After the finish it is a sublime feeling to have completed the triathlon. This feeling gives new joy and strength to go on doing the sport. After a brief recovery you are already asking yourself: What have I learned from this race, what can I do better next time. In triathlon standing still is a step backwards. For me this is a constant challenge and a great incentive.

Through triathlon I get to know my body better and experience it more intensively. Consciously dealing with my body is interesting. Another attraction for me is nature. In training and in races you experience nature and the changing seasons much more intensively than in earlier years without sport.

Another reason I really like this sport is the frequent group experiences. Triathlon is actually an individual sport, nevertheless I experience a great willingness to help, mutual respect and many friendships. These grow through the many long training sessions and races together. I am constantly meeting new people. I believe, whether men or women, young or old, the reasons we do triathlon are always the same.

Triathlon is simply fascinating."

From these three completely different perspectives of women it becomes very clear with how much balance, relaxation and joy women do "their" triathlon. These contributions should give something to think about to many male colleagues who tend to an attitude of grimness.

I find the attitude of these ladies simply exemplary.

About Willtrud B.'s training notes:

When a 10% "credit" is considered, her Canada time of 10:52 h corresponds to a man's time of 9:53 h.

For better orientation, here are her personal details:

Triathlete since 1988. Earlier sporting activity: Swimming

Swimming best time:	1,000 m = 15:25 min.
	1,500 m = 22:45 min.
Running:	10,000 m = 42 min.
Cycling:	180 k = 5:35 h
Special notes:	Winter training: Strength training 3 x per week; Many long runs at low pulse c. 130/140.
	Spring training: Many long cycling trips at high pedalling frequency (low pulse).
	Running training: Less in amount, more in intensity.
	Daily about. 30 min. stretching

Date: From 20.07 to 26.07 — Week: 30

Day	Weight km (mo)	S		C		R		Other sporting activity	Comments	Pulse Rest Strain	Weight kg (ev)
		Dist. m	Time	Dist. km	Time or km/h	Dist. km	Time				
Mon.				60	2:15				"Still felt race in Roth	46	
Tue.				50	2:00				(11.7.)	46	
Wed.		1200	easy:25	60	2:15				a little"		
Thu.						14	1:21 Pulse 143 Ø			48	
Fri.									Day off, very tired	50	
Sat.				10	easy					46	
Sun.						20	2:00			46 / 135	
Total		1200		280		34			14.5 h		

Date: From 27.07 to 02.08 — Week: 31

Day	Weight km (mo)	S		C		R		Other sporting activity	Comments	Pulse Rest Strain	Weight kg (ev)
		Dist. m	Time	Dist. km	Time or km/h	Dist. km	Time				
Mon.				60	2:30	11	1:00 Speed incr. Pulse 120-180		R: 10 x 1 km Pulse 160	47	
Tue.		2500	Technique	110	4:00					48 / 130	
Wed.				65	30 km/h Pulse 150	11	1:10		Somewhat tired	49 / 140	
Thu.		3000	4x700 with/ w.o paddles	81	easy Pulse 135				Feel unwell	53	
Fri.									Sick	75	
Sat.									Angina	64	
Sun.									Feeling better	44	
Total		5500		316		22			≈ 17 h		

Date: From 03.08. to 09.08.   Week: 32

Day	Weight km (mo)	S Dist. m	Time	C Dist. km	Time or km/h	R Dist. km	Time	Other sporting activity	Comments	Pulse Rest Strain	Weight kg (ev)
Mon.									Day off	44	
Tue.				25	1:00					44 120	
Wed.				40	1:30	5	30		Feel better	45 130	
Thu.				50	2:00				Felt it	46 130	
Fri.				60 P130	2:20	10	1:00 P140			46	
Sat.				60	2:45	20	1:45 P150		Feel good	46	
Sun.				115	Easy 5:00					46 130	
Total				360		35				18 h	

Date: From 10.08. to 16.08   Week: 33

Day	Weight km (mo)	S Dist. m	Time	C Dist. km	Time or km/h	R Dist. km	Time	Other sporting activity	Comments	Pulse Rest Strain	Weight kg (ev)
Mon.		2500	Technique			23	2:45			48 130	
Tue.		3000	1:00 Technique							47	
Wed.		2500	Technique	40	1:40 P130	6	36 P130			45	
Thu.				80	3:00				Tired, worn out	46 130	
Fri.									Day off	47	
Sat.		1000						Easy		46	
Sun.				100	4:00 P130					45 130	
Total		9000		220		29				15 h	

Date: From 17.08. to 23.08 — Week: 34

Day	Weight km (mo)	S Dist. m	S Time	C Dist. km	C Time or km/h	R Dist. km	R Time	Other sporting activity	Comments	Pulse Rest Strain	Weight kg (ev)
Mon.		3500	1:30 7x500							44 130	
Tue.		1000	5x200	39	16 km/h P 145	8	:40 P 140			45	
Wed.				150	6:00 P 130-140					44	
Thu.						28	2:30			45 140	
Fri.		3500	Technique 1:30 7x500	50	2:00 P 130					46	
Sat.		2000	Endur.sw. :40			16	1:30 P 145	Speed play	Tired, worn out	45	
Sun.									Depart for Penticton	48	
Total		10000		239		52			18 h		

Date: From 24.08 to 30.09 — Week: 35

Day	Weight km (mo)	S Dist. m	S Time	C Dist. km	C Time or km/h	R Dist. km	R Time	Other sporting activity	Comments	Pulse Rest Strain	Weight kg (ev)
Mon.									Tired, bike didn't arrive	46	
Tue.		1500	:30			5	:30 P 140			44	
Wed.				88	3:30 P 130	6	:30 P 145			42	
Thu.		2000	:40							43	
Fri.					20		40: P 130		Feel really good	42	
Sat.										42	
Sun.		3800	1:06	180	5:44	42.2	4:02		RACE Ultratri.	42	
Total		8800		288		53			Hawaii Qualif.		

From NOVICE to IRONMAN

The Five Stages to Success!

IRONMAN
HAWAII
ULTRA Distance Triathlon
Middle Distance Triathlon
Short Distance Triathlon
NOVICE Triathlon

For most triathletes the "IRONMAN" is simply a magic concept. In a fascinating sport it is a spell that annually causes thousands of triathletes to put everything they have into training in the water, on their bikes or on foot in order to tackle the calculated adventure of the Hawaii triathlon not forgetting the high costs now involved for material and race travel. Even if it is not necessarily Hawaii, a part of the Ironman can be experienced often by any well-trained triathlete on a "normal" ultra triathlon distance in Roth or overseas. Roth, with its unique organisation and its more than 150,000 spectators along the route, has a magic power over many triathletes and those who would like to become one.

Ultra triathlon distances in Roth, Almere (NL), Zürich (CH), Podersdorf (A), Nice and Embrun all have their special appeal and are therefore a "MUST" for many. In order to climb these top rungs of triathlon, systematic training is necessary.

The following chapters answer the understandable question: "How do I reach these rungs and how can I constantly improve myself?" But not only is the Ironman a very appealing goal and one worth striving for, participation in the shorter distance triathlons also has its attractions. This especially applies to those who take up the new challenge of triathlon year after year - whether they be beginners or cross over from another sport.

Triathlon has something for everyone. It presents goals worth committing oneself to.

The five stages of triathlon of course mean that the real beginner in endurance sport should begin with Stage 1 and at the earliest move to the next stage after a year. Depending on the degree of commitment in training it is of course also possible and even sensible to remain on a particular level for several years, develop oneself further and make the most of one's individual potential. This applies particularly to the large number of short distance specialists, i.e. athletes who prefer the distance 1.5 km swimming, 40 km cycling and 10 km running. In other words, a full grown endurance discipline. Even the novice distance with 500 m swimming, 20 km cycling and the closing 5 km run can be interesting for endurance athletes in the mid to long-term. For those who come from other sports, mainly other endurance sports such as running, cycling, swimming or rowing, and have been more or less intensively active in these sports, it is of course possible to begin at Stage 2. Beginning at Stage 3 (middle distance triathlon), which involves 2.5 km swimming, 80 to 90 km cycling and 20 km running, should remain an exception.

Stage 1 Novice Distance 500 m/20 km/5 km

How do I Start in Triathlon?

Perhaps you are a triathlon fan who wants to know more about his or her hobby, or you want to start in triathlon. You are right to ask "How do I start in triathlon?"

Courses in which adults, children and young people can learn swimming, cross-country skiing or alpine skiing are taken for granted these days. The same seldom applies to triathlon. In some few cases it is possible to take courses at adult education centres. One of the first of its kind was run by me in 1988 at the adult education centre in Lüdinghausen in the Münsterland region. At the end of the course, which mainly involved practical training activities, the participants took part in a novice triathlon they organised themselves. Apart from this, the only possibility is to join a triathlon club or a club with a triathlon section. This has definite advantages especially for beginners:

1. Training together
Here triathlon newcomers find people who give their advice to all who need it. Training together is much more fun than always training on your own. When they know that like-minded people are waiting for them, everyone manages to pull themselves together and go to training even when the weather is not so good. Experience shows that those who always train alone quickly find excuses like: it is too cold today, it is too hot today, it is too windy today, it is too dark today etc. Unfortunately under these circumstances most of those keen on sport slowly but surely lose their willingness to do sport. Newcomers should not be shy. Amongst those training you will always find suitable training partners.

2. Flow of information

Club members are regularly informed by notice boards and newsletters, such as where there are events nearby for beginners, when the next party is, what campaigns are on currently etc.

3. Travelling to races together

It is possible that travel to triathlon events can be organised together.

4. Organisation

If you want to take part in official championships you need a starting card. This is only available through clubs. Registration for individual events is usually done through clubs as well.

How Do I Find a Club?

It is often possible to make personal contacts through regional sports reports. In addition the sport office of a town or city can usually provide information on whether there is a club with a triathlon section.

The same applies to the triathlon associations at state level or the state sporting association. If there is no possibilty of joining a triathlon club you should join a running, cycling or swimming club in order to enjoy the advantages of group training in one or two sporting disciplines.

Although there are several thousand such popular sports gatherings, and in spite of all club efforts, not everybody will be able to take part in a running-cycling-swimming meet or club directly near where they live. And above all: not everyone will want to go there, for whatever reason.

The great advantage of triathlon training is after all the fact that anyone can run, cycle and swim when and where they want without an organisation, without paying subs, without sticking to fixed practice schedules. Unlike in a club, they can choose whether they practise their sport alone or with friends and acquaintances. Even membership of a club does not exclude the latter possibilities.

Often one must begin training alone. Therefore, here are some tips for everyone who wants to begin doing triathlon on their own:

1. Make yourself aware that "everyone has been a triathlete since childhood"

Let's remember. As a child you covered several kilometres a day in a playful fashion, learnt to ride a bike before going to school and during your school years at the latest you learnt to swim. Even if these playful movements became static movements at some stage, after decades we can still find our way back to the playful form. Of course the length of this process differs from one person to another, but one thing is certain: It is possible, you just have to want it.

2. Practise with a plan

Let us speak first of practising. Training is the next step. Practising has the effect that you relearn running and swimming. Cycling should not really be a problem for anyone. The most progress is made through systematic practice. Sport learning too is based on the principle of picking something up and then repeating it, whereby frequent repetition leads to greater success.

3. Set yourself goals

With a concrete goal in mind, e.g. being able to run for 30 minutes without a break, or swim 20 minutes without a break, or cycle 60 minutes without a break, or doing the novice triathlon in X minutes, it is easier to practise than with questionable, abstract or even unrealistic targets.

Everyone needs their individual goal, which depends on their talent, their age, their state of health, the amount of training time. Their have their current state of fitness as well as their willpower and their ambition.

The Influence of Talent

Every human is born with talent.

Talented endurance athletes, however, will only get on in triathlon if they have other qualities such as willpower, training diligence, discipline and the right attitude. On the other hand, people with less talent can gain just as much enjoyment from this sport as the small number of winning types by correctly judging their own potential.

The Influence of Age

A young person aged 25 when starting their sporting activity obviously has different perspectives to someone starting at 50. There are, however, plenty of examples which show that at 40 endurance athletes are in no way "on the scrap heap", but on the contrary belong to the world's best.

The Influence of One's State of Health

Only healthy people can pursue their endurance activities of swimming, cycling and running without concern. A check-up at the doctor's is advisable to anyone who is unsure of their health. Many small aches and pains are no reason for not doing calm, even exercises. On the contrary, these days both running as well as the other endurance sports are considered therapy, even for heart attack survivors. The more critical the general condition, however, the more care and medical guidance is needed. Anyone who is not completely healthy should set their goals lower, i.e. they should allow more time to achieve their goals.

Through calm endurance training (exercises) the overall state of health will improve and finally the goal set will be reached after a longer starting period.

The Influence Of Time

No one has time for sport, you make time for sport. Fortunately everyone's day has 24 hours. The question is, what you use them for.

The Influence of Fitness

Being healthy means being free of illness. If you are "healthy" in this sense you still are not necessarily fit. Fitness is a measure of general performance capacity. With the aid of tests it is possible to measure your fitness.

The most popular fitness test is that of Dr. K. H. COOPER. He uses running as a test exercise. The test involves a running time of 12 minutes. A 400 m track on an athletics field is suitable for this. On this track you jog or run without a break for 12 minutes. For COOPER, the distance covered is a measure of your current fitness:

Less than 4 laps (1,600 m)	Very bad level of fitness
4 - 5 laps 1,600 - 2,000 m	Bad level of fitness
5 - 6 laps 2,000 - 2,400 m	Moderate level of fitness
6 - 7 laps 2,400 - 2,800 m	Good level of fitness
more than 7 laps	Very good level of fitness

A higher degree of fitness allows you to set higher goals in triathlon.

The Influence of Willpower

To reach a set goal you need willpower. It is advisable to set your goals in such a way that they can be reached with certainty. Reaching a low goal is better than not reaching a goal set too high. If you know you are a determined person, you should not set your goals too low.

The Successful Road To Novice Triathlon

Congratulations on your decision - to take up sport at last. With this decision you are on the right road. No matter who or what motivated you to take this step - friends, family, work colleagues, press reports, TV programmes, a sceptical look at your increasing girth or pleasant memories of "earlier times" when you were more mobile and more active altogether, with all the advantages of the more sporting impression you made - now it is up to you alone to realise the decision you have taken.

With a little willpower and staying power you can overcome all the small and medium sized hurdles. You will find the further you progress along the road to the novice triathlon, the more fun and enjoyment your sporting activity will bring you. As a total beginner you will be able to follow the guidelines here, even if you have not done any sport for 20 years or more. Beforehand you should, however, make the visit to your doctor mentioned above. Tell him exactly what you plan to do, namely 30 minutes of running or 20 minutes of swimming or an hour of cycling. With medical practitioners, be careful about using the term triathlon. Possibly they will think of the Hawaii triathlon covered so intensively by the media. This event is something for very well trained endurance athletes. But why shouldn't that be possible for you too?

If you successfully cover the individual stages or levels, some day Hawaii will also be your great goal. But do not set your goals too high. Remain realistic. The novice triathlon consisting of 500 m swimming, 20 km cycling and 5 km running is our current goal!

For those who have already been active in sport for some time, the appropriate guidelines are on the following pages.

For the moment let us begin with those totally without experience: Younger and older people, those unused to movement, overweight people, people whose health is not stable - in other words, triathlon beginners.

Training Methods For Beginners

Running
For a not very sporty person who has, however, set his goal as successful participation in a novice triathlon after a few months, running is usually the hardest of the three triathlon disciplines. It is easier if you think back to your childhood and youth.

Back then, a quarter of an hour of running was no trouble at all. In summer you romped around for hours in good weather and in bad, without any particular effort. Riding your bike 6 or even 10 kilometres to the nearest lake or swimming baths was something you did not think twice about. Playing tag and other entertaining activities in the water were as little a problem as playing football or volleyball after leaving it.

With playful ease a triathlon is done without even mentioning it - several times a week. We must and can find our way back to this playful practice. Of course the length of this process differs from person to person and is dependent on our age, willpower, nutrition, occupational activity and many other factors.

If you find the following guidelines too simple, you can orient yourself to the ones that come after.

1st Interim Goal Is: 15 Minutes of Jogging, Not Running.
The 1st step for beginners:
The absolute beginner starts with: 1 minute jogging, 1 minute walking. The whole thing 15 times. So far as there are no other sporting activities, these exercises should be carried out at least twice, better three times per week.

Important: Carry out the exercises with a like minded person. It is easier if there are two of you. During the jogging phase talking to the partner ensures the right pace.

2nd step:
2 minutes jogging, 1 minute walking	repeat 5x.
3 minutes jogging, 1 minute walking	repeat 4x.
4 minutes jogging, 1 minute walking	repeat 3x.
5 minutes jogging, 1 minute walking	repeat 2-3x.

Carry out every intermediate stage until it works out.

3rd step:
7 minutes jogging, 3 minutes walking	repeat 2x.
7 minutes jogging, 2 minutes walking	repeat 2x.
7 minutes jogging, 1 minute walking	repeat 2x.
15 minutes jogging,	1x.

If you can jog 15 minutes in one go, you no longer need to speak of jogging, you are a runner. After this there will be no more practising, but rather training.
You are well on the way to becoming an athlete.

2nd Interim Goal: 30 Minutes Running
If you attempt this goal, you should already be able to run for 15 minutes or demonstrate a certain degree of fitness in other sporting activity.

Large quantities of alcohol, chain smoking and lack of sleep are enemies of good physical fitness.
10 minutes running, 5 minutes walking	repeat 2x.
10 minutes running, 5 minutes walking	repeat 3x.
15 minutes running, 5 minutes walking	repeat 2x.

20 minutes running, 5 minutes walking, 10 minutes running. 30 minutes running.

If you train regularly, you will soon reach this 30 minute goal. If you train less regularly, you will take longer. Important: even after a 30 minute run, if possible conversing with someone, you should have the feeling that you could carry on running. Do not overtax yourself.

Do not turn your entertaining training into a race. If for any reason you stop for more than a week, go back a few stages when you start again. This saves you from overtaxing, failures and disappointments, and at the same time you maintain your enjoyment of running. When you have reached the 30 minute goal, you are well on the way to being able to do more.

The foundation stone for a successful novice triathlon has now been laid. Anyone who can run 30 minutes is soon able to cycle 30 or 60 minutes.

Cycling

In cycling you carry on in a similar fashion to running. Except that here progress will be much easier and quicker than in the third triathlon discipline. To get used to

cycling you do not need an expensive racing bike. A normal touring bike with gears is more than enough.

Goal: 60 minutes cycling

Before you plan the first practice, or training rides, there is often opportunity to cycle in the country with friends or family. If the company is pleasant, even if out of practice on a bike, you barely notice the new strain. Here too you should choose a pace that allows you to converse with your fellow cyclists.

For the first training rides choose a flat or slightly rolling route. Begin with rides of 15 minutes in one direction. After a short break, cycle back.

3 training rides 15 min. + 2-5 min. break + 15 min.
3 training rides 20 min. + 2-5 min. break + 20 min.
3 training rides 25 min. + 2-5 min. break + 25 min.
3 training rides 30 min. + 2-5 min. break + 30 min.
3 training rides 30 min. +   1 minute break + 30 min.
60 minutes easy winding down ride

Swimming

The swimming distance in a novice triathlon is usually 500 metres. In a 50 metre swimming pool five hundred metres means ten lengths. The swimming style is optional. Swimmers out of practice usually prefer breaststroke and should stick to this. Only later on, when sporting ambition increases, should the changeover to crawl or freestyle take place. On the other hand, for beginners there is no reason not to learn the crawl straight away.

So, swim however you swim best. The goal for a swimmer out of practice is: 600 m or 20 minutes non-stop swimming In a 25 m pool begin as follows: swim 25 m, take a break of 15 seconds at the end and then start the second round.

When you have done that 20 times, you have done 500 m.

As a little extra, to show you can still keep swimming, follow with another four lengths. If you have managed this on three different practice days, try the following pattern:

On each of three practice days:

1 x 25 m, 15 sec. break, 1 x 50 m, 15 sec. break. Swim this series 8x. Total distance 600 m.

50 m, 15 sec. break, 5x altogether
50 m, 15 sec. break, 75 m, 15 sec. break, 5x altogether
50 m, 15 sec. break, 100 m, 15 sec. break, 4x altogether
100 m, 15 sec. break, 6x altogether
150 m, 20 sec. break, 4x altogether
200 m, 30 sec. break, 3x altogether
300 m, 30 sec. break, 2x altogether
500 m, 60 sec. break, 100 m, 1x altogether
600 m

During this practice phase try to get into the water 2x per week. On vacation or in hot summer temperatures it is a good idea to practise in a lake. If you are afraid of being in a depth of over 2 m, practice in shallow waters.

As there are no markers or dividers in open water, swim according to feeling or time. An example:

1 minute swimming, 20 sec. break; 20x
2 minutes,   20 sec. break; 10x
3 minutes,   20 sec. break; 7x
4 minutes,   20 sec. break; 5x
5 minutes,   20 sec. break; 4x
6 minutes,   20 sec. break; 4x
7 minutes,   20 sec. break; 3x
10 minutes,   30 sec. break; 2x

15 minutes swimming, 1 minute break, 5 minutes swimming
20 minutes swimming non-stop.

Every interim stage is practised until the distance can be covered without great effort. Only then do you move on to the next interim stage.

Anyone who can swim for 20 minutes will quickly be able to swim 1,000 m and more after further training.

Beginners often prefer breaststroke.

Triathlon Training for Beginners

Now that the triathlon newcomer has established a basis in the three endurance sports swimming, cycling and running over the past months, it is assumed in the following that every budding triathlete can

run 30 minutes,
cycle 60 minutes and
swim 20-30 minutes.

Not all three disciplines one after the other, but each "only" on its own.

Triathlon Specific Training for Beginners

With the three individual achievements the basis has been laid to take part successfully in a novice triathlon.

Now all you need is a race date on which to realise the great goal of finishing in a triathlon for the first time. Find out early and register in time. Event dates are usually known five or six months in advance. Ask other triathletes, sports offices or look in the papers.

Your goal for the first triathlon should be: to finish. For the beginner it is only a matter of getting through all three disciplines one after another, experiencing this challenge consciously and having fun doing it.

Arrange your race in such a way that during the swimming, cycling and running you already look forward to the next event. Do not bother about other participants, just do your own triathlon. Performance oriented triathletes, on the other hand, who want to prove themselves over longer distances, will have the goal of finishing the triathlon with the best possible time and placing

Whatever you do, do not let yourself be discouraged if one or other of the performance triathletes wants to prove himself over the novice distance. There will always be such cases. The term training covers all the measures designed to increase physical performance capacity. Adapting reactions of the body to training stimuli lead to increases in performance.

For beginners, regular and above all calm training leads to definite increases in performance.

The Minimum Quota in Triathlon

Dr. Ernst VAN AAKEN, the "high priest of running", devised the following simple rule: Anyone who runs 42 km in a week is capable of running the distance in one go and without health problems arising. Applied to the endurance sport triathlon that means: if the distances of the planned triathlon are covered in a week, then the triathlon can be successfully completed.

Concretely the following distances would need to be covered in a week: 500 m swimming, 20 km cycling and 5 km running.

How Should Beginners Structure Their Triathlon Training?

Before I show particular examples of how to do beginner training successfully, you should be clear about the main points of endurance sport. The training emphasis in endurance sport is on exertion of low to medium intensity. Anyone for example who after a 6 km run can hardly shower themselves and needs a long rest on the sofa has clearly trained too fast.

Training frequency is the number of sessions per week. With increasing training age the training frequency can be increased.

Beginners train e.g. 3 to 4 times per week, competition athletes 5 to 6 times and performance athletes 7 to 8 times or more.

Exertion and Recovery Belong Together

For every triathlete, in addition to physical exertion, recovery is very important. This is admittedly not a great problem when training 3 to 4 times a week, nevertheless it should always be considered as training develops.

A beginner who trained twice daily and allowed himself no recovery would quickly be over trained. This over training does not result in an increase but rather in a decrease in performance.

An advanced athlete on the other hand can deal with the same exertion because his body regenerates faster as a result of the better training state it is in. Assuming of course that he too has not trained constantly at an intensity that is too high.

To ensure a constant improvement in performance, any training must be carried out regularly and over a longer period of time. Endurance training is always a long-term affair.

Usually a fast improvement in performance can be expected of triathlon beginners. Irregular training, or long interruptions in training, lead to reduced performance.

Creating the Endurance Basis

Every triathlon newcomer should first concentrate on one thing: creating an endurance basis. You can only get this by training for as long and as calmly as possible. Most suitable is your "favourite discipline" or the one you feel strongest in. For a former runner it will most likely be running, for a swimmer swimming and for a cyclist cycling. In your favourite discipline you tend to train a bit longer than recommended, but please keep it light and easy.

A former runner now begins to run regularly 30 to 60 minutes, the swimmer to swim 30 to 40 minutes, and the former cyclist cycles for an hour at least twice a week.

Training in the Three Individual Disciplines

After the "former athletes" and the "real beginners" have trained in their favourite discipline for several weeks to improve their basic endurance, coping with the other sports is next – an initially arduous, but interesting undertaking. Many runners and cyclists have problems with swimming.

But do not think too much about the swimming style, just swim the way you can best. Swimmers often have difficulty with running. By following the guidelines for running beginners given above you will soon have that under control as well. Cycling as a single discipline actually creates very few major problems. If at all, it is usually in the sitting department. A little cream and cycling pants with a leather pad, worn directly on the skin, will quickly let you forget these problems too. Whether a racing bike - but then with a helmet please - or a touring bike is used does not really matter.

On the first training rides you should try to reach 90 revolutions per minute (rpm), later 100. 90 rpm means: 90 pedal turns in a minute.

If you do not manage it straight away, at least keep trying to do it. Your knees will thank you. When cycling you have the possibility of carrying out training with changes of speed, so-called Fartlek.

Combination Training

Regular combination training is recommended every two weeks, whereby for beginners only the changeover from the bike to running is likely to cause problems.

It is important that the last 1 to 2 km on the bike are cycled especially easily.
The weekend is a good time for combination training.
The following combinations are recommendable:

- 20 km easy cycling + 3 km easy running
- 15 km fast cycling + 5 km calm running
- 500 m swimming + 20 km cycling

During these changes you have an opportunity to practise changing clothes without any rush. Save the combination of all three disciplines for your first novice triathlon.

The following training recommendations are really to be understood as such. Please do not make a dogma or a must out of them. I of course do not know your situation.

Plan your training according to family, occupational and other requirements or pressures.

The weather, your enthusiasm and your mood will also play a role. A tip:

if you are in a bad mood carry out a very calm endurance training session. You and those around you will be surprised at the positive effects.

In spite of everything else, you should observe the following rules steadfastly:
- Regular training; only this way are continuous performance improvements possible.
- Low training intensity; conversation must always be possible when running and cycling.
- Train with joy, not with force.
- If possible train at least every 2nd day.
- Begin each training session very loosely and easily and end it the same way.
- Do not forget stretching exercises when training is finished (see chapter Stretching for Triathletes).
- Increase training strain or exertion only slowly.
- Eat consciously.
- If you have feelings of exhaustion or inner unrest, train especially calmly or preferably have one more rest day than planned.
- Do not consider training recommendations a "must".

Training Recommendations for Triathlon Beginners

The training recommendations relate to the last three months before the start of a novice triathlon.

We differentiate between four groups:

All have the goal: successful participation in a novice triathlon with the distances: 500 m swimming, 20 km cycling and 5 km running.

Group 1: Endurance sport newcomers, who can already swim 15 minutes, cycle 60 minutes and run 30 minutes, however in each discipline on its own.

Group 2: Former runners.

Group 3: Former swimmers.

Group 4: Former cyclists.

Training recommendations for group 1:

Week 1, 2, 7, 12

Tue.	Swimming:	15 minutes
Thu.	Running:	30 minutes
Sat.	Cycling:	40 minutes

Week 3, 4, 8, 10

Tue.	Swimming:	20 minutes
Thu.	Running:	25 minutes
Sat.	Cycling:	30 minutes
Sun.	Favourite discipline	

Week 5, 6, 9, 11

Tue.	Swimming:	25 minutes
Wed.	Running:	30 minutes
Thu.	Swimming:	20 minutes
Sat.	Cycling:	40 minutes, followed by 10 minutes running
Sun.	Favourite discipline	

Notes: The individual training days can of course be swapped around, but try to keep to the amounts of training.

With regard to the coming event: do not train on the last two days before the start.

Training recommendations for group 2:

Week 1, 2, 7, 12

Tue.	Swimming:	15 minutes
Thu.	Running:	30 minutes

| Sat. | Cycling: | 1 hour |
| Sun. | Running: | 30 minutes |

Week 3, 4, 8, 10

Tue.	Swimming:	20 minutes
Thu.	Running:	35 minutes
Sat.	Cycling:	1 hour
Sun.	Running:	40 minutes

Week 5, 6, 9, 11

Tue.	Cycling:	40 minutes
Wed.	Running:	30 minutes
Thu.	Swimming:	20 minutes
Sat.	Cycling:	40 minutes + 20 minutes running
Sun.	Swimming:	20 minutes

Training recommendations for group 3:

Week 1, 2, 7, 12

Tue.	Swimming:	1,000-1,500 m
Thu.	Running:	30 minutes
Sat.	Cycling:	40 minutes

Week 3, 4, 8, 10

Tue.	Swimming:	25 minutes
Thu.	Running:	30 minutes
Sat.	Cycling:	40 minutes
Sun.	Running:	30 minutes

Week 5, 6, 9, 11

Tue.	Cycling:	40 minutes
Wed.	Running:	30 minutes
Thu.	Swimming:	25 minutes
Sat.	Cycling:	30 minutes + 20 minutes running
Sun.	Swimming:	30 minutes

Training recommendations for group 4:

Week 1, 2, 7, 12

Tue.	Swimming:	20 minutes
Thu.	Running:	30 minutes
Sat.	Cycling:	1 hour

Week 3, 4, 8, 10

Tue.	Swimming:	25 minutes
Thu.	Running:	30 minutes
Sat.	Cycling:	1 hour
Sun.	Running:	30 minutes

Week 5, 6, 9, 11

Tue.	Cycling:	40 minutes
Wed.	Running:	30 minutes
Thu.	Swimming:	25 minutes
Sat.	Cycling:	40 minutes + 20 minutes running
Sun.	Swimming:	20 minutes

The notes regarding Group 1 apply to all the groups.
A few words on training intensity:

When cycling and running you should almost always train at the pace at which you can easily converse with your training partner. At this speed, also known as "Training 130", your pulse rate should be 130 beats per minute. When cycling it can be below that. With this method you improve your basic endurance. This later enables you to handle longer distances.

Equipment for Beginners

Triathlon beginners should not bother themselves with thinking too much about their equipment. For swimming you really only need a bathing suit and swimming goggles. When buying a new bathing suit you should consider whether to get one with a soft inlay in the crotch. It makes cycling considerably more comfortable, and when the weather is warmer the change from bathing suit to cycling pants is not necessary.

The run at the end can also be comfortably concluded in such a bathing suit. You should in any case make sure there is no large seam in the middle. This can be real torture when cycling. Every triathlon shop or well stocked sports shop has such bathing suits with a soft inlay. The swimming goggles need to be adjusted to the particular face type. There are no special triathlon goggles. In the price range 15-30 DM there are no good or bad goggles, only ones that fit and ones that do not fit. To find out if goggles fit or not when buying them, carry out the following small test: Adjust the width over the bridge of the nose appropriately and press the glasses firmly over the eyes. You have found goggles that fit if, when you let go, the low pressure within the glasses causes the goggles to "stick" for a moment.

But try out several different models and brands. Because sunshine can often be expected in the open air season it is a good idea to get tinted goggles. One or two bathing caps protect against losing too much body heat when the water temperature is low. If you have problems with your sense of balance doing the crawl, you should wear ear plugs. A neoprene suit is not recommended for beginners. It only becomes necessary often when longer distances are involved. For the novice distance beginners do not necessarily need a racing bike. A well-oiled and pumped up touring bike does the job just as well. For information on buying a racing bike see the chapter "Equipment for Triathletes". One thing in advance: if you ride a racing bike, whether in training or competition, for your own safety you must wear a helmet.

For the final discipline you need running pants and shirt and a good pair of running shoes. The running shoes in particular are of great importance. More about that under "Equipment for Triathletes"

Now that you are well prepared and have tested your equipment many times in training, you can step up to the starting line well at ease. Every triathlete can understand your feeling of excitement as you do this for the first time. Others felt exactly the same or similarly. Stay loose and try to experience and enjoy consciously your premiere. If you have done your homework, there is no need to fear the exam. Before the triathlon find out about the route, especially the cycling section. Walk the changeover zones swimming-cycling and cycling-running so that you know how to get from the water to your bike, where your clothes are and where you have to ride or run out again.

The official announcements before the race are important. There you hear all the details about the race and can ask questions yourself.

And now: HAVE FUN and GOOD LUCK!

Remember: you do not recognise a triathlete by their equipment but by their attitude.

A WOMAN, A MAN who swims 500 m, cycles 20 km and runs 5 km is SOMEONE WITH GUTS!

Experiences

38 year old Paula DIEKMANN and her 12 year old daughter TANJA describe their first triathlon experiences.

First the lively TANJA: "As a spectator I watched my mother in triathlon. I was so enthusiastic that I even accompanied my mother on the 5 km running section. Next year I'll do it too, I decided. Then I actually forgot about it all, until the new date was announced. Although I hadn't practised much, I wanted to enter. I jogged a few times with my mother, and in summer I went swimming three times a week. I also went cycling four or five times.

At the starting signal I swam like mad. After 200 m I thought, you'll never make it. But my father stood at the side of the pool and crossed both fingers for me. The first 250 m were the worst, after that I thought: I've already done more than half. The first two cycling laps were harmless, the other two were tough. When I got off the bike I had really wobbly knees. I walked the first 100 m, then ran and walked some more now and then. While running I talked, although I wasn't supposed to. My Dad cheered me on again and again. Without him I would never have made it. At the finish I was over the moon and above all really proud that I had done it. The certificate was the greatest experience at the time. I would recommend it to anyone to try it some time, you just have to have this experience."

How unprejudiced children are. Who else but a child could say so much with so few words?

The 38 year old mother began triathlon this way:
"Two months before a novice triathlon I just wanted to find out why my brother was such an enthusiastic triathlete. I could only do that if I entered one myself. As I had been running 4 km twice a week with other women for a year, and swimming regularly in the summer, and often going on bike tours with my family of four, I figured I should be able to handle it.

Four weeks before the race was the dress rehearsal for me on my own, 500 m swimming, 20 km cycling and another 5 km running. I was satisfied, but noticed that I needed to practise the changeover cycling-running a few more times. In good spirits I took my place at the start and also reached the finish in one piece. My family was thrilled and extremely proud of their mother, especially Tanja.

For four years now I have been taking part in one or two novice triathlons and have constantly improved. It is simply a great feeling, and it gives you a feeling of security when you can prove that you are fit", says beginner P.D.

There is nothing to add to that.

Stage 2 Short Triathlon 1.5/40/10 km

The second triathlon stage offers all triathletes opportunities to reach their goals, or even interim goals:
• The "beginner" who wants to raise his or her sights a little after a year of training and completing one or more novice events.

- The athlete entering from another discipline who already has experience in other endurance sports and now wants to experience the fascination of the three endurance sport types.
- The "competition athlete" whose nature it is to be a sprinting type in the triathlon sense and who feels at home over the short distance.
- The "performance athlete" who seeks and finds success over the short distance because of his high basic speed and training volume.

In addition, ambitious long distance specialists use the short distance to test and improve their basic speed as a training measure. Experience clearly shows: Athletes who perform excellently over long distances are also up front over the shorter distances. The number of events per season a triathlete can comfortably enter are as follows for the short distance:

Beginners 3 - 5

Competition athletes 5 - 8

Performance athletes 10

Short Triathlon Training for Beginners

Here we mean those who want to move up from the novice class to the short distance triathlon class as well as athletes from other sports.

Those who have successfully completed one or more novice courses and experienced for themselves the great fascination of the non-stop triple sport usually raise their sights a little higher. Rightly so!

In Germany and central Europe the novice season ends in September. On the one hand those who have tasted blood are so highly motivated that the time until May of the following year is much too long, namely seven months, on the other hand we all know that there are other things in life more important than good results in triathlon. Let us assume that, because of the enjoyment you got from being in motion from your own performance which you would never have thought possible earlier, because of the feeling of being fit and knowing your body better than you ever did before, and because of your success, you are highly motivated to become even more active in triathlon. But hold on a minute, even the best work horse needs its winter break. This applies especially to triathletes, who in addition to their job usually have a family and a strenuous hobby, namely strength-sapping triathlon. So, in the months of October, November, December and possibly also January, active rest is needed. This means that three easy training days per week are enough for one or two months, after that a fourth session is recommendable. As long as the weather is still good you should keep going on 60 to 90 minute bike rides. You should in any case go on two runs a week. To liven up training a little you can occasionally participate in a popular run, but please, not at full speed; 90 or 95% is more than enough. If you want to use the winter to improve or even change your swimming style, you should do this under guidance if possible. Experienced triathletes are usually helpful. It would of course be even better with the guidance of an experienced swimming coach. Another variation, in order to change from breaststroke, is to spend your summer holidays near a swimming lake. You can read how to do this successfully in my "Handbuch für Triathlon".

A week in the period October to January could be like this:	
Tue. Swimming:	30-40 minutes
Wed. Running:	10 km easy Fartlek
Sat. Cycle tour:	60-90 minutes
Sun. Running:	12 km loosely
Alternatively:	
Tue. Swimming:	30-40 minutes
Wed. Running:	10 km
Fri. Swimming:	40 minutes
Sat. Running:	12 km
Sun. Running:	8 km Fartlek

If you have the opportunity to go cross-country skiing in winter, do so. It is an excellent complement to triathlon, strengthening the upper arm and leg muscles. If the weather no longer allows cycling, it is advisable to go for an extra run. Even with just more running and swimming you further improve your fitness.

If there is then a good weekend weatherwise and timewise in March or April, an intensive cycling phase is recommended, e.g. Fri. 20 km, Sat. 40-50 km, Sun. 30-40 km.

The Last 12 Weeks before the First Short Distance Triathlon
1st short distance triathlon in late May

Week 1, 2, 5, 8, 11	
Tue. Swimming:	1.5 km interv. on, off, 2 x 5 x 50 m
Wed. Running:	10 km Fartlek, 25 km cycling easily
Fri. Swimming:	1 km endurance
Sat. Cycling:	40 km calmly pedalling, 100 rpm
Sun. Running:	10 km calmly
Total: 2.5 km S/40 km C/20 km R	

Week 3, 4, 9, 10

Tue.	Swimming:	1.5 km interv. 50/100/150/200/150/100/50 m
Wed.	Running:	10 km calmly
Thu.	Cycling:	30 km, 90% very quickly
Sat.	Swimming:	1 km
Sun.	Running:	12 km with quick sections, cycling 35 km calmly

Total: 2.5 km S/65 km C/22 km R

Week 6, 7

Tue.	Swimming:	1 km interv. on, 5 x 100, off
Wed.	Running:	12 km calmly
Thu.	Cycling:	40 km with quick sections
Sat.	Swimming:	1.5 km endurance
Sun.	Running:	30 km calmly + running 5 km quickly

Total: 2.5 km S/70 km C/17 km R

Competition Week 12

Tue.	Cycling:	40 km, quickly 80%
Wed.	Running:	10 km, loosely 70%
Thu.	Swimming:	1 km intervals
Fri.	Cycling:	20 km calmly 65%

Sat.-Sun. 1.5/40/10 km short triathlon

The following two weeks are for regeneration. In each week just swim, cycle and run once only. After that, repeat buildup of weeks 3, 4 and possibly 5 then another short triathlon. Go into this, your first short triathlon and those that follow completely without a care. You have nothing to lose and everthing to gain.

Another tip: let the others swim, cycle and run how they like, run your own race. Enjoy the diversity of triathlon.

Congratulations!

You have successfully reached the second stage on the way to the summit. In spite of the even greater motivation, keep a clear head. Now you need to regenerate. You have earned an active rest for one or two weeks. Catch up with other things that may have been neglected.

After that you can start building up for the second short triathlon. Triathletes who already have experience from other events and want to further improve themselves do not have it as easy as beginners. These triathletes are advised to start thinking about the coming competitive season early if they wish to make the most of their sporting opportunities.

The following basic thoughts, training suggestions and ideas, can only be recommendations, which you will need to adapt to your individual situation. In my "Handbuch für Triathlon" (German edition) I have written about the all important "total situation" of triathletes and shown why this is so decisive in creating your training schedules.

If you want to be successful in triathlon you will need to take all other individual influences apart from sport into consideration when planning. These are mostly work, private and family pressures. On top of this comes regeneration, which is so essential. Unless of course you are a triathlon professional, who only needs to bother about training in the main training period. Such athletes can and must of course train more and can therefore not serve as a yard stick for the 99.9% of triathletes who can only practise their hobby in their free time.

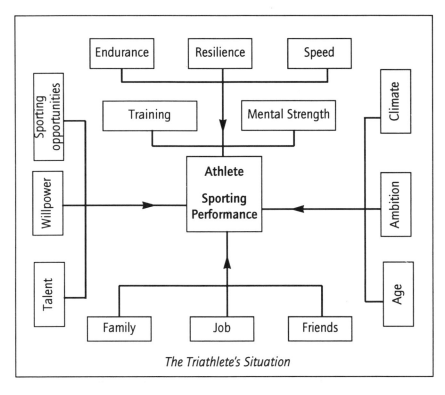

The Triathlete's Situation

Many sporting and non-sporting factors have an influence on the sporting performance of a triathlete. The more "performance supporting" elements come together in an athlete's life, the better the sporting performance.

Short Triathlon for Competitive Athletes

After having gathered experience over the short distance, it is now mainly a matter of improving the individual disciplines.

First guidelines have already been given in the chapter "Training and Competition Tips" for each of the sports swimming, cycling and running. Here we will deal with the combination possibilities and with suggestions as to how you can get by with an annual average of an hour of pure training time per day.
Number of triathlons per season: 5 to 8

The following annual structure is recommended:

October, November, possibly also December:
Transitional period. All training measures are carried out in a relaxed and playful manner, mostly by feeling, with little use of the stopwatch. Slow and entertaining runs, refreshing swimming and stretching are on the agenda. If you want to change your swimming style from breaststroke to crawl, which I strongly recommend, now is the time to do so. Ideally it should be done with expert guidance, otherwise with the help of experienced triathletes or swimmers.

December:
At the beginning of the first part of the preparatory period the amount of training is increased, at medium strain, pulse rates of 130-140. Opportunities to go cross-country skiing should be used. It is an excellent way of training the arm and rump muscles.

January:
The development of basic endurance begun in the previous month is continued at the same intensity. With the help of stretching and strength training the diverse development of the body is supported. January could be the "swimming month".

During the swimming month the idea is to improve the swimming time. Some ways of doing this: Amount - about 3 x 2,000 m = 6,000 m per week.
Warming-up and cooling down should involve about 300-400 m in each case.
Examples:
a) 5 x 50 m with 20 sec. break +
   6 x 100 m with 30 sec. break +
   6 x 50 m with 20 sec. break
b) 3 x 400 m with 2 min. break each time
c) 2 series 6 x 100 m with 30 sec. break, 3 min. break between series
d) 1,500 m endurance swimming, test

February:
The amount of training increases further. The odd cross-country or popular run can make training less monotonous. If you have not yet moved your bike, you should use a home trainer or rolling device to prepare for the cycling month of March. Cycling excursions on the weekend support this. It is important to do one long steady run per week of initially 20 km and later 25 km at a pulse of 130.
Ways to improve running times:
    Always follow the format: 10-15 minutes warm-up running, stretching, training programme, 15 min. cool down running.
a) 5 - 6 x 1,000 m at 10 km best time speed, e.g. 40 min = 4:00 min./km
   Each time the same distance as jogging break with pulse up to 110.
b) 3 x 1,000 m 10 sec. per 1,000 m faster than before
c) 10 - 12 x 400 m, same distance as jogging break
d) 1 x 1,000 m, 1 x 2,000 m, 1 x 3,000 m, 1 x 2,000 m, 1 x 1,000 m,
   Each time 1,000 m jogging break with pulse up to 110.
e) 4 x 2,000 m, each time 1,000 m jogging break
f) 2 x 5,000 m
g) 10,000 m test run in framework of a race
   The frequency of these intensive training sessions should be 1 x per week. In the running month possibly a second time.

March:
If March is to be the "cycling month", then running is only trained at a reduced level. The bike has priority. It can perhaps be used on the way to and from work. Over Easter you can really put the emphasis on cycling. Get on the bike as often as possible and peddle easily. A rounded tread is trained at 100-110 rpm, which is not easy to reach. The amount of training is greatest in March and April. Now at the latest during cycling the winter fat will melt away. Speed sessions on the bike follow later. At this stage training is with the small chain cog.

April:
On the weekends the changeover bike-running should be practised. Ways of doing this:
a) 40 km calm cycling + 5 km quick running,
b) 20 km quick cycling + 10 km calm running,
c) 20 km quick cycling + 5 km quick running.
    From the second half of April onwards a speed session on the bike 1 x per week is recommended in order to slowly get used to the triathlon cycling speed.
    Here too: 15 min. easy warming-up cycling at 100-110 rpm, intervals, 15 min. easy cool down cycling.

The following alternative intervals are recommended:
a) 1, 2, 3, 4, 5, 4, 3, 2, 1 minutes fast cycling, each time the same length of time easily pedalling with the small cog. i.e. 1 min. speed, 1 min. relaxed, 2 min. speed, 2 min. relaxed, 3 min. speed ...
b) 8 x 1 km, each time 1 km between pedalling easily
c) 2 x 10 km with 5 minutes active break
d) Fartlek on the bike, e.g. racing to place name signs.
   The long steady 20-25 km run can be replaced by a steady 70-80 km cycle tour.

May:
Last test phase before the first race. The amount of training is reduced, the intensity increases. But be careful: only one hard session cycling and running per week. Reduce the interval training in swimming once a week in favour of an endurance session. When the water temperature allows it, swim in a lake instead of a pool. Here the endurance method is useful, i.e. 1,500 m or 2,000 m. Short intervals can be swum in the lake by counting the strokes. These could be like this: 50 strokes at speed, 25 relaxed strokes, 50 strokes at speed, 25 relaxed etc. Now is a good time to couple cycling training with swimming training.

June - September:
Competitive season. Training in these interesting months, which after all we have been waiting for long enough, depends mainly on the frequency of short triathlons and the length of time between them. Between two events that take place two weeks apart and which are covered at full effort, there should only be light regeneration training.

The number of training sessions is to be reduced, (see training schedules.) If there is a three or four week gap on the other hand there can be several days of normal training before in the last three days training is either not done at all or at very low intensity.

A holiday during this period provides for new training motivation through the change of scene. You may even find that the possibly inevitable training free days do you more good than you thought. Of course you should not constantly expose yourself to the full heat of the sun, and do your training in the morning or evening hours.

Training Recommendations for Competitive Athletes
As already mentioned, the following training suggestions should not and cannot be simply accepted as they are by every athlete. These schedules represent a concrete way of successfully covering short triathlons. Every athlete should now check the amounts and the intensity of training with regard to his or her situation

and change them accordingly. One should, however, keep to the weekly amounts. After the first event, training should be regenerative only for 10-14 days, i.e. swimming, cycling and running very easily 1-2 x per week. After that, normal training can begin again, until the week before the next triathlon (see 2nd week of June).

Distribution of Monthly Amounts: (approx. in km)

Swimming/cycling/running					
Jan.	32/70/140	May	20/600/120	Sept.	8/420/100
Feb.	18/100/200	June	28/500/140	Oct.	8/260/80
Mar.	18/660/160	July	18/500/160	Nov.	24/100/100
April	24/400/120	Aug.	14/600/120	Dec.	24/80/120

Total 230/4290/1560 km in a year

Training Schedules: The last four weeks before a short triathlon
Date: from ___ to 3rd week of May   Week:

Day	Weight km (mo)	S Dist. m	S Time	C Dist. km	C Time or km/h	R Dist. km	R Time	Other sporting activity	Comments	Pulse Rest / Strain	Weight kg (ev)
Mon.								Gymn./ Stretching			
Tue.				40	Fast	10	Easy		Alternate tr. C + R		
Wed.		2000 Endur. sw									
Thu.						12	Fartlek				
Fri.		1500 Interval									
Sat.				50	Easy						
Sun.		1500		40		10			Test race 90 % hard		
Total		5000		130		32					

Date: From ___ to 4th week of May   Week:

Day	Weight km (mo)	S Dist. m	S Time	C Dist. km	C Time or km/h	R Dist. km	R Time	Other sporting activity	Comments	Pulse Rest / Strain	Weight kg (ev)
Mon.								Stretching			
Tue.				50	Fast						
Wed.		1500 Interv.		10	Easy						
Thu.											
Fri.				30	Hard	8	steadily				
Sat.		2000 Endur.									
Sun.				40	Easy	10	Very fast		Alternate tr. C + R		
Total		3500		120		28					

Date: From	to 1st week of June								Week:		
Day	Weight	S		C		R		Other sporting	Comments	Pulse	Weight
	km	Dist.	Time	Dist.	Time	Dist.	Time	activity		Rest	kg
	(mo)	m		km	or km/h	km				Strain	(ev)
Mon.								Stretching			
Tue.				50 km	2x100 Speed				C: 100 rpm		
Wed.		2000	Interv.			12	Easy				
Thu.				40	Easy						
Fri.						8	Fast				
Sat.		2500	Endur.	30	Fast						
Sun.						10	Fast run				
Total		4500		120		30					

Date: From	to 2nd week of June								Week:		
Day	Weight	S		C		R		Other sporting	Comments	Pulse	Weight
	km	Dist.	Time	Dist.	Time	Dist.	Time	activity		Rest	kg
	(mo)	m		km	or km/h	km				Strain	(ev)
Mon.								Stretching			
Tue.				40	20 km/h fast				C 100 rpm		
Wed.		2500	Interv.			12	Easy				
Thu.				20	steadily						
Fri.		1000	steadily								
Sat.									"Bike check in"		
Sun.		1500		40	10				TRIATHLON		
Total		5000		100		22					

Short Triathlon for Performance Athletes

Experienced triathletes, winning types, simply put: "experts in their field", do not draw their ability only from above average talent or from favourable family or job situations regarding training, they too must train a great deal for their special performance. For these triathletes sport is a major part of their lives. For the total strain a healthy balance of strain and recovery is important, i.e. the right proportion of training sessions and training intensities.

Particulary because of the high training strain it is important always to consider other job and family requirements. These things cannot be solved with good advice and recommendations to athletes from others. Only the athletes themselves can and must consider their situation when firmly planning their training. Therefore the following recommendations should be understood as one of many possibilities to plan triathlon training. Basically the annual plans are little different from the recommendations already made for "competitive athletes". Altogether though, a greater amount of training and a higher intensity is practised already in the preparatory period.

The basics for improving individual performances are also to be taken from the area of competitive athletes, but of course with different individual speeds. This is possible because triathletes who train at this level have more talent and are thus also capable of higher performance. Naturally, under favourable time and other conditions even greater amounts are possible. The following amounts and intensities do not represent the "end of the line".

Distribution of Monthly Training Amounts: (approx. in km)

Month	Swimming/Cycling/Running	
Jan.	50/100/180	swimming month
Feb.	30/150/250	running month
Mar.	30/700/200	cycling month
April	40/900/230	
May	30/800/180	
June	30/700/200	
July	25/600/180	
Aug.	20/800/200	
Sept.	15/700/180	
Oct.	15/400/100	
Nov.	30/150/120	
Dec.	36/100/150	
Total:	351/6,100/2,170 km	

The Last 4 Weeks Before The First High Point Of The Season
Date: From   to 3rd week in May   Week:

Day	Weight km (mo)	S Dist. m	Time	C Dist. km	Time or km/h	R Dist. km	Time	Other sporting activity	Comments	Pulse Rest Strain	Weight kg (ev)
Mon.								Stretching			
Tue.				40	Fast	10	Easy		Alternate tr. C + R		
Wed.		3000	Endur.sw.				Fartlek				
Thu.				50	Fast						
Fri.		2000	Interval			15	steadily				
Sat.				70	Easy						
Sun.		1500	Hard	40	Hard	10	Hard		Test race 90 %		
Total		6500		200		47					

Date: From   to 4th week in May   Week:

Day	Weight km (mo)	S Dist. m	Time	C Dist. km	Time or km/h	R Dist. km	Time	Other sporting activity	Comments	Pulse Rest Strain	Weight kg (ev)
Mon.								Stretching			
Tue.				50	Fast						
Wed.	3000	Interv.				15	Fast				
Thu.		1000	2x500 Speed								
Fri.				40	Hard	8	Easy				
Sat.		3000	Endur.								
Sun.				60	Easy	10	Very fast		Alternate tr. C + R		
Total		7000		150		33					

Date: From				to 1st week in June						Week:	
Day	Weight	S		C		R		Other sporting	Comments	Pulse	Weight
	km	Dist.	Time	Dist.	Time	Dist.	Time	activity		Rest	kg
	(mo)	m		km	or km/h	km				Strain	(ev)
Mon.								Stretching			
Tue.				70	50 km/h Hard						
Wed.		3000	Interv.			12	Easy				
Thu.				50	Easy						
Fri.		1200	Interv.			10	Speed run				
Sat.		2500	Edur. sw.	30	Very fast						
Sun.						18	Speed play				
Total		6700		150		40					

Date: From				to 2nd week in June						Week:	
Day	Weight	S		C		R		Other sporting	Comments	Pulse	Weight
	km	Dist.	Time	Dist.	Time	Dist.	Time	activity		Rest	kg
	(mo)	m		km	or km/h	km				Strain	(ev)
Mon.								Stretching			
Tue.				50	30 km/h very fast						
Wed.		1500	Interv.			15	Easy				
Thu.				25	Very easy						
Fri.		1000	Easy								
Sat.									Care of bike		
Sun.		1500		40		10			Race		
Total		4000		115		25					

For the performance athletes in this group the previous chapters are especially applicable. Even a performance athlete should limit the number of events in a season to about ten, and if possible always have at least two weeks between races. If this is not the case, great care must be taken to ensure sufficient regeneration.

At the end of the season performance athletes doing the short distance who have already successfully raced it for several years may have the goal of racing in a middle triathlon. Because of their comprehensive training they are fully able to do this. By including even longer sessions, but steadily please, reaching the finish over the middle distance should not be a problem.

More information can be found in the next stage.

A Triathlon Race Day

After the main training phase has been concluded a week before the event, and with only minor exceptions training is relaxed and limited, the athlete can spend more time dealing with the "external" aspects of the event.

In order to ease your conscience about so little training you should plan to use these days to take care of things that have been left undone lately, e.g. visits to friends and acquaintances, family matters or occupational things.

Amongst the external triathlon preparations I include the glycogen exhausting run on Tuesday, if Saturday is the big day, or Wednesday if the event is on Sunday. After this run of about 5 km at 95-100% + 25 hard cycling training you begin the three day high carbohydrate diet to overfill the glycogen stores.

Now you can put the running gear aside. If there is to be another brief loosening run it can be done in other clothing than that for the race.

At the beginning of the week there is still time and opportunity to clean and inspect totally the racing bike. Check:

The frame for hairpin cracks, the handlebars, saddle supports, peddle cranks, peddles, brake lever, chain mover, tension of the spokes, wheel rims for cracks, replacement of the tyres, tiny cuts, brakes on cables, functioning of the brake cables, tightness of the chain, grease on the chain mover, chain and cogs, tyre pressure goes down by up to 10% in 24 hours, test ride, spare tubes, helmet, sunglasses, possibly cycling gloves etc. Every little screw should be checked to see if it does its job. Now there is still time to change faulty parts. Swimming gear should also be checked through in the course of the week. Are the goggles watertight? Take a second pair to be on the safe side. You might like to go for a test swim in your neoprene suit.

In the last week you should also put the final polish on your mental preparations. Since announcement of the race date you have had plenty of time to string lightly your "race bow", and now is the time to tighten it again slightly, without, however, over tightening it. As a result of good endurance training of the last months your confidence of reaching the goal you have set yourself has been constantly growing. In the first race of the season this should be: finish, experience a good race, have fun and enjoy triathlon. Later in the season you can set your sights higher. In spite of all requirements, it is important to make sure you more or less correctly estimate your sporting condition, otherwise the triathlon can become a fiasco. Think positively in the last days before the race. Whatever you do, avoid seeing a conspiracy or similar in all the things that can happen during a triathlon. So, full of self-confidence you pack together your swimming, cycling and running things a day before the event at the latest. Be prepared for unexpected weather conditions, especially if you leave home a few days earlier and visit a few people beforehand.

For this reason it is worth a longer trip to an especially attractive triathlon.

You might want to think about the following:

For swimming: Bathing suit
                         2 pairs of swimming goggles
                         Neoprene suit
                         Bathing caps and ear plugs

	Vaseline, possibly nose peg
	Triathlon suit
For cycling:	Racing bike with pump, tubes, drink bottles
	Energy bars, banana, start number ribbon
	Helmet, towel, sunglasses
	Cycling jersey, possibly cycling pants
For running:	Run in running shoes with velcro fastener (Tanka)
	Running jersey and running pants
	Light coloured hat
After the triathlon:	Dry clothing, towel, shower accessories,
	Comfortable shoes, massage oil
	Drinks
Before the triathlon:	Starting papers
	Safety pins, rubber bands
	Taking in liquids, banana

When everything has been packed you can look forward to the event with inner calm, self-confidence, anticipation and the right amount of inner tension. This includes a healthy dose of sporting ambition so I can use the means available to me to exploit my personal potential. Race day, the day "my" race takes place, begins at least three hours before the start. Calmly go about your morning ablutions and breakfast. Make sure you eat easily digestible carbohydrates. Be careful with dairy products. Not everyone can handle dairy products when they have to swim in salt water shortly afterwards.

As a rule registration for the triathlon takes place well in advance. Nevertheless it is advisable to arrive at the location at least two hours before the start signal in order to go through the rather comprehensive starting preparations calmly.

Much trouble can be saved if you read the race details not once but twice. Here often, questions about the course can be answered: route description, refreshment spots, difficult sections etc.

Order of preparation activities:

- Collect starting papers. Check start numbers for the racing bike, for cycling and for running.
- Assemble bike, check tyre pressure, carry out short test ride. In doing so decide on most suitable gear for the first 500 m. Attach filled drink bottle and energy bar to the bike.
- Put your cycling things in the assigned bag. Cycling shoes, socks, helmet, sunglasses, towel, jersey, top, short-long jersey according to weather, pants. In warm weather a bathing suit with soft inlay plus top are sufficient. Prepare rubber band with start number in front and behind. You may wish to put the start numbers in a transparent film sleeve and fasten these to the rubber band with three safety pins.
- Pack your running bag, shoes with velcro fasteners or Tanka, possibly running pants, running shirt, running hat.
- Make sure you attend the race briefing, where the complete race course is explained and questions are answered.
- So, with your bathing suit and possibly your neoprene suit, your swimming goggles and the bathing cap provided by the organisers you head for the starting area to have your upper arm marked.
- For 15 minutes warm-up as usual, in warming clothes. Loose jogging, easy stretching and loosening exercises.
- Put on your swimming gear, neoprene suit, swimming goggles, bathing cap with start number.
- Position yourself in the starting bunch according to your ability.
- START
- In the first 300 m do not panic. Find your own rhythm as quickly as possible.
- If you are fortunate enough to have the right person in front of you, follow them closely but without touching their feet. It is easier to swim in the wake of someone in front, and also saves you constantly raising your head to be sure of where you are heading.

- But be careful. Trust is good, checking is better. Sometimes the person in front of you may have problems finding the right direction.
- In the last 20 metres swim a few strokes of breaststroke.
- In the changeover zone remember what was said at the briefing. Perhaps the bathing cap must be handed in, changing may only be allowed in certain tents, wash off salt water, free your feet of sand, in cold weather dry yourself and get changed. Put on and fasten your helmet.
- Push your bike into the changeover zone, only get on when you have passed a certain marking and start off in a low gear until your muscles have warmed-up.
- Never ride in the slipstream of others. Keep 10 m distance from the person in front and 2 m from anyone on the side. The person overtaken has to ensure the gap is kept to.
- Do not take too many risks when cycling. Your health is more important than a few seconds.
- Drink regularly, possibly eat a banana.
- Ride the last kilometres in a low gear again in order to loosen the muscles for running.
- Push your bike into the changeover zone. Only now undo and remove your helmet.
- Put your bike in the right place.
- Running shoes with velcro or Tanka fasteners can be fastened quickly even in cold weather.

- If it is hot wear a hat.
- Use the refreshment posts. Use sponges to cool pulse and head.
- After reaching the finish drink large quantities of fluids and later eat.
- Gather up your clothing bags and your bike. Check that your gear and equipment is complete.
- Later cycle easily for 15 minutes and have an easy cool down swim.
- Do not forget regeneration measures (see Recovery and Regeneration).

Stage 3 Middle Distance Triathlon Training 2/80/20 km

Triathletes have it in their blood to seek out and take up further challenges. For athletes who have so far successfully handled the short distance of 1500 m swimming, 40 km cycling and 10 km running and now want to realise the dream of an "ultra triathlon", the middle distance is a decisive interim goal on the way to the IRONMAN:
The distances of the middle triathlon are:

1.9 - 2.5 km swimming,
80 - 90 km cycling,
20 - 21.1 km running,

this is also called the half distance. The reason is very simple. The Ironman, as the measure of all things in triathlon, is considered the "single" distance. Half of it is then the half distance, a quarter of the Ironman is called the quarter distance. The last term roughly applies to the short distance.

In the middle triathlon we are dealing with three fully grown endurance sports which all require regular training. These distances are not suitable for absolute beginners. The number of those here who come from other sports is low. It is most possible for marathon runners, whose muscles are well developed and display a high degree of mobility. Running and cycling are typical endurance training at these distances. These athletes can often bridge problems in swimming through high performance in cycling and running. On this middle distance you will find either triathletes who in the mid to long-term want to tackle the ultra distance, or simply full blown ultra distance athletes. The latter like to do these 2.5/90/20 km four weeks before an Ironman distance as a dress rehearsal. On the other hand the middle distance has a high standing both nationally and internationally. In addition to various state championships there are also German and European championships.

Good prerequisites for successful participation in middle triathlon events are:
• Two years regular endurance training
• Participation in one or more marathons
• Cycling rides of 80-100 km in length
• Swimming sessions of 2,000-2,500 m.

It is very difficult to say precisely how many events one should enter in a season as they are often raced alternatively with short or ultra distances. As a guide for triathletes who only do short and middle distances I would say:

Newcomers: 2-4 short distances + 2 middle distances, Competitive and performance athletes: 2-4 short and 2-3 middle distances.

Training for Newcomers

Here those triathletes are those who want to "move up" from the short distance to the next highest, the middle triathlon class. For many the great goal "Ironman" gets even closer with this move, thus further increasing their motivation.

We must, however, be quite clear that in spite of all this motivation and thirst for action, in normal situations our triathlon training is not the only thing in our life. Work, family and friends should not be neglected. If our training is to be fun we must determine the importance our sporting activity has accordingly. Early on at the beginning of the year, when the exact dates of events are known, competition planning for the new season should begin. Before the first middle triathlon, which is not before the end of June, at least one short triathlon should be included in planning. This can be done in the middle of full training. Simultaneously it serves as a real fitness and material test. A second middle triathlon is then possible in August or early September to finish the season. In between there will be time and opportunity to participate in a number of short events.

The prerequisite for such a triathlon programme is a regular winter training with the emphasis on running and swimming. From January onwards this could consist of swimming training once or twice a week, in addition to this steady endurance runs. If your sporting background is in running you may plan a spring marathon for March/April. After a three week regeneration period in which mainly swimming and cycling are trained in an easy manner, alternating training then begins.

Without the marathon run mentioned a training schedule could look like this - per week in each case:

January: 1-2 x swimming, 1,500 m endurance,
                  1,500 m intervals, 3 x 100 m; 3 x 200
                  Running, 1 x 25 km steadily at the weekend,
                  1 x 14 km Fartlek, 1 x 12 km easily, stretching.
February: 2 x swimming, 1,500 m each time, endurance and intervals
                  2 x running, 1 x 2 h steadily, 1 x 1:15 h with Fartlek.
March: 2 x swimming, 1 x 2,000 m with intervals 6 x 100 m, 4 x 200 m
                  1 x 1,500 m 1 length quickly, 1 length easily, endurance
                  3 x running, 1 x 20-25 km steadily, 1 x 1:15 h easily, 1 x 10 km

Fast endurance run at 90-95% intensity, or every two weeks participation in 10-15 km road runs, stretching.
Use the weekends for cycle tours.
Take a week of regeneration, training only lightly and 60% of usual amount.

| April: | On weekend and holidays emphasis on cycling
40, 60 and 80 km or sometimes 100 km steady tours,
easy pedalling, total of 3 x cycling per week.
In addition 1-2 x swimming, intervals 3 x 500 m;
10 x 100 m, 5 x 200 m, pyramid,
2 x running, 1 x 20-25 km steadily, 1 x speed play 15 km,
Stretching. |
| May: | 2 x swimming, 2 x running, 2 x cycling, stretching
Last six weeks before 1st middle triathlon, see daily
schedules. |

If you train for your first middle triathlon in a way similar to that described by me here, you can enter it with a good conscience. Clearly with this small amount of training you will not be among the leaders, but you will definitely enjoy it. The goal you set yourself is of course to finish, not to win.

If you want to invest more time in training, go ahead and do so. In this case you should pay particular attention to the basic training principles, i.e. regeneration weeks, training in groups, generally choosing a training pace at which you can easily converse and many other things. In the last weeks before a middle triathlon, as with the short triathlon, you should train so little that you have a bad conscience. Nevertheless you should have at least a couple of easy sessions. The preparations directly before the event and the race day itself have already been extensively covered in the section on short distance triathlon.

The middle distances do, however, have a great advantage over the short distances. The changeover need not be so hectic, and in cold weather, drying and changing after swimming is not just sensible, it is essential. What are a few minutes when weighed against potential health problems such as kidney trouble or similar.

Training for Competitive and Performance Athletes

Those who want to do better than just finish over the middle distance already have extensive experience in the three sports swimming, cycling and running. A large proportion of the age class athletes are in this group. They usually have the advantage of having been active in sport for many years and therefore have a good to very good level of basic endurance. Younger triathletes on the other hand usually have their advantage in speed endurance and resilience.

It is well-known that it is easier to train endurance than resilience. The following is therefore a rough guideline for training for middle distance:

Middle Distance Triathlon: The Last 6 Weeks For Newcomers
Date: From   to   Week: 1

Day	Weight km (mo)	S Dist. m	Time	C Dist. km	Time or km/h	R Dist. km	Time	Other sporting activity	Comments	Pulse Rest Strain	Weight kg (ev)
Mon.				40	Easy						
Tue.		1000	Interv.					Stretching			
Wed.				80	Fast						
Thu.						15	Easy				
Fri.											
Sat.				50	Easy	20	Fast		Alternate tr. C + R		
Sun.		2000	Endur.								
Total		3000		170		35					

Date: From   to   Week: 2

Day	Weight km (mo)	S Dist. m	Time	C Dist. km	Time or km/h	R Dist. km	Time	Other sporting activity	Comments	Pulse Rest Strain	Weight kg (ev)
Mon.						25	Easy	Stretching			
Tue.		1500	Interv.	60	Fartlek						
Wed.						15	steadily				
Thu.				70	Easy						
Fri.											
Sat.						15-20			Race Road run		
Sun.		2000	Easy								
Total		3500		130		60					

| Date: From | | to | | | | | | Week: 3 | | |

Day	Weight	S		C		R		Other sporting	Comments	Pulse	Weight
	km	Dist.	Time	Dist.	Time	Dist.	Time	activity		Rest	kg
	(mo)	m		km	or km/h	km				Strain	(ev)
Mon.					8			Stretching	Regeneration run		
Tue.		2000	3x500 Endur.								
Wed.				70							
Thu.						15					
Fri.											
Sat.				50	Fast	12	Easy		Alternate tr. C + R		
Sun.		2000	Interv.								
Total		4000		120		35					

| Date: From | | to | | | | | | Week: 4 | | |

Day	Weight	S		C		R		Other sporting	Comments	Pulse	Weight
	km	Dist.	Time	Dist.	Time	Dist.	Time	activity		Rest	kg
	(mo)	m		km	or km/h	km				Strain	(ev)
Mon				40	3x10 km Speed			Stretching			
Tue.		1500	Interv.			5	Fartlek				
Wed.				60	Easy						
Thu.						25	steadily				
Fri.											
Sat.				110	steadily	+5	Fast				
Sun.		2000	2x1000 Endur.								
Total		3500		210		45					

Date: From			to						Week: 5	
Day	Weight	S		C		R		Other sportin	Comments	Pulse	Weight
	km	Dist.	Time	Dist.	Time	Dist.	Time	activity		Rest	kg
	(mo)	m		km	or km/h	km				Strain	(ev)
Mon.				40	30 km/h Speed			Stretching			
Tue.		1500	Endur.			15	Fartlek				
Wed.				60	Easy						
Thu.						25	steadily	Pulse 130			
Fri.											
Sat.				80	Fast	10	Easy				
Sun.		2500	Interv.								
Total		4000		180		50					

Date: From			to						Week: 6	
Day	Weight	S		C		R		Other sporting	Comments	Pulse	Weight
	km	Dist.	Time	Dist.	Time	Dist.	Time	activity		Rest	kg
	(mo)	m		km	or km/h	km				Strain	(ev)
Mon.				50	Fartlek			Stretching			
Tue.						15	Fartlek				
Wed.		1500	Easy								
Thu.				30	Easy						
Fri.											
Sat.		2000		80		20			Middle Triathlon		
Sun.				40	Very steadily						
Total		3500		200		35					

In order to improve themselves all round, sprinters should also do long calm training, while endurers should supplement their training with short quick sessions. The success of these efforts is greatly dependent on whether or not the individual can be bothered making such a change to their training habits. This problem more or less solves itself when there is a training group of roughly the same ability, assuming of course, that the group has the same goals. Otherwise it is advisable to carry out the different training forms with different groups.

This really necessary faster training only applies to a certain extent to older athletes. Those who want to achieve good results over the middle distance should try to achieve the following:

2,000 m swimming	< 42 minutes
40 km cycling	< 1:12 h,
10 km running	< 42 minutes.

From this base you can build up. With regard to the following training recommendations, I must point out that every triathlete must consider their whole personal situation when planning and carrying out their individual training, if they want to enjoy their sport and be successful in it. Details for swimming, cycling and running can be found in the respective chapters "Training Tips for ...".

Structure of the Year's Activities

Transitional period:	October, November, possibly December and January. 2 x weekly easy jogging 1-1:15 h, if possible easy cycling tour, 2 x weekly playful swimming. Analysis of the previous, planning of the coming season.
Preparatory period:	Until the end of May.

January:
First part of the preparatory period. The amount of training increases while the intensity of physical exertion remains low, pulse rate 130. Use any opportunities to go cross-country skiing. With the aid of stretching and light strength exercises you can support comprehensive blood supply to all of your body.

Run about 50-60 km, even endurance runs, 1x weekly a long, steady run of 25 km, if you want to run a spring marathon do 28 km. Occasionally participate in popular runs but not at full exertion. If the weather is good at the weekend go on an easy one hour cycling excursion. Those who want can do their cycling training on a rolling device. Swimming: 2-3 x per week, technique training, endurance swimming and intervals.

February: Swimming month 1,000 m best time=100%

Swim as often as you can. Someone who lives near swimming baths, or has an opportunity to swim in their lunch break, will do so more often than someone who first has to drive 20 km.

2,000-2,500 m 4 x per week would be ideal. Under instruction, 1 x endurance swimming, 1 x 2,000 m or 1 x 2,500 m at a time at 85%.

Otherwise intervals: on/off 2 x 6 x 100, 2 x 4 x 250 with a one minute break each time, pyramid swimming.

Running: one each of 1 x 12 km, 15 km with Fartlek, 20 km steadily.

Cycling: according to the weather easy tours, 100 rpm.

March: Running month

In addition to swimming training 3 x per week, 1 x endurance and 2 x intervals, cycling tours are scheduled at the weekend and once a week. After all, you have to prepare for the cycling month in April. Cycling to work would be ideal.

The emphasis this month is on running. Also possible is of course: January swimming month, February running month, March cycling month and mid to late April the spring marathon run.

Detailed guidance on marathon runs in 3:15 h, 2:59 h or 2:44 h can be found in the chapter Running Training.

Stretching parts of the body that have been especially strained is important here too.

April: Cycling month

If you have done a spring marathon run, in addition to easy running during marathon regeneration, you can dedicate yourself extensively to swimming and cycling.

The emphasis on cycling will be at weekends and over Easter.

Tours of up to 100 km at 100-110 rpm on the small cog are important, e.g. Friday 70 km, Saturday 100 km + 8 km running, Sunday 90 km, Wednesday 50 km.

Cross -country skiing is an excellent sport for improving ones' basic endurance during the preparatory period.

The main thing here is basic endurance in cycling, therefore the first intervals should be done at the end of the month at the earliest. Racing to place name signs livens up this month.

Of course a two week Mallorca trip would be ideal. Then there would be plenty of time for a full private life as well as the training itself.

May:
On the weekends train the changeover cycling-running. In each case one easy session and one fast one. 1 x per week speed training on the bike. E.g. on/off 8 x 1,000 m interval, same distance in between pedalling easily; alternatively 4 x 3 km with 3 km easy pedalling; 3 x 8 km with 5 km easy.
Weekly rhythm: N H R (normal/hard/regenerative)

Swimming as in April, intervals, 1 x endurance swimming.
Running: 1 x per week intervals: on/off 2 x 5,000 m 95%, 6-8 x ,000 m at 10 km running pace 100%. Jogging break 1 km, pulse 110.

Short triathlon race as dress rehearsal.
Competition period: Late May to late September.

June: See training schedules pages 152/153

July:
After the middle triathlon two weeks of regenerative training, after that normal, i.e. R R N. Further short and medium triathlons in the months of August and September.

Stage 4 Ultra Triathlon Training 3.8/180/42 km

Practically every triathlete nurtures one thought: "One day I'll go for the ironman distance and then ...". Yes, and then the dream of the real Hawaii Ironman.This massive sporting hurdle can, however, only be successfully tackled by those who are exceptionally well-trained in endurance. Anyone who has managed the first three stages and is prepared to tackle the fourth will be able to do it. Let's approach it together. As everyone knows there is strength in unity. Anyone who thinks they are the only one who has problems mentally with this bull "ultra triathlon" is totally wrong. Everyone who wants to go for this distance first has problems and difficulties mentally. Me especially. If you don't believe me because I have already done such distances several times, you can read all the details in my first book "Mein Abenteuer Hawaii-Triathlon". It goes without saying that every athlete going into this 226 km long calculated adventure must be well prepared.

Middle Triathlon For Performance Athletes
Date: From   to   Week: 1

Day	Weight km (mo)	S Dist. m	Time	C Dist. km	Time or km/h	R Dist. km	Time	Other sporting activity	Comments	Pulse Rest Strain	Weight kg (ev)
Mon.								Stretching			
Tue.		2000	Interv.			15 5 min. jogging breaks	6x1000				
Wed.				100	Easy 75 %						
Thu.				80	Hard						
Fri.						24	Pulse 130	Stretching			
Sat.		2000	2x1000 Endur.	70	90 % Hard	12	Easy		Alternate tr. C + R		
Sun.		2500	Interv.			15	Fartlek				
Total:		6500		250		66					

Date: From   to   Week: 2

Day	Weight km (mo)	S Dist. m	Time	C Dist. km	Time or km/h	R Dist. km	Time	Other sporting activity	Comments	Pulse Rest Strain	Weight kg (ev)
Mon.								Stretching			
Tue.		2500	Interv.			15	10 km speed Hard				
Wed.				100	Easy						
Thu.		2000	Interv.	50	4x10 km/h Hard						
Fri.				60	Easy	24	steadily	Stretching			
Sat.		2000	Endur.	90	Fast	5	Fast		Alternate tr. C + R		
Sun.		2000	Interv.			15	Fartlek				
Total		8500		300		59					

Date: From to							Week: 3			
Day	Weight km (mo)	**S** Dist. m	Time	**C** Dist. km	Time or km/h	**R** Dist. km	Time	Other sporting activity	Comments	Pulse Rest Strain / Weight kg (ev)
Mon.								Stretching		
Tue.		2000	Interv.			15	6x1000			
Wed.				110	Easy					
Thu.		2000	Interv.	50	4x10 km Hard					
Fri.				60	75% Easy	24	70% steadily	Stretching		
Sat.		2000	Endur.	80	Fast	12	Easy			
Sun.		2000	Interv.			12	Fartlek			
Total		8800		300		63				

Date: From to							Week: 4			
Day	Weight km (mo)	**S** Dist. m	Time	**C** Dist. km	Time or km/h	**R** Dist. km	Time	Other sporting activity	Comments	Pulse Rest Strain / Weight kg (ev)
Mon.	✓							Stretching		
Tue.				50	25 km/h 95%	15	5 km 100%			
Wed.		2000	Interv.	10			steadily			
Thu.				60	Easy			Stretching		
Fri.		1000	Easy			5	Jogging			
Sat.										
Sun.		2500		80		20			Middle Triathlon	
Total		5500		190		50				

Anything else would not be sensible, or to put it more bluntly, would be idiocy. No one can cover this distance unprepared. Fortunately this sporting adventure cannot be bought. These laurels must really be personally earned through careful, balanced and steady endurance training.

The following pages show how every athlete who has managed the first three stages can successfully prepare themselves for these 226 km.

You can make the undertaking "ultra training" relatively simple by integrating your training programme into your daily life. In other words, by skillfully planning swimming, cycling and running into your normal daily routine. I have already made plenty of suggestions elsewhere in this book. Anyone who manages to do this has already created the best prerequisites to reach their great and worthwhile goal. To increase your motivation I would just like to mention that such a triathlon over 226 km will never be routine. After 13 ultras including a double ultra with a wide range of experiences, the three ultras planned for next season will certainly not be routine. They will be another sporting adventure with unpredictable outcome, of that I am sure. It is exactly this that makes it interesting.

For example I have planned to do the Australian ironman next season, because for the first time it takes place during my Easter vacation. Up until the end of March, however, there is little opportunity for cycling training in our latitudes. In previous years I was always glad to have reached 700-800 km as preparation for Mallorca. There will not be much more as preparation for Australia. And in this I find the new challenge, the great incentive, the passion for the ultra distance. In addition to this, for me, is of course the touristically interesting aspect. In spite of the many unknown variables, an ultratriathlon should never become a risk. But anyone who abides by the basic rules of this event will be fascinated by it. Covering the 226 km triathlon distance is definitely considered performance sport. For this reason the following pages will show how triathletes who have already done several years of systematic endurance training can cover the ultra distance in times of about.

   a) 12 hours
   b) 11 hours
   c) 10 hours
or d) in 8:45 - 9:00 hours.

In doing so I am not so much making use of theoretical schedules but quoting schedules that have been used in practice and have led to the desired results. In other words, they can be followed by any committed triathlete. If you have fulfilled the sporting prerequisites of at least three years endurance training and the achievements detailed later, and arranged your personal situation accordingly, you are ready to start planning your ultra triathlon. It is sensible to start this planning during the transitional period. In these autumn and winter months the expectation of the great event next summer begins. Motivation is decisive, and three time Hawaii finisher Georg KROEGER recommends the book "Adventure Sports – Ironman – Der Hawaii Triathlon" to help keep up your motivation. It describes in detail how an athlete in his late thirties grows into the ultra triathlon, what problems and difficulties can arise and how these can be mastered as far as possible. The book is not a training book but a report on experience about preparing and going through the calculated adventure of the Hawaii triathlon.

Race Time Targets

Anyone entering an ultra triathlon for the first time will most certainly give much thought to their potential finishing time. The following can give a rough indication. Knowledge about another triathlete of similar ability can also be helpful. But be careful about such comparisons: Triathlete X is the same speed as I am over the short distance, so I must be as fast as he is over the long or ultra distance. A direct comparison between short and ultra distances is very, very difficult. A good sprinter over the short distance is not necessarily a good stayer over the ultra distance, whereby in triathlon short distance runners and sprinters can usually be considered excellent endurance athletes. Even a short distance of 1.5/40/10 km with race times of about two hours for the top athletes is a true endurance discipline.

Many athletes can already achieve an ultra time of twelve or even eleven hours in their first event of this kind over the magical 226 km. The prerequisites are systematic training and an appropriate personal situation. To go for the ten hour mark usually requires more training, good sporting opportunities, more stamina, willpower, talent and a positive all round personal situation. I emphasise "usually". Every year in Roth you can see relatively young athletes finishing their first event of this type in well under ten hours. These young lads have a fantastic sporting future if they are able to do further training tailored to their individual needs. Unfortunately one sees again and again that many athletes are simply too impatient where the great goal of Hawaii is concerned. The result is high power training, several excellent races and then an abrupt – too abrupt – end to their sporting ambitions. Triathlon, the linking of three endurance sports, requires several years of constant training. You can therefore only plan for triathlon success in the mid to long-term, and only those with the patience to train systematically for several years can be sure of success. A comparison with a marathon runner illustrates this. Every experienced marathon runner knows that the marathon itself does not begin until Kilometer 32. Everything that went before no longer counts. After 32 km it gets down to the nitty-gritty. Anyone who has used all their energy in the first 10, 20 or 30 km will suffer dearly after the 30 km mark. Until km 30 you should wait patiently. In an ultra triathlon the strain on your patience is even longer, both in the race and especially in the year-long training build up.

Anyone wanting to do an ultra triathlon in nine hours or even less must – if not a professional – be able to combine practically all positive influences to make it work. These include: talent, determination, willpower, good opportunities for training, time, ambition, training effort, physical and psychological strength, motivation. In other words a very positive environment. A typical example of such a successful person is Karl-Heinz NOTTRODT, usually known as Kalli NOTTRODT, the "weather frog" from Oberursel near Frankfurt. At the age of 40 he managed to finish in Roth with a time of 8:49 h. How he managed that and more can be read later.

Partner Friendly Training

My realistic training recommendations are based on the assumption that for every working triathlete, success or lack of it in triathlon will depend on how well he manages to integrate his very comprehensive training into his daily routine. And this in such a way that the amount of time involved is justifiable. Long driving distances to training make conditions much more difficult. On the other hand, every athlete should check to see if they cannot make use of one or other of the following possibilities:
- Cycle to work daily, in the afternoon detours provide the desired training distance.
- Visit a swimming baths before work.
- Go swimming or running in the lunch break.
- Run to work some days.
- When visiting friends or relatives, let the family take the car while you cycle there and back.
- Go to work by public transport or car sharing, and run home.
- Get one or more of your family to accompany you on a bike while you run.
- On vacation do cycling training from 7 to 9 a.m., then there is little traffic, the temperature is pleasant and you have the whole free day ahead of you.
- While swimming in a lake have a family member accompany you in a boat.
- Visit the open air swimming pool together.

So you see there are a number of possibilities to arrange your training in such a way that it hardly disturbs the family at all. You will, however, occasionally have to get up an hour or two earlier. Especially on vacation I don't find this easy.

On the other hand I find it glorious in my summer holidays when every second day I can sit on my bike at 7.15 a.m. and pedal 50 to 60 km. Hardly anyone is on the road at this time and the pleasent temperature saves me cycling in the heat and in particular on full roads. On top of that it is training that really trains the fat metabolism because I only take along a banana and my Kanne Brottrunk apple juice mixture.

In addition to this skilful way of incorporationg training into holidays I consider involving family-girlfriend-boyfriend as a decisive matter. If one's girlfriend, boyfriend, partner or family does not just grudgingly put up with sport but actively supports it, this can only be positive for one's sporting development. In return we should take our partners along on the often pleasant trips, short holidays and long weekends. In this case, triathlon needs not be the only centre of attention. With a little imagination you can extend this partner friendly triathlon catalogue.

So, enough of general advice. Now let's turn to concrete training recommendations for the four different ultra targets:
a) 12 hour target
b) 11 hour target
c) 10 hour target
d) 8.45 to 9:00 hour target

In another part of the book I have already written about the important and often decisive mental preparation for the goal to be worked on now, successfully competing in the ironman distance. Particular information about structuring annual training and the individual kinds of training can be read in the chapter "Basic Principles of Triathlon Training". Now I will cover actually doing the three very different types of endurance sport.

Training Recommendations for the Ultra Triathlon

Requirements for the 12 and 11 Hour Target

The following pages show a way which, if more or less adhered to, will definitely fulfil the physical requirements to finish successfully the ultra triathlon.

The target times are:
a) 3.86/180/42.2 km in 12 hours
b) 3.86/180/42.2 km in 11 hours

Approximate race times necessary		12:00 h	11:00 h
Swimming:	1:30 h	23 min./1,000 m	1:20 h 21 min./km
Cycling:	6:30 h	27.7 km/h	5:55 h 30.5 km/h
Running:	4:00 h	5:40 min./km	3:45 h 5:20 min./km

Requirements for:	12:00 h	11:00 h
2,000 m swimming	42 min.	39 min.
80 km cycling	2:40 h 30 km/h	2:30 h 32 km/h
10 km running	41-42 min.	37-38 min.
25 km running	1:50 h	1:42 h
Marathon run	3:15 h	3:00 h

Recommendations for 6½ months before the event (28 wks)

Swimming	106 km = 3.8 km/wk	150 km = 5.4 km/wk
Cycling	4,000 km = 143 km/wk	5,000 km = 180 km/wk
Running	1,176 km = 42 km/wk	1,350 km = 48 km/wk
Req. time per week on average (nett training time)	11 h + stretching + strength training	13 h

Transitional period:
October, November, possibly December, January
2 x wk easy jogging for 1-1:15 h
2 x wk easy swimming
Analysis of previous season, planning for coming season
Preparatory period:
January, February, March, April, May
Basic training; Emphasis on running + swimming
At the start of the preparation period the amount of training increases at low effort, pulse rate 130. Use opportunities to go cross-country skiing in order to train arm and torso muscle groups. With the aid of stretching and strength training, comprehensive supply of blood to the body is supported.

January: Running about 60 km/wk resp. for the 11 h target running c. 60-70 km/wk, even long runs at pulse 130. 1 x per week long, steady run of 25-28 km. Occasional participation in popular runs, 90%.
In good weather 1 – 1:30 h cycle tour. If you enjoy the rolling device, do that.
Swimming 4 km/wk, swimming 5-6 km/wk.

February: Swiming month 1,000 m best time = 100%
The aim here is to swim as often as possible, e.g. 4 x 2-3 km about 10 km resp. 4 x 2-3 km, about 10 km.
If possible under guidance of a trainer.
1 x per week endurance 1 x 2,000 m; 2 x 1,000 m.
Intervals: 2 x 8 x 100 m; 2 x 4 x 250 m with 1 min. breaks between.
4 x 500 m, pyramid swimming 50 m to 250 m to 50 m.
Running: 2 x 15 km, 1 x 25.

March: Running month
Normal swimming training.
4 km/wk endurance+interv. 5-6 km/wk.
Cycle tours on weekends 60-80 km easy pedalling, 100 rpm. Cycle to work.
Focus on running; objective marathon run late March/early April 3:15 h resp. 3:00 h.
Training schedules see chapter "Training Tips for Running".

April: Cycling month
Swimming: 4 km/wk. 5-6 km/wk.
Running: 40-50 km/wk. 50 km/wk.
 After the marathon run, two weeks of easy running only. The emphasis is on cycling training. At the weekends an even round pedalling style is practised using the smaller cog. In doing so, make sure you have rpm of 100-110 per minute, e.g. Friday 70 km, Saturday 100 km+8 km running, Sunday 120 km, Wednesday 60 km. If you have the opportunity to go to a training camp in Mallorca or elsewhere, take it. A good foundation is 900-1,200 km in two weeks. In addition 2-3 x 1 h easy running. In Mallorca swimming is seldom possible.

May: At the weekends practise the changeover cycling-running, in each case one session easy, the other fast, e.g. 100 km cycling + 12 km running; 60 km cycling + 20 km running.
1 x per week intervals on the bike, e.g. 5 km fast, 5 km steadily, 5 km fast .....; 2 x 10 km at 90-95% intensity,
Normal, hard and regenerative training weeks alternate; N H R.
Swimming as in previous month, intervals, 1 x endurance.
Running: 1 x per week interval training 6 x 1,000 m, at 10 km race speed, each time then lightly jog 1 km up to pulse of 110; 2 x 5,000 m 90%, 10 minute break wth light jogging. Running amount 50-60 km, making sure to keep up weekly long steady run of 25–28 km.
Late May: Short triathlon as test race.
Competitive period: Late May to October.

Training Schedules for 12 Hours
June, July see detailed training schedules Pages 161-163

Training Plans For 11 Hours
Target 11 h see training schedules on Pages 164-166

Early **June** perhaps a medium triathlon to check form.
During all physical preparation do not forget about mental training.

July/August ULTRA TRIATHLON

My hearty congratulations to all finishers! Wasn't it a fantastic experience?
Here's to another one next year!

Now every finisher has earned their regeneration period. For 3-4 weeks just completely relax and only train lightly, in spite of the now even greater motivation. Time to catch up on things you have been neglecting.

September:
After 2-3 normal training weeks 1-2 short or medium triathlons to end the season.

Target 11:59 h Date: From to 4th week of May										Week: 1	

Day	Weight	S		C		R		Other sporting	Comments	Pulse	Weight
	km (mo)	Dist. m	Time	Dist. km	Time or km/h	Dist. km	Time	activity		Rest Strain	kg (ev)
Mon.								Stretching			
Tue.				100	Hard	20	Easy				
Wed.		2500	Interv.	60	Easy						
Thu.				40	steadily	10	Jogging				
Fri.		1000	Endur.								
Sat.											
Sun.		2000		80		20			Middle or short distance		
Total		5500		280		50			Hard week		

Date: From to										Week: 2	

Day	Weight	S		C		R		Other sporting	Comments	Pulse	Weight
	km (mo)	Dist. m	Time	Dist. km	Time or km/h	Dist. km	Time	activity		Rest Strain	kg (ev)
Mon.								Stretching			
Tue.				50	Easy						
Wed.		2000	Endur.			12	Easy				
Thu.											
Fri.						20	Easy				
Sat.				80	Easy						
Sun.		1500	Interv.								
Total		3500		130		32			Regeneration		

Target 11:59 h
Date: From   to   Week: 3

Day	Weight km (mo)	S Dist. m	Time	C Dist. km	Time or km/h	R Dist. km	Time	Other sporting activity	Comments	Pulse Rest Strain	Weight kg (ev)
Mon.								Stretching			
Tue.				40	Easy	12	Fartlek	Alternate tr.			
Wed.		2000	Interv.								
Thu.				60	Fartlek						
Fri.						25	steadily				
Sat.				100	90 %						
Sun.		2000	Endur.				10				
Total		4000		180		47			Normal week		

Date: From   to   Week: 4

Day	Weight km (mo)	S Dist. m	Time	C Dist. km	Time or km/h	R Dist. km	Time	Other sporting activity	Comments	Pulse Rest Strain	Weight kg (ev)
Mon.								Stretching			
Tue.				50	Easy	18	6x1000				
Wed.		2500	Interv.	40	Fartlek						
Thu.						28	steadily				
Fri.				80	90 % Hard						
Sat.				120	Easy	15	Fartlek		Alternate tr. C + R		
Sun.		2500	Endur.								
Total		5000		290		61			Hard week		

Target 11:59 h
Date: From   to   Week: 5

Day	Weight km (mo)	S Dist. m	Time	C Dist. km	Time or km/h	R Dist. km	Time	Other sporting activity	Comments	Pulse Rest Strain	Weight kg (ev)
Mon.								Stretching			
Tue.				100	Easy	12	Fast		Alternate tr.		
Wed.		2000	Interv.								
Thu.						18	10 km Speed		Mental Training		
Fri.				80	90% Hard						
Sat.		3000	Endur. +Interv.	140	Easy						
Sun.						25	steadily				
Total		5000		320		55			Hard week		

Date: From   to   Week: 6

Day	Weight km (mo)	S Dist. m	Time	C Dist. km	Time or km/h	R Dist. km	Time	Other sporting activity	Comments	Pulse Rest Strain	Weight kg (ev)
Mon.								Stretching	Mental Training		
Tue.				40	25 km Hard	15	5 km Hard		"Glycogen Training"		
Wed.		1500	Easy								
Thu.				30	Very steadily						
Fri.											
Sat.		3800		180		42.2		<11:59	Good luck You can do it		
Sun.				30	Very steadily						
Total		5300		280		57					

Target 10:59 h
Date: From   to   Week: 1

Day	Weight km (mo)	S Dist. m	Time	C Dist. km	Time or km/h	R Dist. km	Time	Other sporting activity	Comments	Pulse Rest Strain	Weight kg (ev)
Mon.								Stretching			
Tue.				100	90% Hard	18	Easy				
Wed.		2500	Interv.	60	Easy						
Thu.				40	steadily	12	Easy				
Fri.		1000	Endur.								
Sat.											
Sun.		2000		80		20			Middle or short distance		
Total		5500		280		50			Hard week		

Date: From   to   Week: 2

Day	Weight km (mo)	S Dist. m	Time	C Dist. km	Time or km/h	R Dist. km	Time	Other sporting activity	Comments	Pulse Rest Strain	Weight kg (ev)
Mon								Stretching			
Tue.				60	Easy						
Wed.		2000	Endur.			12	Easy				
Thu.											
Fri.						22	steadily				
Sat.				90	steadily						
Sun.		2000	Interv.								
Total		4000		150		34			Regeneration week		

Target 10:59 h
Date: From   to   Week: 3

Day	Weight km (mo)	S Dist. m	Time	C Dist. km	Time or km/h	R Dist. km	Time	Other sporting activity	Comments	Pulse Rest / Strain	Weight kg (ev)
Mon.								Stretching			
Tue.				60	Easy	15	Fartlek		Alternate tr.		
Wed.		2500	Interv.								
Thu.				60	With fast sections						
Fri.		1500	Endur.			25	steadily				
Sat.				100	90% Hard						
Sun.		2500	Interv.			10	Easy				
Total		6000		230		52			Normal week		

Date: From   to   Week: 4

Day	Weight km (mo)	S Dist. m	Time	C Dist. km	Time or km/h	R Dist. km	Time	Other sporting activity	Comments	Pulse Rest / Strain	Weight kg (ev)
Mon.								Stretching			
Tue.				50	Easy	18	8x1000				
Wed.		2500	Interv.	40	Fartlek						
Thu.						28	steadily				
Fri.				80	90% Hard						
Sat.		2000	Endur.	140	Easy	15	steadily		Alternate tr. C + R		
Sun		3000	Interv.								
Total		7500		310		61			Hard week		

Target 10:59 h
Date: From   to   Week: 5

Day	Weight km (mo)	S Dist. m	Time	C Dist. km	Time or km/h	R Dist. km	Time	Other sporting activity	Comments	Pulse Rest Strain	Weight kg (ev)
Mon.								Stretching			
Tue.				100	Easy	15	Fast		C + R		
Wed.		2500	Interv.								
Thu.						18	10 km Speed l.				
Fri.				80	90% Hard				Mental Training		
Sat.		3000	Endur.	150	Easy						
Sun.		1500	"Bathing"			25	steadily				
Total		7000		330		58			Hard week		

Date: From   to   Week: 6

Day	Weight km (mo)	S Dist. m	Time	C Dist. km	Time or km/h	R Dist. km	Time	Other sporting activity	Comments	Pulse Rest Strain	Weight kg (ev)
Mon								Stretching	Mental Training		
Tue.				40	25 km/h	15	6 km Hard		"Glycogen Training"		
Wed.		2000	Endur.								
Thu.				30	steadily	6	Easy jogging				
Fri.											
Sat.		3800		180		42.2			<10:59	Have fun "Finisher" Congratulations!	
Sun.				30	Cycling						
Total		5800		280		63			Ultra triathlon		

Target Time 10 Hours/Target Time 8:45 - 9:00 Hours

c) 3.86/180/42.2 km in 10 hours
d) 3.86/180/42.2 km in 8:45-9:00 hours

Approximate race times required:	10:00 h	8.45-9.00 hh
Swimming:	1:10 h 18 min./1,000 m	52-55 min. 14 min./km
Cycling:	5:20 h 34 km/h	4:50 h 37 km/h
Running:	3:30 h 5:00 min./km	3:05 h 4:20 min./km
Requirements for:	**10 h**	**8:45-9:00 h**
2,000 m swimming	35 min.	29 min.
80 km cycling	2:15 h 36 km/h	2:00 h 40 km/h
1,0000 m running	35 min.	33 min.
25 km running	1:35 h	1:30 h
Marathon run	2:50 h	2:35 h

Recommendations for the Last 6 months before the event (28 wks)		
Swimming	200 km = 7 km/wk	300 km = 10-11 km/wk
Cycling	6,000 km = 215 km/wk	8-9,000 km = 300 km/wk
Running	1,500 km = 54 km/wk	1,800 km = 64 km/wk
Req. time per week on average (nett training time)	15 h + stretching + strength training	20 h

Transitional period: October, November, possibly December, January
Recovery, physically and mentally. 2-3 x wk easy running for 12-15 km, easy swimming without timing. Analysis of previous season, improvement suggestions and planning for coming race season.

Preparatory period: December to mid May.
Basic endurance training: Emphasis on running + swimming.

At the start of the preparatory period the amount of training increases at low strain. Pulse rate 130. Use opportunities to go cross-country skiing in order to train arm and torso muscle groups. Through stretching and strength training comprehensive supply of blood to the body is supported.

Running: 3-4x wk 70-80 km   4-6x 70-120 km
Even long runs 1-2.5 h. One long steady run per week at pulse 130 over 25-30 km.

Cycling training: In good weather 1-1:30 h, possibly rolling device 2x45 min.

Strength training:	1 x per week	2 x per week
Stretching:	2 x 20 min.	3 x 20-30 min.
Swimming:	3-4 x 8-9 km/wk	4-5 x 15 km/wk

Technique + intervals + endurance swimming
Interval on/off e.g. 10 x 100 m + 10 x 50 m
5 x 500 m; 8 x 250 m; pyramid swimming
50/100/150/200/250/300/250/200/150/100/50   Swimming programme
1 x endurance 3 x 1,000 m, 2,000 m, 3,000 m various combinations

February: Swimming month
While keeping up normal training, swim as often as possible. Coaching is desirable.

Amount:	12 km/wk	20 km/wk

Every 3rd week should be a regeneration week with low
intensity and amount.   If possible 1 week
Cycle trips in good weather.   training camp.

March: Running month
Normal swimming training: 7-8 km/wk   12-15 km/wk
Keep up stretching, strength training.
Cycling training: Tour pedalling easily at 110 rpm using small cog. Prepare for cycling month April. Include cycling training in marathon run preparations.
Emphasis: Running with the objective of running a marathon in late March/early April in a time of: 2:50 h   2:30-2:40 h

Training guidelines in chapter "Training Tips - Running".

April: Cycling month
Alternatively: March cycling month/February running month/January swimming month.
Possibly reduce swimming: 5-6 km   6-10 km
Running: After a successful marathon run two weeks of light training only, 3 x 15 km, afterwards back to normal.
Cycling training: Emphasis on weekends and holidays. If possible two weeks training in warmer regions. Italy, southern France, Spain, Mallorca.
                1,200 km/2 wks   1,400-1,500 km/2 wks
Train round even pedalling and endurance. At this time only easy swimming and running. See "Training Tips - Cycling".

May:
At the weekends train changeovers:

Fast cycling training (80-100 km) + steady 15-20 km run,
Steady cycling training (120-150 km) + fast 10 km run.

Swimming: As well as intervals, do endurance swimming in open water.

Running: 70 km   70-100 km

1 x per week interval training e.g. 2-3 x 5,000 m, 8 x 1,000 m, 1, 2, 3, 2, 1 km quickly with 1 km easy jogging between each time.

Competition period: Mid May – mid October.

Stabilisation of top sporting form.

Deliberate competition preparation.

Reduce the strain in the last 10-12 days before the race. Participate in 1-2 short-middle triathlons as build up events. Do not underestimate mental training with a view to the high point of the season.

After the event ensure sufficiently long regeneration:
> low strain, days of rest, only 1 x per day easy training, sauna, massage, plenty of fluids, minerals, vitamins.

Avoid over-straining through too many triathlons.

After an ultra triathlon regenerate for three weeks, only 50% amount of training.

Training Schedules for 10 h (see Pages 170-175)

Notes on the Training Schedules for 10 Hours
The training schedules shown here were carried out exactly like this by me. In 1990 I achieved a time of 10:10 h after the training described. In 1992, following a completely different training and race strategy, I achieved 10:06 h. With a slightly different race strategy and warmer weather in 1992 a time of just under 10 hours would have been realistically possible. In 1993 this "threshold" was then crossed with a time of 9:54.

Amount of training in the last six months

Before Roth 1992 incl. changeover times		Times in Roth
Swimming	103 km = 3.7 km/wk	1:15:18 h
Cycling	6,024 km = 215 km/wk	5:24:59 h
(2,500 of them going to work)		
Running	1,749 km = 62 km/wk	3:26:15 h
		10:06:32 h
Roth 1990		
Swimming	140 km = 5 km/wk	1:11:26 h
Cycling	4,980 km = 177 km/wk	5:37:05 h
Running	1,800 km = 64 km/wk	3:21:53 h
		10:10:24 h

Date: From 01.06 to 07.06 — Week: 23

Day	Weight km (mo)	S Dist. m	S Time	C Dist. km	C Time or km/h	R Dist. km	R Time	Other sporting activity	Comments	Pulse Rest / Strain	Weight kg (ev)
Mon.									30.05 Ultra triathlon Lanzarote		
Tue.				50	Very easy	10	Jogging				
Wed.	1000										
Thu.	2100		2x1000 19:30 18:45						Swimming in neoprene		
Fri.				18 18						45	
Sat.											
Sun.				10.6/60/10.6 After 1:40 didn't have the necessary strength			3:20		Duathlon WC Frankfurt		
Total		3100		146		31			Worn out		

Date: From 08.06 to 14.06 — Week: 24

Day	Weight km (mo)	S Dist. m	S Time	C Dist. km	C Time or km/h	R Dist. km	R Time	Other sporting activity	Comments	Pulse Rest / Strain	Weight kg (ev)
Mon.				40							
Tue.						10	Easy				
Wed.		2100	4x500	18 18							
Thu.				18 18		10			Running difficult		
Fri.		2100	Pyramids	18 18							
Sat.		2500	2x500 5x100 5x50	100	27.5 km/h						
Sun.											
Total		6700		248		20					

Date: From 15.06 to 21.06 — Week: 25

Day	Weight km (mo)	S Dist. m	Time	C Dist. km	Time or km/h	R Dist. km	Time	Other sporting activity	Comments	Pulse Rest Strain	Weight kg (ev)
Mon.		2000	Lake	18 48	3x3 Fast						
Tue.				18 45		14	4x1000 3:25 min		Running great Pulse up to 165	46	79
Wed.		1000		18 18							
Thu.	77					11	50 min		Depart for Portugal		
Fri.											
Sat.				40	25 km/h average						
Sun.		1500	28:30	42	1:17	10	39.25		Seniors EC Villnouva		
Total		4500		247		35			9.AK45		

Date: From 22.06 to 28.06 — Week: 26

Day	Weight km (mo)	S Dist. m	Time	C Dist. km	Time or km/h	R Dist. km	Time	Other sporting activity	Comments	Pulse Rest Strain	Weight kg (ev)
Mon.									Return from Portugal		
Tue.		2000	Not timed			12					
Wed.		1500	Interv.	18 60							
Thu.				18 18		28			Running very difficult after 20 km		
Fri.				18 120					C Trip to Minden		
Sat.		1000		40					Worn out		
Sun.				150	29.7 km/h	17			C Great		
Total		4500		442		57					

Date: From 29.06. to 05.07 — Week: 27

Day	Weight km (mo)	S Dist. m	S Time	C Dist. km	C Time or km/h	R Dist. km	R Time	Other sporting activity	Comments	Pulse Rest / Strain	Weight kg (ev)
Mon.				18 18		28	2:15				
Tue.											
Wed.		3500	Lake			12			Found swimming rhythm		
Thu.				18 18		24	1:46			48 125-140	
Fri.				18 110	28 km/h						
Sat.		4000	3x1000 19:30 18.30								
Sun.		2000				28	2:14 Pulse 130				
Total		9500		243		92					

Date: From 06.07. to 12.07. — Week: 28

Day	Weight km (mo)	S Dist. m	S Time	C Dist. km	C Time or km/h	R Dist. km	R Time	Other sporting activity	Comments	Pulse Rest / Strain	Weight kg (ev)
Mon.				18 18		12	1:00				
Tue.				18 75	Fartlek				Cycling: Fast sections		
Wed.		2000	Lake			12	1:00		Blood test, too little		
Thu.									protein 6.6 %, Ferritin		
Fri.									extremely low 17.1		
Sat.		3.8	1:15	180		42		Rain, cold!	Roth 10:06 h		
Sun.											
Total		5800		309		66					

Date: From   to   Week: 23

Day	Weight km (mo)	S Dist. m	Time	C Dist. km	Time or km/h	R Dist. km	Time	Other sporting activity	Comments	Pulse Rest Strain	Weight kg (ev)
Mon									For 1 week now don't feel like cycling tr..		
Tue.				30		12	59				
Wed.		2500	With neo.								
Thu.		2500	With neo. 10x100 1:45			15	1:10				
Fri.											
Sat.		1000	17:40	42	1:13	10	38	2:12 h	Short triathlon Harsewinkel		
Sun.											
Total		6000		72		37			Vacation		

Date: From   to   Week: 24

Day	Weight km (mo)	S Dist. m	Time	C Dist. km	Time or km/h	R Dist. km	Time	Other sporting activity	Comments	Pulse Rest Strain	Weight kg (ev)
Mon						15	1:16.				
Tue.											
Wed.						23	1:50				
Thu.								Listless	Depart on vacation		
Fri.											
Sat.		1000				17.2	1:06		Run at Lake Wörth, Pulse up to 184		
Sun	79.4	1000									
Total		2000				55					

Date: From   to   Week: 25

Day	Weight km (mo)	S Dist. m	S Time	C Dist. km	C Time or km/h	R Dist. km	R Time	Other sporting activity	Comments	Pulse Rest / Strain	Weight kg (ev)
Mon .				59	2:01 km/h	17	1:25		Started cycling training		
Tue.		2000	lake	60	30.5 km/h				Swimming in lake with neoprene		
Wed.				68	29 km/h						
Thu.		2000				26	2:02				
Fri.		2000		60					Cycling training mornings before breakfast		
Sat.						26	1:59				
Sun.		2800		59	32.2 km/h						
Total		8800		306		69			Vacation		

Date: From   to   Week: 26

Day	Weight km (mo)	S Dist. m	S Time	C Dist. km	C Time or km/h	R Dist. km	R Time	Other sporting activity	Comments	Pulse Rest / Strain	Weight kg (ev)
Mon		2000	Lake	50	30.0 km/h	25	2:00		⌐		
Tue.	78	2900		58	33.0 km/h						
Wed.		2900				17	1:22				
Thu.		2000	Lake	60	30.3 km/h				Very hot		
Fri.		2000				9.6	35:50		Street run		
Sat.		2000	Lake	60	30.2 km/h	5					
Sun.		800		55		29			⌐		
Total		14600		283		57			Vacation		

Date: From		to							Week: 27		
Day	Weight	S		C		R		Other sporting	Comments	Pulse	Weight
	km	Dist.	Time	Dist.	Time	Dist.	Time	activity		Rest	kg
	(mo)	m		km	or km/h	km				Strain	(ev)
Mon.						17	Easy		Swimming with neo		
Tue.				58		28	2:20				
Wed.				60	31.5 km/h						
Thu.		5000	1:35	60	31.3 km/h				Swimming super		
Fri.		2000				25	steadily				
Sat.		2900		68	30 km/h	19	Fast				
Sun.		2900		52	28 km/h				VACATION		
Total		12800		298		89					

Date: From		to							Week: 28		
Day	Weight	S		C		R		Other sporting	Comments	Pulse	Weight
	km	Dist.	Time	Dist.	Time	Dist.	Time	activity		Rest	kg
	(mo)	m		km	or km/h	km				Strain	(ev)
Mon.		5000	1:32	26	30.7 km/h	20	1:28	⌐			
Tue.				70	60 km 32.8 km/h						
Wed.		1000				12	55	Very hot			
Thu.									Returned from vacation		
Fri.								⌐			
Sat.		3.8	1:11	180		42		Hot	ROTH 10:10 No problems		
Sun.		2000									
Total		11800		276		74					

Sporting Profile of Myself:
Born 17.1.47, triathlete since 1983

1,000 m swimming best time:	17:20 min. with Neo; 18:20 w.o. Neo
1,500 m	27:00 min.
10,000 m running best time	34:50 min. on track 1988
Marathon run	2:44 h
40 km cycling	1:05 h
180 km	5:21 h

Peculiarities: October to January four months regeneration.
Winter training: Swimming 4 km/wk (yes, yes, I know, not enough!)
Running from February onwards 70 km
Cycling, from October to February not at all.
From March onwards, 18-19 km daily to work and back by bike.
2 weeks cycling training in Mallorca with a total of 1,200 km and 100k m running.
Exception 1990; three weeks California with only 30-40 km running per week.
Spring marathon with 70 km/wk in c. 2:48 h.

Personal Weaknesses:
Strength training and stretching only sporadically. From October to mid February no cycling training, not even on the rolling device: Altogether too little swimming training. Hardly any interval training when cycling or running.

Personal Strengths:
Constant training; mental strength; very good feeling for race planning, this is confirmed by very even sector times. For me personally a comparison of the training notes from 1990 and 1992 is interesting. Here it is clear that the two schedules cannot really be compared. Peculiarities in 1990: Because of a trip to California I left out the cycling block completely. My idea of doing some of it when I got back worked for three weeks, then I couldn't stand the sight of a bike for two weeks. Finally, three weeks before Roth, I again realised the necessity of cycling training and while on holiday trained two hours a day before breakfast. I simply was not prepared to do more during my vacation. I comforted myself with my more comprehensive swimming training.
About 1992:

Six weeks before Roth I managed a total time of 11:22 h in the Lanzarote Ironman on an extremely difficult cycling section. Because I had registered very early for the Duathlon World Championship in Frankfurt, but only received confirmation very late, I did not want to pull out, and a week after Lanzarote I started over 10.6 km running/60 km cycling/10.6 km running. Not to be recommended. Furthermore, the European seniors championship in Portugal only two weeks later were also not exactly favourable for my Roth preparations. The many public holidays, and a number of flexibly plannable vacation days, just happened to allow me to start there. From a sporting point of view the two events were certainly not sensible. On the other hand I am sure that it will be some time before I get such a favourable programme of interesting events and free time again. So, if two ironman distances are to be covered within only six weeks of each other, one should not enter any other triathlons in between. After three weeks of regeneration there are only two weeks left anyway for normal training before you spend the 6th week getting ready for the new ultra triathlon.

Notes on Kalli NOTTRODT's Training Schedules (see pages 179-182)
In spite of being 40 and working full time, Kalli NOTTRODT, a weatherman with a degree in meteorology, is a 'top' world-class athlete. He has won his age categories in Hawaii and Roth many times. In 1992 in Roth he broke the 9 h threshold for the third time with 8:49 h. How do you do that? Here the motto applies: From nothing comes nothing!

His training notes from the period late April – early May (see page 179) show what a "normal" and a "hard" training week of such a successful man look like.
Amount of training 1992 in lead up to race in Roth: Race time:
Swimming   320 km = 11.4 km/wk   52:32 h
Cycling   8,200 km = 293 km/wk   4:48:10 h
Running   1,600 km =   57 km/wk   3.09:09 h
                                                                            8:49:51 h
In the years before the amount was much higher:
1991:   Swimming   350 km = 12.5 km/wk, average over 28 weeks
            Cycling   9,600 km = 343 km/wk
            Running   2,000 km = 71.5 km/wk

The amazing thing is that in addition to all this, Kalli works a normal 38 hour week. It is possible that being on shift work helps: early (6 a.m.–2 p.m.), late (12 a.m.– 8:30 p.m.), night (7:30 p.m.–7:30 a.m.) and two day shifts from 9 a.m. to 6 p.m. His underlying principle is: three days exertion, one day regeneration or rest. A day of rest still includes 2.5 km of easy swimming. It goes without saying that such a training programme requires many years to build up. In addition there are other characteristics necessary to handle such a rigorous programme: Talent, staying power, willpower, training effort, mental strength, physical robustness and many more. The complete personal environment must be just right.

Triathlon professionals like Thomas HELLRIEGEL and Jürgen ZÄCK demonstrate that training of up to 50 hours per week is possible. Only daily training of six to eight hours for several months a year make times of 8 hours possible. Since I watched these two in 1990 in California over just one swimming sector of 3.6 km I know what they are capable of. I am really glad they are successful because they have had to work extremely hard for it. Only very few people are able to achieve such training programmes and the race results they can lead to. In order to better understand Kalli NOTTRODT's training notes, here is his sporting profile briefly: Born in 1952, triathlete since 1984, before that swimmer with best times of 1:09 in 100 m breaststroke and 2:31 min. in 200 m breaststroke.

1,000 m swimming best time:	13:00 min. w.o. Neo.
1,500 m	19:30 min. w.o. Neo.
10,000 running best time:	33:50 min.
40 km cycling best time:	60 min.
180 km	4:48 h

Winter training: Emphasis	Running 70-120 km/wk
	Swimming 15-20 km/wk
	2 x strength training
	2-3 x aerobics/gymnastics

Spring training: Cycling training when dry and temperatures are above +5. In March two weeks in Mallorca c. 1,400 km cycling.

Absolutely world class for more than ten years now.

Kalli Nottrodt									
Date: From 27.04to 03.05								**Week: Hard week**	

Day	Weight	S		C		R		Other sporting	Comments	Pulse	Weight
	km	Dist.	Time	Dist.	Time or km/h	Dist.	Time	activity		Rest	kg
	(mo)	m		km		km				Strain	(ev)
Mon.	73	2500	:45	143	30.4 km/h	11	:50				
Tue.	72	3500	1:10	74	31.1 km/h	17	1:15				
Wed.	71	2200	:40	87	29.7 km/h	15	1:05	Strength training			
Thu.	71.5	4000	1:10						40th birthday "Crashed"		
Fri.	70.5					25	1:50				
Sat.	71	3000	1:00	93	30.8 km/h	5-6	:25				
Sun.	72			121	Hills 29.0 km/h				C: RTF		
Total		15200		518		74			≈29 h		

Date: From to								Week: Normal week			
Day	Weight	S		C		R		Other sporting	Comments	Pulse	Weight
	km	Dist.	Time	Dist.	Time or km/h	Dist.	Time	activity		Rest	kg
	(mo)	m		km		km				Strain	(ev)
Mon.		2100	:40						"Day off"		
Tue.		3000	1:00	58	30.4 km/h	10	:45	Rope pulling			
Wed.		3200	1:00	77	30.4 km/h	14	1:00				
Thu.		1800	:30	97	30.6 km/h	14	1:00	Rope pulling			
Fri.		2500	:50	Easy					"Day off"		
Sat.		3400	1:00			20	1:30	Strength tr.	No cycling because of rain		
Sun.				73	29.0 km/h	5					
Total		16000		301		64			≈20 h		

Date: From 01.06.to 07.06 Week:

Day	Weight km (mo)	S Dist. m	Time	C Dist. km	Time or km/h	R Dist. km	Time	Other sporting activity	Comments	Pulse Rest Strain	Weight kg (ev)
Mon	72	3300	1:00	105	33.1 km/h	14	1:00	Rope pulling			
Tue.		3300	1:00	50	1:30	14	1:00				
Wed.	72	2200	:40	66	Easy 27.0 km/h	10	:45				
Thu.	72								Day off		
Fri.	72	1600	Easy :30								
Sat.	72			15	:30	2					
Sun.	72			60	1:32	10.6 10.6	38:40 39:10		Duathlon WC		
Total		10400		296		60			16-17 h		

Date: From 08.06 to 14.06 Week:

Day	Weight km (mo)	S Dist. m	Time	C Dist. km	Time or km/h	R Dist. km	Time	Other sporting activity	Comments	Pulse Rest Strain	Weight kg (ev)
Mon.		1000	Easy : 20:00						Day off		
Tue.	72	2000	:40	67	Easy : 2:20						
Wed.		2600	:50	58	Easy : 1:50						
Thu.		2200	:40			13	1:00				
Fri.	72	3000	:60	75	Fartkek 31.9	7	:30				
Sat.				115	3:30	14	1:00	Rope pulling			
Sun.		1500	Easy						Day off		
Total		12030		315		34		Easy week because of Duathlon WC			

Date: From 15.06 to 21.06   Week:

Day	Weight km (mo)	S Dist. m	Time	C Dist. km	Time or km/h	R Dist. km	Time	Other sporting activity	Comments	Pulse Rest Strain	Weight kg (ev)
Mon.	72	3000	1:00	114	Hard 32.1 km/h	13	1:00		2 hard days		
Tue.		2200	:40	89	31.5 km/h	14	1:00				
Wed.									Travel to Portugal		
Thu.		500	:15	45	Easy 1:30	9	:45				
Fri.		500	:15								
Sat.				25	Easy 1:00						
Sun.		1500		42		10			EC Seniors Villanouva		
Total		7700		315		46			15-16 h		

Date: From 22.06 to 28.06   Week:

Day	Weight km (mo)	S Dist. m	Time	C Dist. km	Time or km/h	R Dist. km	Time	Other sporting activity	Comments	Pulse Rest Strain	Weight kg (ev)
Mon.		800	:20						Day off		
Tue.				70	3:00						
Wed.		2400	:40	72	32.0 km/h	7	:30				
Thu.	71.5	2200	:40			11	:50	Rope pulling			
Fri.	72	3200	1:00	77	32.6 km/h	13	1:00	Rope pulling			
Sat.	72	1800	:30	64	Easy 31.1 km/h	7	:30				
Sun.				80	Hills 29.1 km/h	11	:50	Rope pulling			
Total		10400		363		50			19 h		

Date: From 29.06 to 05.07   Week:

Day	Weight km (mo)	S Dist. m	Time	C Dist. km	Time or km/h	R Dist. km	Time	Other sporting activity	Comments	Pulse Rest Strain	Weight kg (ev)
Mon.	72	2000	:40	77	32.0 km/h	30	2:10		Hard week!		
Tue.		1600	Easy :30						Day off		
Wed.		2900	1:00	175	30.7 km/h	11	:50	Rope pulling			
Thu.		3200	1:00	117	Hills 29.5 km/h	13	1:00				
Fri.	71.5	3200	1:00	73	Easy 30.5 km/h	10	:45	Rope pulling			
Sat.				72	30.7 km/h				Worn out		
Sun.									Day off 10 h work + rain		
Total		12900		514		64			26-27 h		

Date: From 06.07 to 12.07   Week:

Day	Weight km (mo)	S Dist. m	Time	C Dist. km	Time or km/h	R Dist. km	Time	Other sporting activity	Comments	Pulse Rest Strain	Weight kg (ev)
Mon.	72	2000	:40			13	1:00		Rain, so no cycling		
Tue.		2300	:45	88	33.5 km/h	7	:30				
Wed.	72	1800	:30	55	32.3 km/h	9	:40				
Thu.	71	1500	Easy :30						Day off		
Fri.									Rained, so no cycling, 30 km planned		
Sat.									ROTH 8:49!		
Sun.		3800	:52	178	4:48	42	3:09				
Total		11400		321		71					

Stage 5 – Hawaii Qualification and the Crowning Experience Hawaii

Anyone who has already gone through the four stages, and – I hope – always finished, is not only many experiences richer but has also really lived the passion and the challenge of the ultra distance.

At the same time they have prepared the way for Hawaii.

During the transitional period every athlete now has time to plan quietly the two absolute triathlon highlights for the coming season.

1. Hawaii – Qualifying Event
2. IRONMAN – HAWAII

The main thing is to incorporate one's own experience into the planning, and also to consider one's weaknesses. It may be necessary to include even more training in the normal daily routine.

Generally you should work according to the motto:

"Work on your weaknesses, maintain your strengths."

Using your own training notes, and the suggestions in this book, it should be possible to draw up a concrete plan for the next season. The important coordinates are the two ironman distances. Do not make the mistake of thinking there should also be another 8–10 events. Put all your concentration and attention into the two season highlights. And if you do not manage the Hawaii qualification, never mind, there is always next year. I would like to express a warning about too early and too exuberant motivation. The coming season will be very, very long. Even if the first ultra triathlon worked out great, no one should consider leaving out the regeneration period. In December at the earliest slowly begin the steady endurance training described. One more thing about planning the new season. Get your vacation planning done early. After successfully qualifying for Hawaii you will need to allow for at least two weeks, three if possible, especially if after the Ironman you would like to visit one or other of the charming islands. Certainly you should arrange the financial aspects as early as possible. To those in central Europe who want to see not only the sporting but also the touristic side of Hawaii, I recommend joining up with Hannes BLASCHKE. In German we have a saying "Hannes, der kann es", meaning "Hannes can do it", and this applies to Hannes BLASCHKE in more ways than one. In 1985 he demonstrated his sporting prowess with his fourth placing. For some years now he has been organising trips to Hawaii and knows the region very well, spending some months of each year on Big Island. You will need to plan for the following costs: Starting fee c. 300 $, payable when registering. On top of this come about 2.000 $ for airfares and accommodation, additionally there will be costs for food and possibly flights to other islands. If you are not too demanding you can thus get by with about 3.000 $ per person.

A lot of money; for high school pupils, apprentices or students perhaps too much. On the other hand, this Ironman in Hawaii is simply the biggest thing there is for a triathlete. Also, triathlon is an endurance sport which one can indulge in for a very long time and you do not "have to" have been to Hawaii in your early twenties. Whether or not to go to Hawaii a second or third time is a matter of opinion.

Personally, today, I strongly doubt that I will go a third time. Without a doubt my first start in 1985 – see the book I wrote afterwards: "Adventure Sports - Ironman - Der Hawaii Triathlon" – was the most impressive. In my second race in 1989 much had already become routine and I spent too much time looking at my watch. Although I was almost an hour faster in 1989 (10:44), my 1985 race made a greater and more profound impression on me.

On the other hand, I cannot deny an especially pronounced tingling in my limbs when the Ironman month October begins. Especially because in 1992 I had qualified for Hawaii, both in Roth and in Lanzarote, but for job reasons could not travel to Hawaii. Back to the qualifying event. Theoretically there are a whole range of opportunities to qualify for Hawaii. In March in New Zealand, in April in

Australia, late May in Lanzarote, mid July in Japan and Roth/ Germany, in August in Canada. All of these races cover the full ironman distance. In addition there are a number of American events in the middle distance category. Dates can be read in the Triathlon magazine "Triathlete".

Hawaii

These are the seven locations in which it is possible to qualify over ironman distances:
Ironman Europe, Roth, Germany
Ironman Lanzarote, Club La Santa, Tinajo, Lanzarote, Spain
Ironman New Zealand, Auckland
Ironman Australia, P.O. Box 153 Tuncurry NSW 2428
Ironman Austria, Klagenfurt
Ironman Canada, Penticton, B.C.
Iroman Zürich, Switzerland and Ironman Brasil

For us in central Europe the events in Roth and Lanzarote are most practical. Both give us time to gather enough cycling kilometres in our own latitudes in order to do the 180 km in a reasonable time. If, however, you want to have a good time as well as qualifying, then Roth is better. The wind, and the immensely difficult cycling route in Lanzarote, just do not allow good times. In the 10 hour region the cycling times in Lanzarote are a good hour more than those in Roth.

Only very experienced athletes can do both events and then go to Hawaii in October to start there. In "Adventure Sports – Ironman – Der Hawaii Triathlon" you can read in detail how every athlete organises and does his training, prepares himself mentally for the various events, gets his gear together for the big day, how the day of reckoning passes, what one experiences, thinks and feels during such a long race. All that is missing to give a complete overview is the impression an outsider has of the the whole spectacle known as "Ironman". Who better to give this than 52 year old Gudrun SCHMIDT from Suhl who accompanied her 18 year old son Jan through his first ultra triathlon in Roth in 1992 both externally and "internally". She herself is a committed triathlete, successful Olympic cross-country skiing participant and feeling triathlete mother.

She writes: "Triathletes are used to having their sanity questioned. After all, even after ten years of triathlon history in Germany and five Ironman events in the triathlon capital Roth, the average citizen considers swimming 3.8 km, cycling 180 km and running 42 km in one go to be organised madness. The most recent example: A programme on Spiegel-TV titled "Ironman, Final Victory In the fight Against One's Own Body".

Admittedly, the triathlete is a bit different to the average citizen. Somewhat livelier, a little more modern, perhaps a bit more dynamic. What other athletes wear neon sunglasses, navel-free tops and bathing suits on a bike even in rain, wind and temperatures of 10 degrees Celsius? But anyone who plunges into this undertaking, pays 300 $ starting fee and spends months of targeted training within the limits of their possibilities, is taking a calculated risk. They know what they can demand of themselves and what their limits are. Of course they will pay their dues, especially if still very young and doing it for the first time. And the coach, too, who thought he had already experienced everything possible in sport, has to correct himself: The Ironman is the greatest. Swimmers, cyclists and marathon runners will excuse me, but what is a victory in long distance swimming, cycling 180 km or a marathon worth when here men and women are doing them all non-stop in fantastic times?

An ironman actually begins the day before. Piles of noodles are cooked and eaten, the heroes rest up and gather strength. Then the bags for the various changeover areas are packed. Neoprene suit and swimming goggles, helmet, cycling shoes and goggles, running shoes and various items of clothing - everything has to go somewhere else! In the afternoon the bike has to be handed in. That is a spectacle in itself. You meet and can see the stars right up close. Every participant has to hand in his bike at the bike park area. Finally there are 1,700 bikes parked there, all closely guarded till next day. And this begins for us at 4 a.m. At 6:30 a.m. we are at the swimming start and I cannot believe my eyes: Thousands of others are there already. Now we leave the heroes on their own, for entering the changeover areas is only allowed for active participants. Now everyone is occupied with themselves. Somehow there is a strange atmosphere, quiet music plays, this is the calm before the storm that begins at 7 a.m.

In the first group of starters 850 athletes gather in a wide group, 750 men in red bathing caps, 100 women in white caps. At the starting signal I get goose pimples and have to hold back the tears. This is an amazing scene!

Swimming start in Hawaii

In the water everyone looks the same, it is hardly possible to make out people you know, even when following directly along the shoreline.

The cycling course has to be covered three times. Unfortunately it is now beginning to rain and does not stop before evening. But the rain can do nothing to stifle the enthusiasm along the course. In throngs the spectators cheer the athletes up the hills. They literally shout them up, with chalk and paint they have written encouraging messages on the asphalt. No one out there dare let up a single step - and here I am sure not only the coach has goose bumps. The boys are freezing. A string vest and bathing shorts on wet skin are more than enough over a long period of time. After more than six hours of exertion the marathon begins – a long way around Roth and along the Main-Danube canal. This is where age and experience start to pay off. 38 year old Matthias has overtaken Jan after 15 km and has a 26 minute lead by the finish. This is not just a marathon – this is what Ironman is all about.

At the finish everyone raises their arms, then for most there are tears of joy, including the coaches." Those were the words of a feeling coach and mother, standing on the sideline and not able to influence what was going on before her. Every finisher can congratulate themselves at the finish. A day of deeply moving experience has just come to an end. Anyone who has also qualified for Hawaii can be proud of themselves. You do not necessarily have to show this pride to others. It gives self-confidence, confirms willpower and creates further motivation

Qualified, and Now What?

There are usually three full months between Roth and Hawaii, i.e. twelve weeks. After the European Ironman every triathlete needs a sufficiently long period of regeneration. For physical and psychological recovery two to three weeks of light, easy training are absolutely necessary. Despite a possibly unexpectedly good result, no one should consider adding training kilometres and intensity.

This is certain to be repaid in the form of injuries which at the last minute may even prevent participation in Ironman Hawaii, or in the form of over training with the resulting reduction in performance.

Training planning can by all means allow for a quality improvement (increase in the amount) in September. This should not, however, cause any additional stress, particularly as both occupational and personal commitments will need to be fulfilled.

Regenerative measures are important, such as: Sauna, massages, stretching and sufficient sleep. If you have the opportunity to attend a training camp in September, take it.

Special Aspects of Hawaii

Hawaii is not Roth!

Certainly, the experience gained in the qualifying event in Roth will be very useful for Hawaii, but do not overestimate it. Even taking the completely different climatic conditions into account, there is hardly a course that is so incalculable as Hawaii's lava desert. A formula such as Roth Time + X Minutes = Hawaii Time does not work. Especially when you are starting on Big Island, the triathlon island, for the first time.

Every triathlete should try to do his Ironman without time pressure. The Americans have a fitting term for this: "Just do it", they say. Which means as much as: "Simply do it and see what happens". This is just the right attitude for this unique event. I must add: "Don't swim, cycle and run against others, but only against yourself."

When should you arrive?

It is not possible to make a general recommendation on this. There are many athletes who arrive in Kailua-Kona two or three weeks before the big day and do no better or worse than those who arrive only five days before.

Many top athletes only travel to Hawaii about a week beforehand, but come from sunny California and only have three hours time difference to deal with.

Those coming from Europe have problems firstly with the hot climate and secondly with eleven to twelve hours time difference, depending on when the daylight saving in Hawaii and Europe ends. If I had enough time, I would travel to Hawaii two weeks before the race and stay on a week afterwards to see some of the other Hawaiian islands.

The first three to four days make up the first critical acclimatisation phase. In the next four or five days there would be time to get to know the course, with the last days being kept free for recovery and preparations.

If you arrive too early you are likely to get tired of Hawaii before the starting signal is fired. It is important that the slowly increasing positive inner tension and the delights of the surroundings are not lost.

The Ironman begins when you land in Kailua-Kona.

Completely exhausted from the 20 hour flight, and a one night stopover, you land on a piece of the great lava desert. In the hot humid air you cannot imagine doing a triathlon over 226 km here. The worries about your luggage may last a while. In particular the transport of the bike from Honolulu to Kona sometimes takes a few days. In the first days it is therefore a matter of keeping calm. The most difficult phase of the Ironman has begun. In the next few days careless mistakes can change the race from a crowning to a torturous event.

Because of the climate and the long trip the body is more than stressed. Anyone who thinks they have to catch up on missed training now is betting on the wrong horse. Catching up on sleep, occasionally going for a 40 minute run or swimming in the Pacific is more sensible. Stay in the shade as much as possible and slowly get used to the intense sunshine.

Use suncream with a high sun protection factor, especially on the relaxed cycling outings. The fluid requirement when cycling is extremely important. Always take two full cycling bottles with you. During the day you should also always carry a full cycling bottle.

In Hawaii you just cannot get enough fluids. At night you should also have a bottle near your bed. Alcoholic beverages would only increase the need for fluids. For this reason you should avoid them, and also drinks with caffeine or sugar.

Always carry a large cycling bottle when doing running training. Along the course there are a number of drinking stops even in the weeks before the great race. If you dehydrate during training, you risk not recovering for several days.

If you regularly measure your pulse at rest with a pulse measurer you will notice that it is several beats faster than at home. In 1989 my pulse at rest of 47-48 at home rose to 55 beats in Hawaii.

How Should You Train in Hawaii?

The specific difficulty of peak fitness is of course related to the time the athlete arrives. In this phase you should train in the manner that has proven effective for you personally. Concrete amounts and intensities can no longer be generalised. In these days directly before the race each athlete should act according to his gut feeling rather than a fixed plan. Listening to your body is now more important than ever in order to know what you can ask of it and what not. After a few days your body will gradually adjust to the heat.

Nevertheless you should spend the most time relaxing near the pool. No one should let other triathletes drive them crazy. In Kona you see athletes swimming, cycling and running from dawn till dusk. It is often hard not to join them. Now, however, is the time to remain firm.

Swimming is the least demanding. At 7 a.m. the Pacific Ocean is still relatively calm and inviting.

Mental Preparation

As physical preparation is more or less complete a week before the event, there is even more time available to devote to mental preparation. This mental training has of course mainly been developed during the long training sessions of the previous months. Now it is a matter of activating these abilities and applying them at the right moment.

The first step is not to develop any fear of the Ironman, but at the most, respect. If in your mental preparation you assume high waves during the swimming, extreme headwinds over 180 km in the cycling and absolutely unbearable heat during the running, it can only get easier in the actual race itself. You have to have the will to struggle with this nature experience, determined to cover these notorious 226 km despite all the troubles involved.

In your mind you must experience these difficult situations as often as possible so that when it comes to it you can also conquer them physically.

Here again is the most important tip from the chapter "Mental Training": I am participating in my Ironman, not against or for others, but only for my race. Therefore I do not orientate myself to others, but only to myself, my own capabilities.

I want to experience consciously my Ironman.

As an athlete I must then remain "stubborn" and not go along with the attacks of other triathletes, in the certainty that at the finish line I will be waiting for many of those who at the beginning, apparently irresistably, go past me. This whole thing should be fun, shouldn't it?

Those who miss out on their dream "Hawaii" should choose another worthwhile way to end the season, e.g. the historic marathon run to Athens, which also takes place in mid October.

Equipment for Triathletes

Even as a triathlon insider you will find something new in the way of equipment at practically every event you attend.

Interested spectators at triathlon races never cease to be amazed. A glance at the cycle park in the change-over area leaves no doubt what kind of "material battle" is about to be fought. Is triathlon therefore just a sport for the rich and for mad "Rambos"?

Fortunately this is not the case at all. When carried out in a way suited to one's personal ability, triathlon is an extremely healthy endurance sport. And, thank goodness, one sees again and again that an ultramodern, aerodynamically styled super racing bike does not ride itself. In the German Middle Distance Triathlon championships in 1991 the winner, Olaf RENNIKE, beat the whole elite on their top bikes with his old, standard racing bike.

A beginner will certainly need no more than what he already owns as a sportingly active person. Bathing suit, racing bike and helmet and a pair of running shoes together with a running shirt.

An ambitious triathlete who goes for the short, middle and ultra distances will need more than this in our climate zone.

Swimming Outfit

Bathing Suit
When buying a new bathing suit, you should consider getting one with extra lining in the crotch. This makes cycling after the swim more comfortable. The change from bathing suit to cycling pants need to be done over the short and middle distances. The run afterwards can also be done in this fast drying material.

Swimming Goggles
These ensure a clear view and protects the eyes from salt when swimming in the ocean or from chemicals (e.g. chlorine) in public baths. The choice should be made individually. It is advisable to try various models from a number of manufacturers. To do this, press goggles with the appropriate nose width firmly over the eyes.

If the low pressure within the glasses causes them to stay in place for a brief moment, then they fit. To avoid unpleasant fogging it is often sufficient to wash the goggles out with a little shampoo or saliva when dry. Tinted goggles improve visibility when swimming in the open.

Bathing Cap
Usually provided by the event promoter. Absolutely necessary for people with sensitive ears. In cold weather two bathing caps prevent excessive heat loss.

Neoprene Suit
Not recommended for swimming distances in open air baths and up to 1,000 m length. Neoprene suits are cold protection suits which according to German Triathlon Union regulations may only be worn up to a water temperature of 23 degrees. They offer excellent protection against hypothermia in low water temperatures. The suits are made in thicknesses of between 2 and 5 mm. According to thickness and arm length they cost between 200-500 $. An optimum fit should be ensured in order to guarantee complete freedom of movement and good blood circulation. The light rubber material improves buoyancy and thus one's position in the water and the swimming times achieved.

Ear and Nose Plugs
Both are used by athletes allergic to chlorine or who find water entering the nose and ears unpleasant. Ear plugs also prevent feelings of dizziness as our sense of balance is located in our ears.

Paddles
Swimming paddles are small rectangular plastic boards which are attached to hands and wrists using rubber bands. They are used to improve arm stroke technique because unfavourable hand positions under water are noticed much more. Swimming with paddles requires more strength and thus trains the muscles.

Swimming Board
Used for learning and training leg movements.

Neoprene suits: indispensable for long distances and cold water temperatures

Pullbuoy
Used as a swimming aid when training arm strokes, as when squeezed tightly between the thighs it improves the position in the water.

Triathlon Watch
A watertight watch which allows frequent time and thus performance checks during swimming training is a useful purchase for every triathlete. If, however, constant time checking makes you feel pressured, you should swim without a watch and rely on your feeling.

Vaseline
Protects against rubbing of the neoprene suit on the neck and in the armpit area.

Cycling Equipment

It would be easy to write a whole book just on this topic. In the framework of this book I will just try to give some help in purchasing bikes and parts. In any case, it is recommended to go to a dealer with his own workshop and repair service. Prompt service is more important than saving a few DM in a department store.

Buying a racing bike is a matter of trust. Competent and honest advice on the part of the dealer is called for where such a costly purchase is involved. When you ask for a bike that perfectly matches your individual needs, you need to know what demands must be met and how much you can spend.

A beginner can get away with 700-800 $. If you look at the bike park of a medium to large event on the other hand, you will see that in some cases much different amounts can be invested in the "triathlete's favourite baby" — but need not be. The triathletes' well-known flair for trying out new things has led to many innovations in recent years, all aimed at improving the aerodynamics to reduce air resistance and at the same time reduce weight.

Frame
The reactor, the core of a racing bike, is the frame. It must have high stability coupled with low weight. For several years there have been experiments with various materials to improve these aspects. In addition to steel frames made of Reynolds (England) or Columbus (Italy) tubes, frames made of steel with a high carbon content and high quality aluminium alloy have been used to reduce weight.

In recent times carbon frames have contributed mainly to the futuristic appearance of the bike parks. Here I mention only the Giotto Cinetica tubeless frame for the saddle. More important than saving a few grams is the correct height of the frame. A useful formula for this is:

Frame height = length of stride x 0.66, e.g. 87 cm length of stride x 0.66 = 58 cm frame height. The length of stride can be measured in this way:

Stand with your back to a wall without shoes. Feet about 10-20 cm apart. A broom-handle is raised horizontally to the crotch until a slight pressure is felt. Measuring the distance from the top of the broom-stick vertically to the ground gives the length of stride. The suitable frame height can only be measured exactly in a proper cycle shop, on a so-called measuring horse. The same applies to the sitting position, which depends on these factors:

• Saddle height
• Setting of the safety pedals
• Positioning of the saddle (American position)
• Length of front section and
• Height of handle bars.

Triathlon Handle Bars

Triathlon handle bars should be obligatory for beginners too. They reduce air resistance and relax the muscles of the upper body.

The following also ensure aerodynamically favourable effects:

• low stretched out positioning of the triathlete caused by low front section,
• arms on the handle bars close together,
• lower arms positioned pointing upwards.

Usually the gear levers are mounted on the triathlon handle bars, of which innovations and new developments are constantly appearing. In this way the triathlete can maintain his aerodynamically favourable position even when changing gear. This in turn means that one changes gear more often and can thus maintain a favourable pedalling frequency longer.

Wheels

Here particular attention should be paid to quality, for friction arises in all moving parts. Many athletes have a set of especially high quality wheels for races. Normal wheels have 36 spokes. For races there are wheels available with only 16 spokes, or also carbon fibreglass designs with only three spokes,Tri-Spoke) or disc wheels. By reducing the number of spokes and also their form (blade spokes), the creation of wind eddies, and thus air resistance, is reduced. The same applies to radial spoking. The front wheel should therefore definitely be radial spoked. The rear wheel can stand radial spoking on the side opposite the gear rim if good double thick end spokes are used. Because of the transfer of energy the rim side should have triple crossed spokes.

Gear Rim

Here we differentiate between screw rim, screwed onto the hub as a block and can only be changed as a unit. Cassette rim (clip rim), the pinions can be changed individually.

It can be used in variations according to the type of country. The gradation of the rims varies: On flat land 12-21 is sufficient, otherwise 13-23, for hilly sections 14-28 teeth.

Chain

Under normal conditions the chain should be changed every 3,000-4,000 km. Many hill climbs require more frequent changing.

If a chain is used too long it spoils the gear rims. You can check if a chain is ready for changing as follows: Place the chain forwards on the large chain disc. If two fingers can raise it more than 2 mm from the chain disc, a renewal is necessary.

Gear Change

The SIS, or grid gear change, common these days allows clean and fast gear changing even when concentration is weak. Even experienced athletes change gear more frequently with the SIS or click gear change and can maintain their pedalling frequency at an almost constant rate.

Tyres

There are two basic types: tube tyres and wire tyres. In a tube tyre the tube and the tyre are a unit. This is stuck to the wheel rim using double-sided tape or tyre adhesive. With a little practice the tyre can be changed very quickly if there is a defect. Spare tubes should, however, be prestretched. This is easiest if the tube tyres have been on the rims for a few weeks.

Wire tyres consist of a tyre and a separate tube inside. The wire tyre is held in place by a wire ring in the bead.

Advantages of wire tyres:

a) Very long life, 2-3,000 km
b) Easy to change and to repair
c) Much cheaper than tube tyres
d) Spare tubes are easier to carry.

Disadvantages:

a) Usually have lower pressure
b) On average slightly lower rolling capacity.

Advantages of Tube tyres:
a) Excellent rolling capacity
b) Ridden at very high pressure
c) Best riding characteristics in curves
d) Not as stiff as wire tyres.

Disadvantages:
a) Short life
b) Much dearer than wire tyres
c) Changing the tyre requires considerable practice
d) The correct tyre pressure plays an important part
e) Spare tubes take up a lot of space.

Pedals

Safety pedals, e.g. Look, Time, AeroLite etc. allow fast insertion and extraction of the shoes. This fact has proven itself above all in falls. After the helmet, safety pedals are the next most important feature on a racing bike and should be worth the roughly 100 $ even to triathlon beginners.

Saddle Support, Saddle and Saddle Height

For safety reasons the saddle support must penetrate the saddle tube by up to at least 6 cm. Depending on the frame height and body size, athletes with longer legs may need a longer saddle support than usual. The correct saddle height is calculated as follows: The athlete sits on the bike motionlessly and puts a heel on the pedal that is lowest. If the saddle height is correct, this leg should be fully stretched out.

To take up the "American position" on a racing bike you need special saddle supports.

To keep weight down, these days plastic saddles with a leather cover are mostly used. They weigh only 200-300 g.

Cycling Helmet

Today's very light and fashionable cycling helmets are an absolute MUST for every triathlete in competition. Without a helmet you will not even be allowed to mount your bike after the swimming.

This rule has already saved many athletes from nasty head injuries. In today's traffic volumes head protection is absolutely necessary for racing cyclists.

Of course this also applies to every training ride. Not only in Hawaii but also at most other international triathlon events the cycling helmets are especially examined at the "Check-in".

Advantages of high-tech equipment:
- *A ride that strains the back less,*
- *optimised aerodynamics,*
- *reduced roll resistance through absorption of ground unevenness.*

Triathlon bikes

Very strong lightweight pedal crankshafts

Zipp's flat disc design

The high carbon rim wheel shortens the spoke length. Advantages: less spokes, lighter and stiffer rims.

Bottle Holder

A triathlon bike should have at least two bottle holders so you can give yourself sufficient fluids during long training rides or in competitions. In the meantime there are a number of drinking systems which save reaching for the bottle.

Without moving from the aerodynamically favourable form you can take in fluids through thin tubes. These drinking systems only become a problem later when cleaning and disinfecting them.

Over longer triathlon distances, however, these systems do not provide sufficient fluids. It is possible to mount additional bottle holders on the handle bars and the saddle support.

Bike Computer

Suitable for checking on performance in training and competition. Current speed, average speed, route length and especially pedalling frequency provide important information.

Athletes who feel themselves constantly under pressure from their bike computer and thus often go above training speed should use it less often.

Rolling Device

Regular training on this device in winter can help maintain the muscles used for cycling. It also serves for build up training after a hard race or for easy pedalling after a hard running session.

You can compensate for the intense monotony of training on this device by listening to music. The same applies to riding on a home trainer. Because of the lack of air resistance one tends to sweat strongly when training this way.

Cycling Shoes

These should have a hard sole and be firmly attached to the pedals. In this way an efficient transfer of energy and rounded pedalling are made possible. Velcro fasteners on the shoes are advisable for fast changes.

Cycling Pants

For longer training sessions and for races, cycling pants with leather in the crotch are recommendable. This ensures comfortable sitting and prevents chafing.

Cycling Jersey

Should fit closely and not hang loosely. Cycling jerseys should not be too tight at the arms and above all they must completely cover the back. The back pocket allows you to carry a banana or energy bars with you.

Cycling Gloves

They should ensure that in spite of sweaty hands you have a good grip, that vibrations are absorbed, that the tyres can be wiped while underway and that in case of a fall your hands are protected.

Running Outfit

Pulse Measurer

These sports devices, which have already been mentioned a number of times, can be used by triathletes in many ways and are excellently suited to checking on one's sporting performance and fitness, whether swimming, cycling or running.

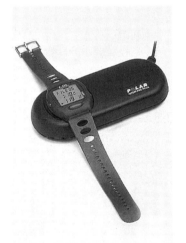

For less than US$ 100 waterproof pulse measuring devices are available.

The Polar Advantage Interface offers a variety of evaluation alternatives for both performance athletes and research.

Summer Outfit

String Vest

In hot summer temperatures a string vest is an advantage. The skin can breath freely and even when one perspires strongly the shirt does not cling to one's upper body. In order to protect the nipples it is a good idea to get a string vest with a smooth inside, or else to tape up the appropriate places inside the vest. Often applying vaseline is enough to avoid chafing in the nipple and armpit areas.

Running/Cycling Tops

Modern running and cycling tops are made of mixed synthetic fibres which absorb sweat and draw it away from the skin.

Running Pants

Athletic shorts with integrated underpants of very soft material have now become very popular. Many triathletes do their running training in a close fitting bathing suit. In this case it is important to make sure that stitching at the seams is not too rough.

Socks

When wearing well fitting running shoes these can be done without. If that is not the case, cotton or woollen socks are absolutely necessary to avoid blisters.

As well as a having good absorption properties, socks should have the right shape and not slip when running.

Underwear

In slightly higher temperatures cotton undershirts, T-shirts and underpants are best suited for absorbing moisture. They should not be too tight.

For women triathletes special sport bras are pleasant to wear. They are made of a single piece of breathing, elastic material.

Headband

Prevents stinging sweat getting in your eyes when you sweat a lot.

Cap

A running cap fulfills the same purpose as a head-band and also protects from direct sunlight.

I personally find that in high summer temperatures, which you do not only encounter in Hawaii, running with a peaked cap gives me the pleasant feeling of running under a small sunshade.

Winter Outfit

Underwear

It is recommended to get so-called nordic underwear, e.g Helly Hansen. This has the excellent characteristic of very quickly transporting moisture to the T-shirts worn over it.

The same applies to longjohns. Of course this nordic underwear is also ideally suited for cycling training.

Gloves

Athletes sensitive to the cold should not be bothered by what others think, but if necessary wear gloves or mittens, which warm even better. The idea that "Ironmen" do not wear gloves is completely out of place.

Hat
Anyone with a sensitive head or ears should not think twice about wearing a woollen hat.

Windcheater
In cold, wet and windy weather a windcheater is indispensable. Recently developed materials such as Goretex are both water resistant and allow perspiration out. Unfortunately such clothing is still very expensive.

Fluorescent stripes
These should be attached to the upper body and the running shoes when it is dark. Meanwhile there are also fluorescent vests one can pull over one's head. In autumn and winter these safety aids are as important as a helmet when cycling. If these fluorescent stripes had been available back in 1967, then most likely the "high priest of running" Dr. Ernst VAN AAKEN would have been saved from a terrible accident. In misty weather he was hit by a car and lost both legs.

Running Shoes
For a triathlete, running shoes are the be all and end all. You can practise your sport with unsuitable shorts and shirts, but if you try that with running shoes you will not get much enjoyment from your sport in the mid to long-term. In fact, by wearing badly fitting running shoes you run the risk of a number of injuries, e.g.:
- Hardening of the calves
- Joint and muscle pain
- Problems with the knees
- Back problems among others.

On top of that comes the fact that these days only one person in three still has perfect feet. Everyone else has to put up with more or less pronounced splayfeet, fallen arches, flat feet or club-feet, often even a combination of these. Therefore every athlete having problems with muscles, tendons and joints, from the head down through the spine, pelvis and knees to the feet, should first have his feet checked for abnormalities. As many people's legs are different lengths, these should be measured too.

Differences of more than 10 mm are usually partially compensated for with heel wedges that can be stuck in the shoes. Fallen arches and flat feet seldom create problems when running. A splayfoot can be supported with special padding. This must, however, be placed correctly.

Joint, and in particular knee, injuries can be caused by a club-foot. These foot defects can be analysed in the following ways:

- standing,
- walking barefoot.
- running in running shoes.

Running in running shoes especially shows clearly that worn out and inappropriate running shoes can considerably increase club-foot symptoms (Pronation). This of course really provokes overtaxing of individual joints. An ideal way of checking this is a running test on a running belt recorded by a video camera. When shown in slow motion the faults can be seen very clearly. Some sports shops with very good running shoe advisers have this diagnosis method available.

With good running shoes these problems can be solved in most cases. If inlays are needed in shoes, these must be complete inlay. Partial inlays slip. A number of orthopaedic shoe makers are able to make inlays for running shoes out of very light material, e.g. cork foam or high density polyethylene foam.

My personal experience in this field was as follows: In order to overcome my splayfoot fault I received complete inlays from an orthopaedic shoe maker with a built in round foam pad. My foot problems were reduced, but the inlays were so massive and heavy that they fitted in very few running shoes, and running with these foot weights was more than uncomfortable. On cycle tours of more than 80 km I could only peddle with one leg for long stretches because I had to massage the other foot. This even happened to me in Lanzarote on the extremely difficult 180 km route.

After that I made frantic attempts to solve this problem with lighter inlays. I actually found orthopaedic shoe maker H. ANSORGE in D-44797 Bochum-Stiepel, Kemnader Strasse 104, who fitted me with very light plastic inlays which removed both my running and cycling problems.

The following example shows what kind of strain an athlete encounters when running:

On a 10 km run, each foot touches the ground 4,000 times. Assuming a medium impact of 2 g (double earth acceleration), for a 75 kg runner that means 75 kg x 2 g x 4,000 paces = 600,000 kg = 60 t. Or power of 6,000,000 N = 6,000 KN = 6 MN.

The running shoe is the link between our feet and the ground. Unfortunately the enormous mechanical strain described here can quickly lead to foot faults. The most common joint and muscle pains are caused by unsuitable or worn out shoes, and also by unevenly worn out shoe heels.

So anyone going to an orthopaedic specialist should definitely take along their running shoes if they have joint and muscle pains. Very often the problems can be solved with new, better fitting running shoes.

Commonly used triathlon running shoes, recommendable for their shock-absorbing properties and stable fitting form, from:

>Brooks,
>New Balance,
>Saucony,
>Asics,
>Karhu

Hawk AP/Plus

GEL-TARTHER DS

Which shoe is right for you?

The right running shoe must fulfill the following criteria:
- shock absorbing,
- supporting, guiding.

When buying shoes you should therefore take the following into consideration:
- Buy shoes in the afternoon as the feet are then slightly swollen.
- Allow at least 30 minutes for the purchase. Walk around the shop in the new shoes and old socks.
- The shoe must fit, not be too loose or too tight.
- The space between the toes and the front of the shoe should be 1 cm.
- The heel must fit tightly and not slip.
- The shoe must support the foot.
- If you wear out the inside of your heels first, you need a sole that has tougher material on the inside than the outside - and vice versa.
- The inner sole must not be too soft. The foot must always have sufficient support.
- Inside, the shoe should be soft, the tongue padded so that the instep is protected from parts that pinch.
- The outer material should be flexible and surround the foot well.
- Racing shoes that are too light have too little absorption, so that even top stars do not run the marathon in an ultra triathlon in pure racing shoes.
- The running shoes should last and the price should be reasonable.
- The most expensive is not always the best. There is a huge choice of running shoes priced between 80 and 230 DM. An athlete can save a lot of money by not always insisting on having the absolute latest model. Often shoes are no longer "all the rage" after only six months and can be had for half the price in specialised stores.

Most important! When buying new running shoes, always take the old shoes along. Many foot faults can be ascertained by looking at the used shoes.

Despite the great choice of running shoes available these days, "the" right running shoe that exactly takes all more or less pronounced personal foot problems into account does not exist. Therefore every triathlete should have at least 2-3 different models. These should be worn alternately.

Nutrition for Triathletes

Hundreds of thousands of people do triathlon of some kind in Germany, millions worldwide. Some of them do it as a hobby to keep themselves healthy and fit, others as performance and high performance athletes to take themselves to the limit.

Today it is known that proper nutrition is essential for maintaining health and fitness. This is of even more significance for triathletes because their body is exposed to the greatest amounts of strain in many hours of training and above all in competitive events.

Top individual achievement in triathlon can therefore only be achieved through systematic training and appropriate nutrition. Inappropriate nutrition is often the reason for early exhaustion and pulling out of races. It can also place one's whole triathlon training in jeopardy with regard to the seasonal highlight(s). Triathlon training and races are linked with increased use of energy and set off a whole chain of metabolism processes. For these the human organism mut be provided with:

a) Nutrients that provide energy
> Carbohydrates
> Protein
> Fat

b) Active substances
> Electrolytes
> Trace elements
> Vitamins
> Fluids.

Nutrients: Carbohydrates, Protein, Fat

Carbohydrates
They play an important part in the energy metabolism of the muscle. Carbohydrates are stored as glycogen in the muscle and in the liver. The amount of muscle glycogen available is a major factor determining performance. A diet rich in carbohydrates can increase the glycogen content in the muscle and thus improve endurance in triathlon. Therefore carbohydrates play a decisive part in all three sports. They are the most important energy suppliers to the body. Generally the distinction is made:

• Simple carbohydrates, from which energy can be won quickly for brief periods. These include household sugars, i.e. glucose, fructose and cane sugar. In the long-term they cause unfavourable blood fat values, i.e. increased triglyceride values.

- Complex carbohydrates or multiple sugars are the various starches contained in grain, grain products, potatoes, muesli, noodles and vegetables. They provide the body with long lasting energy, and at the same time they supply important minerals and vitamins.

For triathletes it is most important to take in the required carbohydrates in the form of complex carbohydrates. With a carbohydrate rich diet, the sugar molecules not currently needed for gaining energy are transformed into glycogen. These are stored in the liver and in the muscles. The muscle glycogen thus serves as an energy reserve store. If, however, these reserves are not drawn on through physical movement, the excess carbohydrates taken in will be transformed into fat and "deposited" in the body.

As energy suppliers carbohydrates have two great advantages:

a) They provide fast energy. Anaerobically they can release energy four times as quickly as our second energy store, fat, and aerobically they release it twice as fast as fat.

b) When they "burn" (oxidation), carbohydrates release on average 8.6% more energy per litre of oxygen taken in than does the oxidation of free fatty acid.

Thus the great significance of carbohydrates for all maximum and highly intensive strain situations becomes obvious. Fat burning on the other hand ensures energy for long lasting performance at low to medium intensity. During these processes sufficient oxygen is available.

Carbohydrate rich and starchy foodstuffs important to triathletes are:

- Grains: oats, wheat, rye, buckwheat, barley, millet
- Natural rice
- Wholemeal products: wholemeal bread, biscuits, pancakes
- Oatflakes, wheatflakes, muesli, cornflakes
- Wheatgerm
- Potatoes
- Noodles
- Legumes: peas, lentils, beans

Muscle and Liver Glycogen

In order to deal with highly intensive endurance exertion, muscle glycogen is needed. Because this is only available in limited amounts, the length of time high effort is possible is also limited. The exhaustion of the glycogen stores leads to a fall in performance. The storage of glycogen reserves in the working muscles can be increased by skilled training, so that the endurance trained athlete has two to three times as much muscle glycogen available as an athlete without endurance training. The downside is that every gram of glycogen binds 2.7 g of water and 19.5 mg of potassium.

Muscle glycogen is stored directly in the muscle cell and is also used up there. Liver glycogen (60-100 g) continuously releases glucose molecules into the blood in order to maintain the blood sugar level. If, however, the muscle cell begins to run out of muscle glycogen, then it will even burn glucose from the blood sugar, which thus drops. A drop in blood sugar puts the central nervous system in danger because it is dependent on the supply of glucose. This state of having too little sugar is marked by sudden lack of strength, dizziness, profuse sweating, trembling, blackness before the eyes and feeling ill. It can be combatted with biscuits, bread or a sugar cube. Badly trained athletes who have not sufficiently trained their fat metabolism risk using up their muscle glycogen too early and then their complete liver glycogen. For triathletes it is important to know that one day of fasting can use up your complete liver glycogen reserves. So be careful with days of dieting before days of long intensive training or even races.

How can the glycogen stores be filled and enlarged?

Top individual performance can only be achieved if the glycogen stores are optimally filled. Only then does the muscle have carbohydrates available for the longest possible time. Triathletes should make use of the principle of super compensation. According to this, the increase in glycogen in the muscle is over proportionately high when one eats carbohydrate rich food straight after (within 2-3 hours) an exhausting training session, i.e. the muscle stores more glycogen than before.

If you eat normal food, the glycogen stores are replenished within two days. If the food is rich in carbohydrates, more than 60%, this replenishment only takes one day. By carrying on with a carbohydrate rich diet the result is an increase in the glycogen stores. It is somewhat more difficult to develop even larger glycogen stores. This requires intensive training to reduce the reserves, then three days of diet rich in fat and protein followed on the 4th to 6th days by carbohydrate rich food. The three days of fat and protein rich foods are likely to be a problem for most endurance athletes as they are used to eating carbohydrate rich foods. In addition, during this time normal training should continue.

This method can raise the glycogen reserves up to 700-750 g. Linked with this, however, is a weight increase of about 2 kg of water. On the other hand, carbohydrate reserves of 3,000 kcal or 12,500 kJ are now available.

A less extreme method which does not quite achieve the high glycogen reserves just mentioned, but is easier to carry out, is something I have been practising for years. On the fourth to last day before a marathon, middle or ultra triathlon I go on a glycogen exhausting run: 5 km warming-up, 5-6 km at a tough pace and 5 km cooling down. During the following three days before the event I eat food especially rich in carbohydrates. That is, even more so than usual.

With the aid of a carbohydrate rich diet the following measures to raise performance in endurance sport are possible:

- Raise glyocogen reserves with a carbohydrate rich basic diet.
- Deliberately raise the glycogen content before a race by hard training followed by carbohydrate rich food.
- Provide muscle groups with sufficient potassium in this period.
- Only the muscles' own glycogen stores influence the performance of the individual muscle. The glycogen reserves of resting muscles cannot be activated and transferred to working muscles, i.e. the glycogen reserves of the upper arm muscles cannot be transported to the running or cycling muscles.
- During longer lasting exertion (middle and ultra triathlon) eat additional easily digestible carbohydrates.

Protein

Proteins (from the Greek: proto, the first) are the most important substances. No protein, no life. In each body cell there are actually up to five thousand different types of proteins, mainly enzymes. These biological catalysts regulate all the biochemical processes in our body.

Many proteins have transporting tasks. The red blood corpuscles (haemoglobin) transport oxygen, the plasma proteins move metabolism by-products and food.

Proteins are thus responsible for building up enzymes and also hormones. These regulate the automatic functioning of all metabolism processes. As a result of these processes of building up and reshaping, every human loses protein daily, in particular performance oriented triathletes. These must be replaced.

Proteins consist of various amino acids. Of the total of 22 different amino acids there are eight which the human body cannot produce itself. These eight amino acids have to be gained through food. The more essential amino acids a protein has, the more valuable it is. The protein content of our food demonstratively illustrates the influence on our performance ability.

Even a not quite sufficient intake of protein leads to a reduction in our performance. Health problems only appear later. In comparison to fat and carbohydrates, protein has a special significance.

The human organism is capable of transforming protein into fat and carbohydrates. In contrast, it cannot transform fat or carbohydrates into protein. The nitrogen required for this is neither in fat nor in carbohydrates. That would be too good to be true for us triathletes, most of whom have problems getting enough protein daily. More on this later.

Generally one differentiates between two kinds of protein:
a) Animal protein contained in:
    Meat, sausage, game, poultry, fish, milk, eggs.
b) Vegetable protein contained in:
    Grain, legumes, nuts, potatoes, vegetables, soya, corn.

Biological Valency of Protein

This indicates how many grams of body protein can be built up by the particular food protein. There is biologically valuable and biologically less valuable protein. The more similar a food protein is to human body protein, the higher the biological valency. Animal proteins always have higher valency than vegetable proteins.

	Biological valency
Egg	100
Beef	94
Fish	94
Milk	88
Cheese	84
Rice	70
Potatoes	70
Wheat	56

Interestingly, however, proteins from various foodstuffs taken in simultaneously can complement each other and mutually increase valency. A protein of low biological valency that is lacking in certain essential amino acids can be compensated and boosted by adding a different protein which has a surplus of these particular amino acids. This especially applies to the combination: Grain protein + milk protein.

Favourable combinations to increase protein quality:

Grain	+ Legumes
Corn	+ Beans
Potatoes	+ Egg, milk, fish, meat
Wheat	+ Egg
Wholemeal flakes	+ Milk, yoghurt, buttermilk, kefir
Bread	+ Sausage, cheese, milk, egg

Protein And Triathlon

In triathlon the amount of protein required depends not only on age and weight, but also on occupational demands and amount of training. Endurance performance of high intensity in triathlon, such as in interval training and in races, leads to wear on muscle fibres and structural changes in the cell membranes. This in turn leads to higher protein consumption in metabolism under exertion. This fact should be taken into consideration with higher protein intake especially in the regeneration phase. Ensuring sufficient protein intake is important for every triathlete, no matter what performance level he is at. Protein rich food supports not only muscle performance as well as concentration and coordination capabilities, but also general readiness to perform, activity and enjoyment of life. A diet with insufficient protein, on the other hand, makes intensive and concentrated performance in triathlon harder.

How Much Protein Does a Triathlete Need?
Triathlon, an endurance sport with high energy input, should have a balance of carbohydrates/fats/proteins in the proportion of 60/20/20 energy percentages: admittedly a purely theoretical value. Of course no triathlete can do much with these figures. Who works out how many per cent fat, per cent protein and per cent carbohydrates they have just eaten? In practice no one can do that. Even a lunch consisting of a large steak, potatoes and a lot of salad only has a protein share of about 10%. It is extremely difficult to achieve a proportion of over 10%.
The solution can therefore only be:

> As little fat as possible,
>
> As much protein as possible,
>
> Carbohydrate proportion comes about of its own accord.

Ideally our basic diet should fulfill these requirements. Dr. Ulrich STRUNZ always stresses that the lentil is the best food for endurance athletes in Europe (23% protein, 1% fat, remainder carbohydrates and roughage).

Dr. STRUNZ has found the ideal blood consistency in a number of Brasilian marathon runners who for financial reasons had mainly lived on beans. In order to achieve the necessary proportion of protein in our diets, we need to apply the above mentioned favourable protein combination on a daily basis, and in the main training and competition period use protein concentrates or supplements. Dr. STRUNZ puts it this way: "We need to eat much more poor people's food." By this he means lentils, beans and peas. In other words, legumes .The widespread belief that meat is identical with protein is quite simply wrong. Pork schnitzel or veal contains only 20% protein. Together with an increased protein requirement comes an increased need for Vitamin B6. It plays a key role in protein metabolism and improves the use of protein in the cell. The pharmacy Schloss-Apotheke in D-91154 Roth/Germany has a protein concentrate of high biological valency with the necessary minerals according to Dr. STRUNZ. This protein concentrate places no strain on metabolism because it contains no cholesterine, purin or saturated fatty acids. The instant powder is neutral in taste and can easily be mixed into drinks and food.

In your daily diet you must make sure that the increased protein intake is not accompanied by an increased proportion of fat. The amount of other undesirable substances such as purin and cholesterine can also increase.

A high proportion of fat leads to quicker tiring and diminishes oxygen exploitation because of the resulting higher oxygen consumption. In metabolism, foods containing purin lead to production of uric acid. This can be deposited in kidneys, joints and tendons, which can result in increased proneness to injury, kidney stones and gout. Offal (liver, kidneys) has a high purin content. Fatty sausages, eggs and offal have a high fat content. Therefore consumption of these foods should be limited. For this reason serious triathletes often need protein concentrates or supplements. These do not have the disadvantages mentioned.

Protein content of animal foods:

100 g Lean meat	20 g
100 g Low-fat curd cheese	17 g
100 g Cheese, 45%	25 g
100 g Milk	3 g
100 g Yoghurt	6 g
100 g Protein concentrate 50% animal/50% vegetable	85 g

Protein content of vegetable foods:

100 g Soy beans	37 g
100 g Legumes	22 g
100 g Oatflakes	14 g
100 g Noodles	13 g
100 g Hazelnuts	13 g
100 g Bread	7 g
100 g Potatoes	2 g

Only a blood analysis can tell us exactly whether we are getting enough protein. For triathletes the total protein proportion should be between 7.6 and 8.2%. The fat content should be under 10%. Protein deficiencies also lead to lower haemoglobin and ferritin values. More about this in the chapter on blood findings for triathletes. If, like me, you have a problem with protein values that are too low, you should eat more "poor people's food" such as lentils, beans, corn and peas, and regularly take protein supplements. You will have the best results with protein supplements or other protein additives if you take them 1-2 hours before training, or in the first meal after training, as protein cannot be stored in the body for a longer period of time.

Fats

Just as protein has essential amino acids, fat has essential fatty acids called linol acids. They cannot be produced in the body itself and must therefore be taken in through food.

Fats, which can deliver twice as much energy as carbohydrates 1 g = 9.3 cal to 4.1 cal, contain energy in concentrated form. In addition fats serve as solvents for vitamins A, D, E and K. Therefore a certain amount of fat is needed in food. Fats are consumed,especially during long lasting endurance performance such as is usual in triathlon, at low and medium intensity.

Typically an endurance athlete will still cover his energy requirements to a relatively large extent by burning fat, even at higher intensity. A good degree of basic endurance training ensures that even at intensive exertion the glycogen stores are spared initially. If a well-trained person runs easily at under 50-60% of maximum ability to absorb oxygen, over several hours exertion up to 70-90% of energy needed will be provided by fat metabolism.

For triathletes good fat metabolism means sparing the limited carbohydrate stores. The carbohydrates thus saved are then available at times of peak exertion. Those with bad endurance training, whose fat metabolism has a lower performance level, will get their energy from carbohydrate metabolism at a low level of exertion.

Their glycogen is used up sooner. Triathletes should therefore take care that if possible less than 25% of their calories come from fat. That only works if you turn to low-fat protein suppliers (lean varieties of meat, low-fat cheese, low-fat dairy products) and eat as few foods with hidden fats as possible.

Hidden fats can be found in:

Meat and sausage, chocolate, cheese, cake, sauces, mayonaises, eggs, all foods fried in breadcrumbs, pancakes, French fries (chips), desserts among others.

Minerals and Trace Elements for Triathletes

Minerals and trace elements are anorganic substances or molecules which contain no carbons and which are dissolved in body fluids. They are also called electrolytes.

One speaks of minerals when the daily requirement of a non-sporting person is over 100 mg: Sodium (Na), Calcium (Ca), Phosporus (P), Chlorine (Cl), Potassium (K), Magnesium (Mg).

Trace elements have a daily requirement of less than 100 mg. These include: Iron (Fe), Iodine (J), Cobalt (Co), Copper (Cu), Zinc (Zn) among others. Electrolytes are of decisive importance for proper metabolism, especially for the process of muscle contraction; furthermore in the supporting function of the bone skeleton, in blood coagulation and in many enzyme reactions in energy and protein metabolism. Because the body does not produce minerals, loss of them through sweating, urinating and excretion must be constantly compensated for.

Even slight variations from normal concentrations lead to major changes in performance. For this reason it is important for performance oriented triathletes to have regular checks.

More on this in the important chapter on blood findings for triathletes. The high performance of serious triathletes requires considerably more of these substances.

The following table shows the average daily mineral requirements of non-sports people and triathletes:

	Non-sporting	Serious triathlete
Calcium	1 g	2 g
Potassium	2-3 g	4-6 g
Phosphorus	1 g	2.5-3.5 g
Sodium	5 g	15-25 g
Magnesium	0.3 g	0.6 g
Iron	10-18 mg	30-60 mg
Zinc	10-20 mg	20-30 mg

Triathletes lose trace elements and minerals as well as other substances through sweat.

Daily sweat loss of 2-5 litres is not unusual in the main training and competition period. For this reason the need for minerals, trace elements and also Vitamin C is almost tripled.

Calcium (Ca)
Important for: Bone development, muscle contraction, transporting excitement from nerve to muscle.
Contained in: Milk, cheese, yoghurt, nuts, wholemeal products, Kanne Brottrunk , fermented grain.
Note: Chocolate, rhubarb and spinach negatively affect calcium intake.

Potassium (K)
Important for: Glycogen replenishment, muscle contraction.

Contained in: Fruit, vegetables, potatoes, vegetable foods, fermented grain, Kanne Brottrunk.
Regulating factor of the cell.

Phosphorus (P)
Important for: Structure of bones, teeth, participation in muscle and brain activity, provision of energy.
Contained in: Dairy products, fish, grain, vegetables, eggs, potatoes.

Sodium (Na)
Important for: Building up water in the body, osmotic pressure, enzyme function.

Magnesium (Mg)
Important for: Muscle function, bones, provision of energy, nerves. Magnesium plays a key role in protein and carbohydrate metabolism.
Contained in: Green vegetables, wheatgerm, legumes, fish, poultry, fruit, fermented grain, Kanne Brottrunk.
Note: Mg is the most important mineral. Symptoms of a magnesium deficiency: Tingling and cramp in the calves, lack of concentration, nervousness, depressions, lack of appetite.

Trace Elements

Iron (Fe)
Important for: Transport of oxygen, development of haemoglobin and ferritin, metabolism, enzyme component.
Contained in: Meat products, liver, wholemeal bread, brewer's yeast, fermented grain, Kanne Brottrunk, legumes, vegetables, beet sugar.
Note: Triathletes' increased iron requirement is explained by: Loss of iron through sweat (1.2 mg/l sweat)
- Apparently, running on asphalt damages the red corpuscles in the foot sole area. The production of new red corpuscles requires iron.
- Increased oxygen requirement and thus a necessary increase in red corpuscles - more haemoglobin - more iron in the blood altogether.
- Loss of iron through menstruation of female triathletes.
Note: Tea and coffee hinder iron absorption. Vitamin C aids iron absorption.

Zinc (Zn)
Important for: Enzyme activation, sexual function, appetite.
Contained in: Cheese, eggs, fish, meat, salads, green peas.

The Most Common Deficiency Symptoms of Triathletes and Other Endurance Athletes

Iron Deficiency
Symptoms: Tiredness, exhaustion, listlessness, reduced performance.
Magnesium Deficiency
Twitching muscles and cramps, trembling hands, cramp attacks of the whole body.
Potassium Deficiency
Weak muscles, general listlessness
Protein Deficiency

Ways To Combat Deficiencies

Be aware of what you eat
In a nutshell:
Wholesome, as little fat and as much protein as possible.
Further practical tips for nutrition can be found in the chapter: "Increasing Performance with Correct Nutrition."

Natural performance supporting dietary supplementation with Kanne Brottrunk and Fermented Grain.
Regular consumption of Kanne Brottrunk, a lactic acid fermented drink, leads to a balancing of the mineral "household" and an increase in oxygen partial pressure. Linked to this is improved metabolism, which leads to improved performance.

Dr.STRUNZ, who has intensively studied metabolism optimisation for several years, has discovered that red corpuscles - so important for endurance athletes - are mainly composed of the following:

a) A basic framework, namely protein

b) The integrated iron

c) A catalysator, ferment or enzyme which links the two.

According to his extensive research this seems to be in Kanne Brottrunk .

In hard training the Kanne Brottrunk provides for better circulation and removal of toxic tissue acid, the consequences are no more aching muscles and no cramps. This makes it possible to train harder and longer.

The regeneration phase is thus considerably shorter. 4-8 teaspoons of mineral rich fermented grain (also available from Kanne)per day as energy food is a natural fuel. I have already described the scientific backgrounds in the "Handbuch für Triathlon".

Substitutes on prescription
According to Dr. STRUNZ, as a rule, conscious eating will balance out the electrolyte "household", with two significant exceptions:
- Iron
- Magnesium

Endurance athletes seem to need additional substitutes of iron and magnesium. This was found out after thousands of blood tests. Only seldom does one find additional deficiencies when people eat a balanced diet, says Dr. STRUNZ Although it is possible to buy magnesium and iron supplements in department stores and drugstores, they should only be taken under medical supervision. More on this in the chapter "On Blood Composition of Triathletes".

Protein Concentrates or Supplements
A wholesome basic diet usually leads to sufficient provision of protein. One should, however, watch out for low protein suppliers, as mentioned. If the necessary total protein value in the blood for triathletes of 7.6-8.2% is not achieved, protein concentrates are a possibility. These should be taken in liquids 1-2 hours before or in the first meal after training as they cannot be stored in the body for longer periods of time.

"Sportaktiv" Mueslis for Endurance Athletes and Bodybuilders
These mueslis from Reform Oelmuehle Weingarten have been adjusted to the nutritional requirements of endurance sport and bodybuilding. Because of the greater proportion of proteins, minerals and trace elements the Sportaktiv mueslis "Kraftsport" (bodybuilding) are best for triathletes.

"PowerBar" Energy Bars
Because of the low proportion of fat (< 2 g) and the relatively high protein proportion of 10 g per 65 g bar, the energy is absorbed by the body very quickly. For this reason these bars are especially suitable for races. Taken in small amounts together with liquids, the bars provide an energy boost which is especially important on long triathlon distances.

"taxofit® Multivitmins + Minerals + Trace Elements Forte Capsules
These serve as a prophylaxis to prevent vitamin and mineral deficiencies. Vitamins, minerals and trace elements are substances which are are essential for life. They regulate the metabolism processes and thus contribute to maintaining performance ability.

High performance athletes in particular, who use an optimum training phase to lay the foundation for a strength-sapping season, can compensate for the loss of micronutrients caused in training by using a high quality vitamin and mineral supplement in order to prevent a drop in performance.

"Basica"

This is a base mineral-trace element product according to the formula of Swedish nutrition researcher Ragnar BERG, which has been available for over 50 years. Basica was developed on the assumption that acid building foods such as meat, fish, cheese, eggs and grain products can lead to excess acidity and the build up of waste products in the organism. Also, in our diets there are not enough minerals and trace elements. According to the composition of our organism of 20% acid building and 80 % base building elements (BIRCHER-BRENNER, HAY, Ragnar BERG) our diets should reflect the same proportions. This is, however, only possible with an almost completely vegetarian diet which in sport would lead to deficiency symptoms. Basica therefore serves as compensation for food with excess acid. The organic fruit acid remains are completely burnt in the body so that the remaining elements (minerals and trace elements) leave a base surplus. After exhausting exertion in particular, athletes have reported fast regeneration through the use of Basica.

The Significance Of Vitamins For Triathletes

For humans, vitamins belong to the food elements essential to life. Vita (latin) means to live. In carbohydrate, fat and protein metabolism, vitamins play a key part. Simultaneously they are decisively involved in building up blood cells, hormones and enzymes. They also protect against infection (Vitamin C).

Vitamins themselves contain no usable energy, yet they are involved in the whole energy gaining process and are used up in this process. Generally one differentiates between: Fat soluble vitamins, which include vitamins A, D, E, K and the water soluble vitamins B1, B2, B6, B12, C, folic acid, pantothenic acid and biotin, niacin.

Average daily vitamin requirements of non-sports people and triathletes (according to literature):

Vitamin	Non-sporting	Triathlete
B1	1.3 mg	7 mg
B2	1.7 mg	10 mg
B6	1.8 mg	12 mg
B12	5 mg	6 mg

C	75 mg	750 mg
E	12 mg	15-40 mg
Niacin	18 mg	30-35 mg
Pantothenic acid	8 mg	8-14 mg
Folic acid	0.16 mg	0.2-0.5 mg

Altogether vitamins improve health, performance ability and accelerate a number of healing processes.

Vitamin B1 (Thiamin)
Important for: Nervous system, carbohydrate metabolism.
Contained in: Nuts, grain, legumes, fermented grain, wheatgerm, oatflakes, pork.
Note: B1 deficiency disturbs the water "household", leads to depressions, tiredness, lack of will to train.

Vitamin B2 (Riboflavin)
Important for: Protein and carbohydrate metabolism, cell breathing.
Contained in: Milk, cheese, grain, vegetables, fruit, fermented grain.
Note: B2 deficiency leads to tears in the corner of the mouth.

Vitamin B6 (Pyridoxine)
Important for: Protein metabolism.
Contained in: Grain, meat, liver, legumes, bananas, milk, potatoes, fish.

Vitamin B12 (Cobalamin)
Important for: Development of blood, growth, development of red corpuscles.
Contained in: Dairy products, meat, fish, fermented grain.
Note: B12 deficiency leads to reduced red corpuscle content.

Vitamin C (Ascorbic acid)
Important for: Resisting infection, bones, blood, improves iron absorption, in its function as antioxidant it seems to be able to neutralise carcinogens (substances that cause cancer) in food and in the body.
Contained in: Fruit, citrus fruit, berries, vegetables, potatoes.
Note: Vitamin C deficiency leads to tiredness, reduction in physical and mental performance. When training at high altitude an additional 1-2 g of Vitamin C is recommended.

Vitamin E
Important for: Cell protection, oxygen supply, fatty acid metabolism.

Contained in: Vegetable oils, wheatgerm, vegetables, fruit, wholemeal products, potatoes, eggs, fermented grain.

It is important for triathletes to know that through long storage and incorrect cooking the vitamin content in food can be lost to a greater or lesser extent. The weak points in the vitamin supply are vitamins B1, B2 and C, especially when you do not take enough care about eating wholesome foods and take in the majority of your nourishment from mainly "empty calories".

Foods containing mainly "empty calories":

Sugar, alcohol, fats, polished rice, white flour products such as white bread, bread rolls, toast bread, cakes made of fine flour, gateaux, lemonades, Coca-Cola, chocolate, sweets, icecream. As a result of biochemical reactions, damaging molecules also arise. These can be absorbed by vitamins C and E, neutralising their negative effects. In this way the aging process of body cells and a drop in performance are delayed. In order to reduce the loss of vitamins and minerals as much as possible when preparing food, triathletes should particularly note the following:
- Store fruit and vegetables in dark rooms.
- Whenever possible eat food uncooked (raw vegetables, fruit, salad).
- Wash food without cutting it up.
- Wash food in cold water and as briefly as possible.
- Cook vegetables in very little water. Use the cooking water again.
- Keeping food warm and reheating it destroys the enzymes.

The following table shows how high the maximum loss through cooking can be:

Vitamin C	100%
Folic acid	100%
Vitamin B1	80%
Vitamin E	55%
Vitamin B6	40%
Vitamin A, D	40%
Vitamin B12	10%

Balanced Liquid Intake for Triathletes

A 75 kg triathlete carries about 45 kg of water around. Half of this water is in the muscles alone. The entire metabolic functions are geared towards this water household, in which the enzymes and minerals can produce their best results.

Small deviations here already lead to changes in the way these processes take place. Water losses lead to stronger concentrations e.g. of blood in the course of the metabolic processes and thus to reduced performance.

Physical performance such as that in triathlon goes hand in hand with a high production of heat. When a litre of water evaporates, about 600 kcal of heat are given off, at the same time the organism uses the evaporation to protect itself against overheating.

Weight losses in triathlon are mainly losses of water and mineral salts. Especially in humid weather, triathletes can lose up to THREE litres of sweat in an hour. The amount of sweat depends on a number of factors, e.g.:
• Intensity of exertion
• Temperature
• Humidity
• Training state
• Individual factors such as lesser or greater propensity to sweat.

The ability to produce sweat is a prerequisite for the performance to be achieved because the increasingly produced heat that goes with increasing sporting performance has to be released from the body.

The great endurance achievements of triathlon are only possible because the body is capable of releasing the by-product of performance - heat - through sweat. In spite of all this, after a triathlon, even a well-trained athlete's body temperature may rise to 40° or even 41°.

Composition of human sport sweat:
All figures are "mg per litre sweat"

Sodium	1,200	Phosphate	15
Chloride	1,000	Zinc	1.2
Potassium	300	Iron	1.2
Calcium	160	Lactic acid	1,500
Magnesium	36	Uric acid	700
Sulphate	25	Vitamin C	50

What Effects Does Water Loss Have?
Through water loss the general ability to perform is reduced. Generally one can say:

The greater the loss of water, the greater the reduction in performance.

With every per cent of body weight lost, the plasma volume (blood volume) sinks by 2.4%, muscle water by 1.3%.
Consequences of water loss:
The loss of fluids means that first in the blood, and then in the whole body, water is drawn away. The body fluids thus become more "concentrated". The blood becomes more viscous and can therefore fulfil many of its transport duties only in a limited way, e.g.:

- Reduced oxygen tranport to the muscles, which means less provision of energy and lower muscle performance.
- Reduced oxygen tranport to the liver, which means less energy for the liver cells and slower elimination of metabolism by-products e.g. lactic acid. As a result tiredness comes on more quickly.
- Reduced oxygen transport to the brain, which means reduced ability to concentrate ,which in turn leads to mistakes in cycling or running technique.
- Reduced transport of heat from inside the body to the skin, which means overheating of the organism and associated reduction in performance.

At 2% water loss, at 75 kg body weight that is only 1.5 l, endurance ability is reduced and a light feeling of thirst arises. For us triathletes this means: Drink before you begin to feel thirsty, i.e. as soon as you get on your bike.

With a water loss of 4%, performance is reduced quite considerably, there is also a reduction in strength.

6% water loss results in exhaustion, irritability and evident weakening. The feeling of thirst is very strong.
In a triathlon race it should never come to this - not even in Hawaii. The same also applies of course to longer training sessions.
Water loss above 6% this leads to illness, psychological disturbance and to lacking motor coordination, e.g. wobbling and staggering instead of running.

Beyond 10% the loss of water is dangerous, something which in sport can no longer be considered sport.

Fluid loss that happens quickly in hot weather is especially difficult. It aggravates the loss of performance. Slow fluid loss on the other hand, as happens in cool weather, reduces the loss of performance. Triathletes, or any athletes, who begin to drink early and drink a lot, sweat less because their blood vessels are full and can thus radiate more heat. Thus less heat has to be released via sweat evaporation.

Unfortunately, with the sweat, minerals are lost too. It is therefore important that not only the lost water but also the lost minerals are replaced. Pure water cannot be absorbed by the body because the minerals necessary for its absorption are not supplied with it.

The pure water will then be excreted again via the kidneys, whereby further minerals will be excreted with it. The whole situation would therefore only get worse.

Tea, lemonade and Cola also provide almost pure water and are therefore not suitable for replacing lost sweat. They lack the necessary minerals. An ideal drink, purely from the mineral aspect, is a 1:1 mixture of Brottrunk barley water + apple juice.

This provides for an improved metabolism, which is after all responsible for there being no low points in an ultra triathlon. I also find that since I have been drinking Brottrunk barley water I get neither cramps nor aching muscles. The reason is probably the lactic acid which purifies the tissue.

The following table shows clearly how a suitable replacement for the minerals and Vitamin C lost through sweat can be made:

Kanne Brottrunk + apple juice + fermented grain

Average contents in 100 ml (mg)	Sodium	Potassium	Calcium	Magnesium	Vitamin C
Sweat	120	30	16	3.6	5
Lemonade	0	0	0˙	0	0
Cola	0	0	0	0	0
Mineral drink 1)	88	160	16	8	0
Mineral water 2)	78	8	211	22	0
Brottrunk barley water 3)	44	25.5	12.2	7.2	0
Apple juice 4)	3	214	9	5.5	10.5
Kanne Brottrunk w.:Apple j. Mixture 1:1	23.5	120	10.6	6.3	5.2

1) Mineral drink Mineral plus 6
2) Rheinfels-Quelle mineral water
3) Kanne Brottrunk
4) Granini apple juice

Improving Performance Through a Proper Diet

In the Pre-Competition Period

Triathlon is a combination of stamina and strength. Because in training a compromise in the ideal relationship between stamina and strength must be found, this means that in one's diet in the spring months a compromise in the relationship between carbohydrates and protein must be found.

According to Dr. STRUNZ the simplest formula is: "As much protein as possible, as little fat as possible." As few triathletes can prepare their meals with the kitchen scales - especially when eating out or in canteens - it is important to know which foods to avoid and which to give preference to.

Foods that only provide "empty calories" should be avoided. The list of foods mentioned already need not be damned so much that triathletes may never eat a white bread roll, a piece of cake or even a pancake. Endurance athletes' love of cake is well known. The idea is not to encourage everybody to become joyless ascetics. Rather it is a matter of being aware of this negative list so that when one has a choice, one eats a wholemeal cake instead of the perhaps seductive looking cream cake. If your diet as a whole is healthy, you are allowed to "sin" now and then. But we should be aware that in the long run a high performance engine cannot run on low quality fuel. A well-trained athlete is not six times more capable than a non-sporting person by nature, but is so because of his endurance training and his conscious eating habits. In choosing the right foods, in addition to the right proportion of carbohydrates, proteins and fats we have to pay just as much attention to getting enough minerals, trace elements and vitamins. The same applies to the right liquids.

Recommended Foods Suitable For Triathletes

a) Carbohydrate rich, starchy foods
- Legumes (beans, lentils, peas)
- Grains (oats, wheat, rye, barley, millet, natural rice, buckwheat)
- Wholemeal products (bread, biscuits)
- Wheatgerm
- Oatflakes, muesli without sugar additive, cornflakes
- Potatoes
- Brewer's yeast, fermented grain
- Pasta (noodles, spaghetti, maccaroni)

b) Protein rich foods (low in fat)
- Low-fat cheese
- Curd cheese, lean
- Low-fat milk, low-fat dairy products
- Yoghurt, cottage cheese
- Lean meat, veal, beef, hare, venison
- Poultry
- Fish
- Legumes

c) Fats (high quality)
- Sunflower seed oil
- Linseed oil
- Soy oil
- Diet margarine
- Mackerels and pollack

d) Fruit
- All kinds of fruit
- Dried fruit without sulphur

e) Fluids
- Milk
- Fruit and vegetable juices
- Kanne Brottrunk, mixture: Kanne Brottrunk, apple juice, mineral water

Timing Of Meals
Five Meals Are Better than Three
Several smaller meals spread throughout the day are better than fewer, larger ones because they put less strain on the digestive organs. Also, the human organism makes better and more economic use of the smaller amounts.

In his book "Die Ernährung des Sportlers" Prof. NÖCKER recommends five meals with the following proportions of energy:

1. Breakfast about 20% of daily energy
2. 2nd breakfast about 15% of daily energy
3. Lunch about 25%
4. Afternoon about 15%
5. Evening meal about 25%

A training session should not begin until at least 90 minutes after a meal. The last meal in the evening should not be eaten too late as this can lead to sleeping problems. As triathletes mainly train endurance, the meals after training should be mainly rich in carbohydrates in order to allow quick replenishing of the glycogen stores. After intensive swimming, cycling or running sessions on the other hand, the emphasis should be on protein rich food.

Altogether triathletes have problems maintaining a 20% protein share in their diet. To achieve this goal it is necessary to be especially attentive to the recommended protein suppliers. In many cases protein concentrates or supplements are required in order to reach the correspondingly high level of 7.6-8.2% protein in the blood.

Anyone not able to eat solid food after a training session should immediately ensure they get appropriate fluids to compensate. It is a simple matter to stir some protein powder into the drink. Afterwards you can eat light foods such as fruit, yoghurt or curd cheese with fruit. As a drink it is recommended to take one of those named above. For the reasons mentioned you should not give preference to Cola, lemonades or other drinks with "empty calories".

Practical Nutritional Tips for Triathletes
The following suggestions should be taken as orientation aids and can be exchanged at will depending on the training situation.

Suggestions for Breakfast
Wholemeal bread with low-fat sausage meat slices, cheese 30-40% fat, sugar beet syrup, honey, lean curd cheese, milk, fruit juice, cornflakes or muesli made of wholemeal flakes with fruit and milk.
Fresh grain porridge made of gound oats boiled briefly in water and garnished with fresh fruit and raisins, with two teaspoons of mineral rich fermented grain and 0.2 l Kanne Brottrunk.

2nd breakfast or afternoon snack
Milk, fruit, yoghurt dishes, wholemeal bread with lean sausage or sugar beet syrup, wholemeal biscuits/cake, sponge, mineral water + apple juice + possibly protein concentrate (50% animal / 50% vegetable).

Lunch
Soups with fermented grain as seasoning, fresh salads, vegetables without thickening, especially beans, corn, peas, lentils, potatoes, rice, noodles, fish, lean meat, egg dishes, all prepared with low fat, 0.1 l Kanne Brottrunk.
Fresh fruit, milk dishes, curd cheese.

Evening meal
Wholemeal bread with cheese or low-fat topping, raw vegetable salads, potato, rice, noodle or grain dishes.
Fruit, stewed fruit.

Drinks
Mineral rich drinks to compensate for sweat loss.
Mineral water, apple juice+Kanne Brottrunk, orange juice.

Performance oriented triathletes should eat 500 – 1,000 g of bread per day during the main training period in order to compensate the minerals, trace elements and vitamins. As a result, the body is then capable of detoxifying the substances (deposits) which lead to muscle cramps and thus performance drops by having inufficient enzymes.

The Kanne Brottrunk contains a great number of minerals, trace elements and essential amino acids as well as vitamins. All this in open form, i.e. available through months of enzyme processing during manufacture. This is known as the "living gelate bond". The gelate bond is also found in vegetables, fruit and in bread, i.e. in "living" foods. In bread it develops through the yeast and the sour dough process in combination with the baking process. Bread enzymes are in turn exceptionally well-suited for eliminatinq e.q. toxins, alcohol and toxic tissue acid.

The biological bread grain lactic acid provides for improved metabolism. 1 ml of Kanne Brottrunk contains 5 million lactic acid bacteria. The optimum weight of a triathlete is a performance factor that should not be underestimated. Especially during running and cycling uphill performance is very much reduced by being overweight. Overweight athletes also sweat more because their fat layers hinder the release of heat, and they require more fluids in hot weather. They only have an advantage when swimming in cold water. Generally the optimum competition weight will develop on its own in the pre-racing season if one sticks to a diet rich in roughage and low in fat and sugar. It is not advisable to go on a diet to lose weight because this usually leads to mineral and vitamin deficiency symptoms. Such diets also hinder a systematic training build up.

Nutrition in the Competition Period

Your motto for the last days before a triathlon should be: Increase carbohydrate intake by reducing fat and protein. The goal is the optimum increase in the glyocgen reserves following the principle of super compensation.
Assumption: Race day is Saturday.

If on Tuesday in the last hard training session (5 km warm-up running + 5 km hard pace + 5 km cool down running + 25 km tough cycling training + 5 km easy pedalling) the glycogen stores are emptied and on Wednesday, Thursday and Friday mainly carbohydrates are eaten, a considerable increase in the glycogen reserves of the running and cycling muscle groups is achieved. By including an additional three days Sunday, Monday, Tuesday of fat and protein rich eating (Saltin diet), an even greater supply of glycogen can be built up. This second dietary variation must be tested in training beforehand to see if one's body can handle it. Such a maximum increase of muscle glycogen only makes sense before a middle or an ultra triathlon because here the glycogen stores are completely emptied. The reason is that a maximum increase of muscle glycogen goes hand in hand with a weight increase of 2-2.5 kg.

The following applies for the final days before the triathlon:

- 5-6 smaller meals spread evenly through the day put less strain on the digestive organs.
- Avoid foods that are difficult to digest and cause wind, e.g. legumes, coarse cabbage, mayonnaise, coarse wholemeal bread. Always rely on your own positive experiences here.
- Raise the proportion of carbohydrates by: Limiting sausage, meat, cheese, eggs, in other words fats. Careful! Hidden fats are also fats! Give preference to easily digested foods such as: Potatoes, noodles, rice, grain products; consumption of carbohydrate rich ready-to-eat products.

Proper foods should also be prepared properly, i.e. lightly

Through improper preparation easily digestible foods can be made hard to digest, e.g. by deep frying. Suitable methods of preparation: Boil, simmer, steam, sauté, simmer in foil, in coated pans or in a clay pot.

Nutrition on Race Day and During the Race

Two to three hours before a triathlon you should eat a light, carbohydrate rich meal, such as e.g. dark bread with jam or sugar beet syrup, noodles, fruit and fuit juice + Kanne Brottrunk. In high temperatures or long races (middle - long distance) drink an additional half litre of fluids half an hour before the start.

In a short triathlon a solid meal is generally not necessary. On the other hand, half a banana will not hurt. The need for fluids depends on the weather. If it is cool a little water or tea is sufficient. In warm weather the promoters usually provide electrolyte drinks. Often these are too concentrated. I therefore recommend taking your own drink in the short distance: 1/2 apple juice + 1/2 Kanne Brottrunk.

In a middle triathlon every triathlete should eat suitable solid carbohydrate and protein suppliers while cycling. Bananas, PowerBars and other energy bars are suitable. The constant intake of fluids is important. You should begin at the beginning of the cycling section, especially in hot summer temperatures; i.e. before you start to feel thirsty. It is always advisable to find out beforehand what kind of drinks will be provided. If these are offered later in the cycling and running sections in too high a concentration, you should also take water and alternate this with the drinks.

In the running section you should try to take in as much fluids as you lose through sweat. This works if you drink 0.1-0.2 l at regular intervals. The higher the temperature, the shorter the time between fluid intakes should be. By regularly drinking mineral drinks you can avoid a great drop in performance and unpleasant muscle cramps.

In ultra triathlons such, as Roth or Hawaii, you must eat solid foods. Preferably this should be easily digestible food in the form of biscuits, bananas, fruit loaf or energy bars. Muesli bars and chocolate are not recommended as the digestive tract is strained by it for too long. In order to find out what agrees with you best, you need to practise eating during long training sessions a number of times. By the way, it should also taste good. On the 180 km cycling sector, part of the energy used up will need to be replaced. This is only possible through regular food intake. In competition you should not take any unnecessary risks in this respect. With regard to fluid intake, the same applies here as in the middle triathlon. In extreme heat there is only one thing to do: drink, drink, and drink again. In Hawaii you can lose up to 2 l sweat per hour of the race, so it is absolutely necessary to take in fluids in the form of electrolyte drinks every 5 miles or 8 km.

So far as I know, only one triathlete has ever tried to do the whole course in Hawaii without taking in fluids. Halfway through the cycling section the dream was over. Unbelievable! In the final running section solid food intake is no longer necessary, though biscuits or a piece of banana do no harm as they are easily digestible. Here fluid intake is again decisive. As providing one's own drinks is not possible for understandable reasons, and is in fact not allowed, you have to take what is offered. Electrolyte drinks, water and cola are offered everywhere. These are also easy to mix. As we have already found, the body absorbs a light electrolyte drink better than pure water. Cola raises the blood sugar level briefly. If cola is not drunk at short regular intervals there is a drop instead of a rise in the blood sugar level. That would automatically lead to a rapid drop in performance. In high temperatures there is a way to reduce sweat loss and still enjoy relieving refreshment. You simply tip water over your head and neck and cool your arms and legs with wet sponges. In this way you conduct away excess heat and refresh your overheated body. Headgear with a cloth to cover the neck increases this positive effect.

Nutrition during Regeneration

For every triathlete regeneration begins directly after crossing the finish line. Now you must replace lost water, minerals, trace elements and vitamins as quickly as possible. You must also make sure that the used up protein structures are built back up again through a regular diet of protein rich food. The same applies of course to your diet after a hard training session.

After intense endurance activity the muscle groups display higher receptiveness to carbohydrates. The recovery process is speeded up by refilling the glycogen stores.

For athletes who have little appetite after a race, carbohydrate rich drinks or soups are best. With these the triathlete can first quench his thirst and at the same time take in electrolytes and carbohydrates, e.g. fruit juice, Kanne Brottrunk. Normalising the electrolyte and protein store can take several days, depending on how strenuous the race was. In this period you should pay special attention to foods containing potassium and magnesium. In other words vegetables, fruit, grain meals, legumes and dried fruits, not forgetting trace elements like iron and copper. These days natural mineral waters are unfortunately no longer suitable for this. For optical and taste reasons these usually have the iron taken out of them. In addition to giving preference to drinks containing trace elements such as low-fat milk drinks, pure buttermilk and kefir it is a good idea to supplement this with a low dosage of mineral and trace element mixture from a health food shop, e.g. Basica with 20 different elements.

As on the race day foods were eaten which only put minimum strain on the digestive tract, in the days that follow it is recommended to eat food with a high roughage content. A large number of triathletes long for a cold beer after a race. Alcohol is absorbed by the body very quickly, but also excreted again quickly. Fluid losses are not replaced by drinking alcohol. That means, before the beer - if possible alcohol free - drink other fluids first.

The Triathlete's Circulatory System

Anyone entering triathlon competitions in an ambitious way needs to include in their preparations not only individual training schedules, performance tests and knowledge about nutrition suitable for sport, but also the certainty that theirsporting activity is all right. This certainty is provided by the results of blood tests, which every triathlete should have done once or twice a year, top athletes more often. This can be done by the family doctor, internist or sport doctor.

The evaluation of these blood tests gives important information regarding the training programme and the dietary plan. While a performance test gives a fairly clear answer, the results of a blood test are usually not so easy to interpret. This is a major reason why to date very few athletes have their blood tested regularly. As visits to the doctor are otherwise rare amongst triathletes we should not have a bad conscience about the costs incurred.

Because of a lack of information many triathletes do themselves out of a chance to make the most of their performancepotential. Until a while ago I belonged to the group of those who either did not know or were insufficiently informed in this respect and thus had a number of problems.

One problem for many athletes is certainly that they have no sport doctors in their club or their neighbourhood. In medium sized cities and major centres this should not be so difficult. A general practitioner can arrange for the necessary blood tests, but because of his training he will probably be out of his depth in sporting questions.

The following is an attempt to explain the blood values of most significance for triathletes and to give corresponding comparative values. If you then get your individual blood values from your doctor or his practice nurse, you should be able to compare them here and discuss with your doctor what to do next.

Optimum Weight

In the preparatory period with its intensive training this usually comes automatically. Especially in the cycling month the winter fat flies off. Otherwise a diet with much roughage ensures the best competition weight, unless the excess weight is in the double digit region.

Then all that can help is a long-term change in eating habits. Regarding optimum weight you should not so much be guided by tables and rules but more by your feeling and reason.

Of course competition weight should be considerably under so called normal weight. Normal weight can be calculated as follows:

$$Normal\ weight = Height - 100$$
$$e.g. \quad = 187 - 100 = 87$$
$$= 170 - 100 = 70$$

Thus a 1.87 m tall person has a normal weight of 87 kg, a 1.70 m tall person's is 70 kg.

Pulse at Rest

The simplest method is to count the pulse beats in your wrist for a half or a whole minute in the morning before getting up. Measurement with a pulse measurer is of course more accurate. The pulse at rest values depend on a number of factors:

Heart size, age, amount of training, climate, diet and physical condition. Untrained persons have a pulse at rest between 60 and 80. Endurance athletes should be under 60. Performance athletes are usually between 40 and 50.

Prof. NEUMANN made an interesting statement that there is no direct connection between the pulse at rest and sporting fitness.

The pulse at rest provides important information with regard to training. If it suddenly rises by more than 10-15 beats per minute, then you are ill or illness is on its way. If the pulse at rest is only about five or more beats higher than the days before, then only light, regenerative training is called for. In Hawaii the pulse at rest is a few beats higher than at home because of the climate.

Blood Pressure

When measuring blood pressure, which is produced by the heart, we differentiate between two features: systole (contraction) is the name for the phase when the heart contracts; diastole (expansion) for when it expands. High blood pressure begins at: systolic above 160 mm Hg, diastolic above 95 mm Hg and is a danger to the organism.

Endurance training as it is mainly carried out in triathlon lowers blood pressure and is therefore of great benefit to the whole organism. Today you can measure your blood pressure at any chemist.

The Blood

The human body contains about 5-6 litres of blood, i.e. blood plasma, blood corpuscles and other elements. Blood plasma is the fluid part of blood. In it are numerous anorganic or mineral substances. Based on years of measurement, reference or NORMAL VALUES for women and men have been established. These apply - how could it be otherwise - to "normal people" and not athletes.

An endurance athlete can be recognised not least by his blood readings. Regular sporting activity already leads to an increase in blood volume. Consequently the relative concentration of red corpuscles is often lower than in non-sporting people. Triathlon training leads to a favourable relationship between "good" HDL cholesterine and "bad" LDL cholesterine. Kanne Brottrunk improves this positive balance further. The risk of early hardening of the arteries is thus very low unless, that is, excessive intake of simple sugars (sweets, fats, alcohol) results in high triglyceride levels. The blood sugar level is generally pleasantly low in endurance athletes. Slightly high uric acid levels are not rare among endurance athletes. In 1982 Dr. Ernst VAN AAKEN noticed uric acid levels of 7.5, 7.9 and even 8.2 in top long distance athletes. Uric acid consists of toxic substances that cannot be broken down any further and are filtered through the kidneys. If they are not excreted sufficiently the concentration in the blood rises.

The "erythrocytes" (red corpuscles) transport oxygen to the cells and carbon dioxide on the way back to the lungs. The "leucocytes" (white corpuscles) are the antibodies of the immune system. The "thrombocytes" (platelets) are for coagulation, particularly important when there are injuries.

Uric acid readings above 50 mg/dl indicate over training. The "haemocrit" shows the relationship between the volume of the red corpuscles and the total blood volume in per cent. The normal reading for men is around 40-50%, for women between 35-45%. Top athletes usually have lower readings without, however, going below the minimum limits. This is presumably because of the general increase in blood volume of a very well trained endurance athlete.

The Key Blood Component Values for Triathletes

The following blood readings are especially important for triathletes and should therefore be checked once or twice a year. Good times for checks are once in the preparatory period and a further check during the competition period.

Haemoglobin (HgB)

The red corpuscles carry a so-called chromium protein around with them, haemoglobin, which contains iron. This haemoglobin looks after the oxygen transport and distribution in the body. This goes from the lungs to the tissues, via the blood. A certain amount of red corpuscles are therefore the basic prerequisite for good performance. Humans have between 3.9 and 5.9 million red blood corpuscles (erythrocytes). About 900 g of haemoglobin are carried around by the red corpuscles, 14-18 g/dl in men and 12-16 g/dl in women. A HgB reading of under 12 g/dl is already classified as anaemia. For a triathlete it is desirable to have a high HgB level in the blood in order to take in and transport more oxygen. The HgB level should be as high as possible, according to Dr. STRUNZ over 16 g/dl. Because haemoglobin is a protein that must be enriched with iron, the doctor from Roth recommends the following to increase the HgB level: Eat plenty of protein + iron substitute + Kanne Brottrunk as a "medium".

Another possibility to get the body to produce more haemoglobin is to train at a high altitude. Above 1,800 m, in the low oxygen air, you can get the body to produce more HgB. For a short period you can then achieve better results in a decisive race down at normal altitudes. According to Dr. STRUNZ, one point in the haemoglobin content means an improved time of four minutes in a marathon run. With regard to the HgB, the link with iron metabolism is important.

Iron

Many endurance athletes have an iron deficiency. This is noticeable in listlessness, lack of motivation and in great drops in performance. To better understand this it is necessary to know that altogether there are about 4 g of iron in the human body. The majority of this (65%) is in the haemoglobin and the myoglobin, 16% is in the ferritin and 10% in the liver. Only 0.1 % of the total iron content is found bonded to a certain protein in the blood itself, so called serum iron. Serum iron therefore provides the least information about the body's "iron reserves", it only lets us know the current amount of iron circulating.

If serum iron is low, then there is an iron deficiency. If this deficiency lasts, first of all the iron in the smaller body "stores" is activated, i.e. in the body cells of the liver, bone marrow, spleen and muscles, to eradicate this deficiency. Only after a longer period of iron deficiency is iron taken from the "large stores", namely the red corpuscles. As a result the haemoglobin level goes down, oxygen intake and transport are restricted. This results in listlessness and lack of fitness. The actual iron level, which can change within hours, should be over 80 µg/dl for triathletes.

Ferritin

Ferritin is a protein which carries iron. The concentration of ferritin in the blood is a reliable indicator of the iron level. The ferritin content has a certain relationship to the amount of iron in the bone marrow.

For triathletes the ferritin level should be over 130 µg/dl.

A note on blood tests: On the day of the test your body must have rest. The two days beforehand there should be no intensive training as this could falsify individual readings.

Total Protein

The importance of protein intake has been discussed in the chapter on nutrition. Sufficient protein intake is also important for the so significant haemoglobin level. The normal values for the serum analysis are between 6.6 and 8.7%. For the reasons mentioned above, triathletes should have try to have values of 7.6 to 8.2%. A difficult undertaking for many. I personally have been "running after" this value for a long time and still have not reached it. A total protein level in the blood that is too low can usually be traced back to a diet not rich enough in protein. The answer is to consciously eat high protein food. The diet should be supplemented with protein concentrates, whereby research by Dr. STRUNZ has shown that 50% animal and 50 % vegetable protein is most favourable. For a long time the role of protein in sport was not considered significant. This view has been corrected in recent years.

At the world conference of sports physicians in October 1991 it was announced that in the first hours, endurance athletes cover 19% of their energy requirements from protein metabolism - an unheard of figure before then. Every participant in the 1992 Munich Marathon was given a leaflet in which for the first time the great significance of protein for endurance sport was pointed out.

Dr. Randy ICE, who accompanies the Race Across America (cycling race right across America covering just under 5,000 km) provided more detailed information: "An athlete who runs 16 km/h for an hour has used up 36 g of protein."

All of this shows that in order to keep fit and healthy, endurance athletes must place more value on high protein foods such as lentils, beans, millet and rice.

After all, the whole human immune system consists of protein.

Magnesium

The normal levels of magnesium for serum analyses are c. 0.8-1.0 mmol/l. Ultra triathletes should make sure that the level is at least 0.9. If the magnesium levels are too low it can lead to negative symptoms e.g. drop in performance, restlessness, irritability, sleeping problems, lack of concentration, weather sensitivity. The above mentioned tests are the most important for triathletes. Often a number of blood tests are carried out whose purpose is disputed.

A well thought out blood analysis is evident, not in the number of individual results,but rather in a limited number of the most important - and meaningful values.

Table of the Most Important Blood Values

	Reference values Men	Women	Required values Triathletes
Haemoglobin	14-18g/dl	12-16g/dl	> 16 g/dl
Iron	80-150	60-140µg/dl	> 80µg/dl
Ferritin			> 130µg/dl
Total Protein	6.6-8.7		7.8-8.2 mmol/l
Magnesium	0.8-1.0 mmol/l		0.9-1.0 mmol/l
Potassium	3.6-5.4 mmol/l		4.6-5.4 mmol/l
Calcium	2.1-2.9 mmol/l		2.5-2.9 mmol/l
Erythrocytes (red corp.)	3.9-5.9 Mill/µl		
Leucocytes (white corp.)	4,000-10,000 Mill/µl		
Trombocytes (platelets)	150,000-350,000 Mill/µl		
HDL Cholesterin	> 35	> 45 mg/dl	
LDL Cholesterin	< 150 mg/dl		Same as ref.values
Triglyceride	< 150 mg/dl		
Urea	10-50 mg/dl		
Uric Acid	< 7	< 6 mg/dl	
Blood sugar	70-110 mg/dl		
Haematocrit	40-50%	35-45%	

Reference levels of Münster University

A minimum programme of blood values for triathletes is:
HgB Haemoglobin
Ferritin
Total Protein
Magnesium
Urea for regulating training (> 50 over training)

What to Do in Case of Injury or Sickness?

Because of its diversity, triathlon is one of the kinds of sport that causes least wear and tear. This applies to the whole human supporting and moving apparatus, that is the muscles, ligaments and tendons. In balanced triathlon training there is a constant change in the muscle strain. In spite of all this injuries can happen. Appropriate precautions can reduce these rare injuries even more. This is in our own interest.

A few remarks first about training with minor illnesses.

The supreme principle must alwas be: "TRIATHLON serves HEALTH" and not "Health serves triathlon".

This means in practice: If you have a cold with a temperature, flu or a stomach and intestine infection, all training should be stopped. Your body is already weakened by these illnesses, a further weakening through training would only make them worse. When the infection has died away, it is a good idea to wait another two days and then begin with easy cycling training.

Running Is the Sport Where the Most Injuries Can Arise

In running the two main causes of injury are:
- Increasing the amount of weekly training too quickly.
- Speed or interval training.

By knowing how such injuries arise it is easier to avoid them.
- The increase in the amount of running per week should not be more than 10%. This applies mainly to basic endurance training in the preparatory period.

In other words, increases for example from 40 to 44, 49, 54, 59, 65, 71, 78, 86 km. Jumps from 40 km to 80, 90 km place you at the risk of injury and should be avoided. If, however, you have built up your level in small stages to e.g. 60 km, then of course greater jumps in the amount of training are possible.

It is important to adapt the supporting and moving system to the increased exertion slowly. Only when this has been done is interval training to be recommended.

Main causes of injury in interval training:
- Insufficient warm-up and cool down. The right order is: 10-15 minutes of easy warm-up jogging with a few brief intensifications, stretching, intervals ..... 10-15 minutes easy cool down jogging, stretching.
- Training days that are too hard, too many races.
- Too high a speed on the long adapting runs. Here the rule is: The longer the run, the slower the pace.

Too many speed weeks. Do not do interval training for more than 10-12 weeks in a row. Afterwards leave out speed training for a few weeks.

- Never train "to the limit".
- Not enough regeneration in autumn and winter.
- Unsuitable running shoes (see chapter on running gear).

Cycling

Apart from falls, cycling is much gentler on the supporting and moving apparatus than is running. The athlete must no longer carry his body weight. When cycling other muscle groups are exerted than in running. Here too you should do a proper warm-up before and cool down after interval rides. It goes without saying that you wear your helmet, both in races and in training. Cycling strengthens the back muscles and stabilises the arm and shoulder areas. Both aid the triathlete in swimming.

When cycling injuries can arise through:

- Racing bike not suitable for your body, e.g. saddle too low or too high, handle bar section too short or too long, wrong frame height.
- Cycling in too low a gear and thus with too few revolutions. This leads to sore knees.
- No safety pedals.
- Incorrect cycling clothing; in cool weather especially the kidneys should be protected; even in races in cool weather cycle in dry clothing.
- Slow down in places where vision is insufficient.

Skin grazes and bruises are the main consequences of falls from bikes, assuming that a helmet was worn. There is a danger of tetanus infection arising from light grazes that bleed little. As this can be very dangerous you should be vaccinated against tetanus.

Cold wraps are usually sufficient to deal with swelling and simple strains. These should be soaked in Kanne Brottrunk. In fact Brottrunk barley water is excellent altogether for removing external swelling. The swollen parts should be rubbed with the lactic acid fermented drink as often as possible. If, however, the swelling and pain continue, you should see a doctor to have possible ligament or tendon injuries treated.

Swimming

Here too the risk of injury is more than low. If you regularly stretch a little before swimming and then do easy warm-up swimming for the first 300-400 m you will be spared potential injuries.

In cool weather, low water temperatures and longer swimming distances, a neoprene suit as protection is absolutely recommended.

If you know the injury causes described above and heed the precautionary measures, in the long run you will be spared injuries in triathlon.

Forbidden Ways for Triathletes to Increase Performance

In another part of the book I have written about the permitted ways of improving performance. These should be used in order to make the most of your individual sporting potential.

The forbidden ways of improving performance are known as doping. Drugs can be used to improve physical performance.

Doping substances have a sustained influence on the functioning of the body. The athlete is only partially capable of independently making decisions. He becomes a "remote controlled running or cycling machine".

In my opinion, this way to achieving performance has absolutely nothing to do with sport.

In doping I cannot see sport as a means of physical training. Man's desire to measure himself against his fellow man also has nothing in common with doping. In my opinion taking doping substances of any kind is reprehensible for the following reasons:

- Doped athletes gain an advantage that is more than unfair.
- With illegal means, so far as they can even be used in triathlon, one is only deceiving oneself. The sporting performance achieved is not achieved by me personally, but by chemical giant XY.
- Performance comparisons and performance lose credibility.
- The most significant argument against doping is the health risk. Even today hardly anyone can tell how great the negative effects will be in 10 or 20 years.

The available performance potential can only be used by willpower by up to four fifths. The other fifth is an "iron reserve" of the body. This only becomes available in extreme situations such as mortal danger, fear or anger. Drugs attack these "iron lifesaving reserves". The consequences can no longer be controlled and can lead to collapse or even death. The effect of medicaments is based on lowering the natural pain threshold dilute the blood.

For all triathletes there can therefore only be the one prescription as the essential means:

TRAINING, TRAINING, TRAINING!

Dealing with Your Personality Structure - A Factor of Success

Prof. Georg Kroeger, Dipl. Soc.

Success - Attempt at a Definition

First let us try to define the term success. You are certainly successful if you achieve the goals you have set in a time frame you also set yourself. We can agree on this perhaps trivial but understandable formula. In other words:

If you begin now at stage zero and in five years climb the summit of triathlon existence - finisher in Hawaii - you can place yourself in the category "success" - at least in this partial sector of your life.

Today there are a number of academic studies which deal with the factor "success". All the studies come to a similar conclusion: that people who are able to estimate realistically their skills and abilities, coupled with calculated risk, will very probably be successful. This applies to all facets of life. Rough sections along the way to the goal should also be calculatable factors.

So much for the theory. Hermann ASCHWER is responsible for the practice.
On the basis of your individual orientation he has pragmatically shown the necessary steps.

Motivation - the Driving Force

There is no single motive, rather your actions will always be triggered by a number of motives. I am sure you can describe your main motivation for doing triathlon. But if you think about it other motives will occur to you.

This in turn has a causal relationship to your social situation. Motives of this kind are usually in deficit, or based on some kind of "lack". That is bound to be a factor that you have often experienced in your life.

Goals reached no longer motivate; this means nothing more than that you must set yourself new goals. When you head for these new goals a positive way of thinking will help you.

Positive Thinking - the Amplifier

You possess almost absolute freedom of your thoughts, therefore you can think what you want.

With the help of your will you can steer, guide and discipline your thoughts. The sum of your thoughts forms your opinion, your point of view, has an influence on moods and over time even influences your characteristics.

The more you think positively in the sum of your thoughts, the more positive influences there will be on your ego.

Your thoughts are inspired by the enviroment. Our environment is relative and in its existence it is dependent on your subjective way of viewing things. Therefore a positive way of viewing the world is a part of positive thinking.

Personality Structure - the Differences

In my personal environment I have come to know the greatest variety of triathletes, i.e. people with varying personality structures. Very few of them have achieved their personal goals.

Most of them have literally "fallen by the wayside", have given up, dropped out, or still dream of the "Ironman" - which will always be a dream.

"Doesn't matter at all", some of them will say, others will - once again - have to put up with the reproach "another thing started and not finished".

Of course you first have to test, try out, in other words make a start. But when you have "sniffed around" enough, successfully finished in one or other novice triathlon, and you have the desire and the time to carry on, then: "Carry through!" Pragmatically dealing with your personality structure should help you.

In the following, for simplicity's sake we will initially restrict ourselves to three personality models:

Introvertedness

Features:

Formality, exactness, planned action, fixed allocation of time, distanced behaviour, tendency to keep to oneself, systematic action, ability to abstract, thinking and action oriented to the future. If you recognise mainly these characteristics about yourself, you should follow your disposition, e.g. by making your training schedules as detailed as possible.

You will probably have no trouble with that, as you usually follow a plan, coupled with fixed allocation of time. Diet plans and lactate measurements etc. will round off your programme planning. Your training journal will mostly accompany you daily, you have no problem with training alone, you are independent of training partners.

Dangers of introvertedness:

You stick too closely to your training schedules and carry out a planned session even when you fell unwell. This leads to possible risk of injury and illness. So: in future when it is cold or rainy, do not get on your bike just to fulfil your kilometre plan. My introverted training partners often had trouble with colds, especially bronchitis. A good way of preventing such "training book dependency" is to have training partners with a different personality structure.

Extrovertedness
Features:
Seeks superiority, often makes decisions spontaneously and emotionally, desire to compare oneself with others, tendency to generalisations, places value on external appearances, thinking and action are oriented to the present.

Your strengths are in improvisation. Training is pleasure based and often done spontaneously. If you feel good, you double your training sessions. If you do not feel good, you "skip" a session and instead go into a triathlon shop and once again buy the latest outfit. The outfit in particular is important for you and your feeling of well being. After all, you want to look good. There is actually nothing wrong with that.

Dangers of extrovertedness:
Every training session turns into a race. In a way you are dependent on your training partners who you need to show "how it is done". Over training with all its unpleasant consequences is bound to happen some time.

My extroverted training partners often had problems with their Achilles heel because of uncontrolled running training and sometimes even fatigue breaks.

You may even end your triathlon because financially you live beyond your means. It is not necessary to get a new racing bike every year.

Ambovertedeness
Features:
Likes to be, and is always, with other people, lives a group oriented life, needs harmony, sociable, avoids radical change, has a feeling for people, often very popular, thinking and action oriented to the past.

You are not the great fighting type but rather you seek balancing compromise. This makes you likeable, but you can only practice triathlon in all its complexity when you are surrounded by like-minded people. It will certainly do you good to belong to a club with a family atmosphere. For you it is important to also maintain contact with your training partners outside the triathlon sphere. While the introvert sees the trainings partner as being there for the specific purpose and the extrovert sees in him a potential rival, you feel yourself bound in friendship and a common destiny.

Dangers of ambovertedness:
If the feeling of togetherness just mentioned is not found - namely building up a triathletic friendship - you may quit, because you are barely interested in or even capable of training alone. It may also be that you prefer to stay in the club house for a chat rather than to get on your bike.

My amboverted training partners were injured comparatively seldom, they only trained when others did.

Quintessence

The information here is a framework for your orientation. My purpose is to show you the possibilities and the limits.

If your personality structure is as clear as what I have described, then you will probably find it easier to trace your personal success back to it. Most people, however, have a personality structure that is a mixture of these types, whereby you will recognise your own individual mixture.

Only those who recognise themselves have the great opportunity of correctly classifying their actions and dealing with these appropriately.

Bibliography

Van Aken, E.:	Das van Aaken Lauflehrbuch. Meyer & Meyer Verlag, Aachen 1997
Aschwer, H.:	Handbuch für Triathlon. Meyer & Meyer Verlag, Aachen 1995
Aschwer, H.:	Triathlon-Training. Vom Jedermann zum Ironman. Meyer & Meyer Verlag, Aachen 1996
Aschwer, H.:	Adventure Sports-Ironman – Der Hawaii-Triathlon Meyer & Meyer Verlag, Aachen 1997
Cooper, H.:	Dr. Coopers Gesundheitsprogramm. Droemar Verlag 1994
Diem, Carl-J.:	Tips für Laufanfänger, Meyer & Meyer Verlag, Aachen 1997
Galloway, J.:	Richtig laufen mit Galloway. Meyer & Meyer Verlag, Aachen 1996
Hahn, K.:	60 Marathonstrecken hat eine Stunde. Jahn & Ernst Verlag 1998
Hottenrott, K.:	The Complete Guide to Duathlon Training. Meyer & Meyer Verlag, Aachen 1999
Lydiard, A.:	Running to the Top. Meyer & Meyer Verlag, Aachen 1997
Lydiard/Gilmour:	Distance Training for Young Athletes. Meyer & Meyer Verlag, Aachen 1999
Schmidt/Hillebrecht:	Übungsprogramme zur Dehn- und Kräftigungsgymnastik. Meyer & Meyer Verlag, Aachen 1996
Schmidt, A.:	Handbook of Competitive Cycling. Meyer & Meyer Verlag, Aachen 1997
Steffny, M.:	Marathon-Training. Schmidt Verlag, Mainz 1994

Specialist magazines:

Triathlon-Duathlon:	Meyer & Meyer Verlag, Aachen
Triathlete:	Triathlete Sport Groupe SA Verlag, B-1050 Belgien